Redefining social justice

MANCHESTER
1824

Manchester University Press

Redefining social justice

New Labour rhetoric and reality

Edited by

VALERIE BRYSON AND PAMELA FISHER

Manchester University Press

Manchester and New York

distributed in the United States exclusively
by Palgrave Macmillan

Copyright © Manchester University Press 2011

While copyright in the volume as a whole is vested in Manchester University Press, copyright in the individual chapters belongs to their respective authors, and no chapter may be reproduced wholly or in part without the express permission in writing of both author and publisher.

Published by Manchester University Press
Oxford Road, Manchester M13 9NR, UK
and Room 400, 175 Fifth Avenue, New York, NY 10010, USA
www.manchesteruniversitypress.co.uk

Distributed in the United States exclusively by
Palgrave Macmillan, 175 Fifth Avenue, New York,
NY 10010, USA

Distributed in Canada exclusively by
UBC Press, University of British Columbia, 2029 West Mall,
Vancouver, BC, Canada V6T 1Z2

British Library Cataloguing-in-Publication Data
A catalogue record for this book is available from the British Library

Library of Congress Cataloging-in-Publication Data applied for

ISBN   978 07190 8220 7   hardback
ISBN   978 07190 8221 4   paperback

First published 2011

The publisher accepts no responsibility for the persistence or accuracy of URLs for any external or third-party internet Web sites referred to in this book, and does not guarantee that any content on such Web sites is, or will remain, accurate or appropriate.

Typeset in Charter
by Servis Filmsetting Ltd, Stockport, Cheshire
Printed in Great Britain
by CPI Antony Rowe, Chippenham, Wiltshire

Contents

Contents

Contributors

James Avis is Director of Research and Professor of Post-compulsory Education and Training at the University of Huddersfield. His research interests lie in post-compulsory education and lifelong learning. He has written extensively on the policy contextualisation of further education. His books include *Issues in Post-compulsory Education and Training* (co-edited with R. Fisher and R. Simmons, University of Huddersfield Press, 2009), *Education, Policy and Social Justice: Learning and Skills* (second edition, Continuum, 2009) and *Teaching in Lifelong Learning: a Guide to Theory and Practice* (co-edited with R. Fisher and R. Thompson, Open University Press, 2010). His current writing addresses localism, governance and community in relation to education and the state and also explores issues surrounding workplace learning.

Valerie Bryson is Emerita Professor of Politics at the University of Huddersfield. She has published widely on feminist theory and gender issues. Her publications include *Gender and the Politics of Time* (Policy Press, 2007) and *Feminist Political Theory* (second edition, Palgrave Macmillan, 2003). With Georgina Blakeley she is editor of *Contemporary Political Concepts: a Critical Introduction* (Pluto, 2002); *Marx and other Four-letter Words* (Pluto, 2005) and *The Impact of Feminism on Political Concepts and Debates* (Manchester University Press, 2007). She co-edited *Sexuality, Gender and Power: Intersectional and Transnational Perspectives* (with Anna Jonnasdottir and Kathleen Jones, Routledge, 2011) and is working on issues of gender, time and political theory.

Anne Chappell is Senior Lecturer in Social Policy at Buckinghamshire New University. Her research interests include social exclusion, social citizenship and disabled people.

Ruth Deery is Reader in Midwifery at the University of Huddersfield. Over a career spanning thirty-four years she has worked continuously as a midwife and academic. Her recent research has focused on the maternity services and women's health in the new NHS, with particular interest in organisational change, public policy, emotions, critical obesity and care. Her work has been widely published in refereed journals, and includes *Emotions in Midwifery and Reproduction* (jointly with B. Hunter, Palgrave Macmillan, 2009); '"Switching and swapping faces": performativity and emotion in midwifery' (jointly with P. Fisher), *International Journal of Work Organization and Emotion* (2010); '"The hardest leap": acceptance of diverse body size in midwifery' (jointly with S. Wray), *Practising Midwife* (2009); 'Public policy, "men's time" and power: the work of community midwives in the British National Health Service' (jointly with V. Bryson), *Women's Studies International Forum* (2009); 'The tyranny of time: tensions between relational and clock time in community-based midwifery', *Social Theory and Health* (2008).

Pamela Fisher is a Lecturer in Sociology at the University of Liverpool. Her main research interests are in the sociologies of health, wellbeing and disability, in particular how these relate to issues of identity and to understandings of citizenship and social justice. She has recently been working with Mencap on a project relating to professional identity. She has been published widely in peer-reviewed journals. Pamela is co-author (with J. McLaughlin, D. Goodley and E. Clavering) of *Families Raising Disabled Children: Enabling Care and Social Justice* (Palgrave Macmillan, 2008).

Chris Gifford is head of the Division of Criminology, Politics and Sociology at the University of Huddersfield. He has finished a project with colleagues from other European universities on citizenship education and is involved in work with colleagues at the University of Huddersfield on the study of Britishness. His publications include *The Making of Eurosceptic Britain: Identity and Economy in a Post-imperial State* (Ashgate, 2008); 'The United Kingdom and the European Union: dimensions of sovereignty and the problem of Eurosceptic Britishness', *Parliamentary Affairs* (forthcoming); '"It's the state, stupid! Utopian realism in a global age' (jointly with P. Woodcock), *Journal of Power* (2008); 'Political economy and the study of Britain and European integration: a global–national perspective', *British Journal of Politics and International Relations* (2007).

Tim Heppell is a Lecturer in British Politics within the School of Politics and International Studies (POLIS) at the University of Leeds. He has published widely on political parties and party leadership, and his books include *Choosing the Tory Leader: Conservative Party Leadership Elections from Heath to Cameron* (Tauris, 2008) and *Choosing the Labour Leader: Labour Party Leadership Elections from Wilson to Brown* (Tauris, 2010).

Lesley Jeffries is Professor of English Language at the University of Huddersfield. Her main research interests are in the detailed workings of language in context and she has published mainly in the stylistic and critical stylistic fields, focusing on the language of contemporary poetry and contemporary politics. Recent publications relevant to the latter include 'Not a drop to drink: emerging meanings in local newspaper reporting of the 1995 water crisis in Yorkshire', *Text* (2003); 'Journalistic constructions of Blair's "apology" for the intelligence leading to the Iraq war', in S. Johnson and A. Ensslin (eds), *Language in the Media: Representations, Identities, Ideologies* (Continuum, 2007); *Opposition in Discourse* (Continuum, 2010); *Critical Stylistics: The Power of English* (Macmillan, 2010).

James W. McAuley is Professor of Irish Studies and an associate dean at the University of Huddersfield. He has written extensively on Northern Irish politics and society, and especially on aspects of Ulster unionism and loyalism. His latest books include *Ulster's Last Stand* (Irish Academic Press, in press); *Abandoning Historical Conflict* (with C. McGlynn, J. Tonge and P. Shirlow, Manchester University Press, in press) and *Ulster Loyalism after the Good Friday Agreement* (edited with G. Spencer, Palgrave, in press). He is researching on conflict transformation and broader aspects of British identity.

Catherine McGlynn is a Senior Lecturer in Politics at the University of Huddersfield. Her research focuses on issues of national identity and citizenship, with special reference to ethnic differentiation and conflict resolution. She is co-author of *Abandoning Historical Conflict? Former Political Prisoners and Reconciliation in Northern Ireland* (Manchester University Press, in press) and the author of *Ethnically Differentiated Citizenship: States and Civil Societies* (Palgrave Macmillan, in press).

Peter Sanderson is head of the Department of Community and International Education at the University of Huddersfield. A sociologist and psychologist, he has written on expert learning and assessment, as well as collaborating with Hilary Sommerlad in her work on gender and the professions, and on training and regulating publicly funded legal advisers. His publications in collaboration with Hilary Sommerland include *Gender, Choice and Commitment* (Ashgate, 1998), a contribution to Greenfield and Osborn's *Law and Popular Culture* (Routledge, 2006) and articles in journals and books on both sides of the Atlantic on the expert knowledge of lawyers, legal advice and access to justice, and gendered professionalism.

Hilary Sommerlad is Professor of Socio-legal Studies at Leicester University and Director of the Centre for Research into Diversity in the Professions. She was trained as a historian and political scientist as well as a lawyer, and since 1991 has researched and written on women and the legal profession, and on citizenship, access to justice and the transformation of legal aid. She has run research projects and consultations for public bodies such as the Ministry of Justice, the Panel on Fair Access to the Professions and the Law Society, and her work on legal aid has been translated into Spanish and Japanese. Her collaborative publications with Pete Sanderson include *Gender, Choice and Commitment* (Ashgate, 1998), a contribution to Greenfield and Osborn's *Law and Popular Culture* (Routledge, 2006) and articles in journals and books on both sides of the Atlantic on the expert knowledge of lawyers, on legal advice and access to justice, and on gendered professionalism.

Paul Thomas is a Senior Lecturer in Youth and Community Work at the School of Education and Professional Development, University of Huddersfield. His Ph.D. focused on the impact of community cohesion policies in Oldham, Greater Manchester, with key findings published as 'Moving on from "anti-racism"? Understandings of "community cohesion" held by youth workers', *Journal of Social Policy* (2007). His research interests are community cohesion, multiculturalism and youth 'identities'; he has recently focused on the 'Preventing Violent Extremism' policy initiative. In relation to this he has published 'Between two stools? The government's "Preventing Violent Extremism" agenda', *Political Quarterly* (2009), and appeared as an expert witness for the House of Commons Communities and Local Government Select Committee inquiry in 2009. He is working on a book entitled *Youth, Multiculturalism and Community Cohesion* (Palgrave Macmillan).

I

Introduction

Valerie Bryson and Pamela Fisher

In 1997 New Labour promised not only an end to eighteen years of Conservative government but also the beginning of a new era of social justice based on contemporary needs and 'commonsense' values rather than 'old-fashioned' ideology rooted in the past. As its 1997 manifesto proclaimed, 'We are a broad-based movement for progress and justice. But we have liberated these values from outdated dogma or doctrine, and we have applied these values to the modern world.' While this rhetorical commitment to justice was clearly central to New Labour's political platform, it has been much less clear what it might mean in practice, and there are ongoing political and academic debates over the ideological nature, purpose and effects of the New Labour 'project' and the vision of social justice that it involved.

Edited by a political theorist, Valerie Bryson, and a social theorist, Pamela Fisher, this volume provides a timely contribution to these debates by bringing together contributions from linguistics, law, education, health, sociology and politics to reflect both on how social justice was articulated in policy and how it was experienced in people's lives between 1997 and 2010. Each chapter's analysis remains highly relevant to post-2010 politics, particularly in relation to David Cameron's aspirations for the 'big society' and his government's rhetorical claims to 'fairness'.

The co-editors' sympathies lie mainly in materialist and feminist perspectives as well as in social theory's 'turn to language', especially the dialectical relationship between the power of discourse and the material conditions of people's lives. Both share the view that the unproductive divisions between macro and micro theories and between theoretical and empirical research need to be overcome, and that conventional understandings of what constitutes 'the political' need to be enlarged. These perspectives inform the book, and the chapters both link macro-level conceptualisations of policies to their micro-level impact on people's lives and explore the ways in which understandings and experiences of social justice are inextricably bound up with language and how words become associated with particular meanings – which may in turn act to exclude alternative visions. Beyond this, each chapter is effectively free-standing; there is no one unifying narrative or editorial 'party line' and the contributions differ in terms of the level of approval or criticism of New Labour policies. While readers can therefore choose to dip in to selected chapters, those who read the full book will find that there are some recurrent themes, and that the whole is more than the sum of its parts.

The first two sections of this editorial 'Introduction' outline the historical background to New Labour for readers unfamiliar with this and identify some key aspects of New Labour's language and ideology. The third section provides an overview of the chapters. Our overall findings are in a final chapter; this also considers how the concept of social justice might develop after New Labour.

The Labour Party – old and new

From its origins, the Labour Party has always been a coalition of groups, with a range of visions and interests jostling for priority. For much of the twentieth century, it was also clearly the party of the working class and the trade union movement, committed to ending poverty and the exploitation of the many by the few and to using state power to achieve this. From 1918 until the dawn of the New Labour era in the mid-1990s this vision of social justice was symbolised by Clause Four of the party constitution, which promised:

> To secure for the workers by hand or by brain the full fruits of their industry and the most equitable distribution thereof that may be possible upon the basis of the common ownership of the means of production, distribution and exchange, and the best obtainable system of popular administration and control of each industry or service.

After the Second World War, the 1945–51 Labour government went some way towards delivering this, with the introduction of the National Health Service (NHS) and a programme of nationalisation that included the railways and the coal, steel, gas, electricity and telecommunications industries. By the late 1950s, however, ideas of public ownership began to seem both old-fashioned and electorally unpopular in an era of unprecedented prosperity in which the Conservative Prime Minister, Harold Macmillan, could plausibly claim that most people had 'never had it so good'. Although Hugh Gaitskill, then party leader, failed in his attempt to amend Clause Four in the aftermath of the party's second successive election defeat in 1959, internal debates about the party's direction continued, and from the late 1970s there were a series of major battles between left and right for control of the party under the successive leaderships of James Callaghan, Michael Foot, Neil Kinnock and John Smith. By the time that Tony Blair became leader in 1994 these battles had been largely won by the party 'modernisers', although it was left to Blair in 1995 to replace Clause Four's commitment to common ownership with the statement that:

> The Labour Party is a democratic socialist party. It believes that by the strength of our common endeavour we achieve more than we achieve alone, so as to create for each of us the means to realise our true potential and for all of us a community in which power, wealth and opportunity are in the hands of the many, not the few.

By the mid-1990s major social, economic, political and cultural changes had eroded the Labour Party's 'natural' bases of electoral support and seemed to make its earlier vision of social justice outdated. A steep rise in living standards had removed the squalid mass poverty of the early twentieth century and meant that even the poorest groups were relatively well off, while the shift from manufacturing to the service sector meant that the size of the industrial working class had shrunk dramatically. Well under a third of the population described themselves as working-class (Dolowitz, 2007), and trade union membership had fallen from a peak of 50 per cent of all workers in the late 1970s to around 30 per cent (Lindsay, 2003). In this context, Labour's traditional language of class and redistribution had little resonance, and seemed to offer no scope for countering the neo-liberal thinking that dominated political debate from the Conservative election victory in 1979.

This thinking meant that Thatcher's successful curbing of union power in the 1980s was widely seen as a necessary restraint on an overpowerful sector rather than an assault on the rights of ordinary citizens. More generally, the post-war consensus that had accepted both the mixed economy and the responsibility of governments to promote social welfare was rejected in favour of a stress on free markets and individual freedom that favoured low taxation, tight restrictions on public spending and the privatisation of nationalised industries. This in turn was based on a belief in the virtues of competition and individual responsibility that refused to blame 'society' for social problems – an approach encapsulated in Thatcher's now infamous statement that 'There's no such thing as society. There are individual men and women and there are families.' From this perspective, state intervention to tackle inequality was both undesirable and economically harmful (Walker, 1997), while poverty was generally linked to individual moral failure by the 'undeserving poor', rather than to economic restructuring or recession (Smart, 1996: 303). This thinking drew heavily on the ideas of the influential neo-liberal thinker F. A. Hayek, who condemned governmental attempts to pursue social justice as an assault on individual liberty; the increasingly widespread acceptance of such neo-liberal assumptions meant that many came to agree with his view that Labour was a redundant force that would never rule again (see Gray, 2004).

Despite the apparent strength of its ideological position, by the late 1980s the Conservative Party was experiencing a number of political difficulties and divisions that resulted in the replacement of Thatcher by John Major in 1990, and that appeared to present the Labour Party with a new chance of electoral success. Meanwhile Neil Kinnock, party leader from 1983 to 1992, had secured a series of reforms, including the expulsion of the 'Militant Tendency', a weakening of the party's traditional commitment to redistributive taxation and an acceptance of privatisation, which many believed would accommodate the Labour Party to changed conditions. Nevertheless, in 1992 Major was able to brand Labour as a profligate 'tax and spend' party in thrall to trade unions and militant extremists, and he won the election, albeit with a much reduced majority.

The Commission on Social Justice

This fourth consecutive election defeat suggested to many in the Labour Party that success required more drastic modernisation and a thoroughgoing reassessment of its key principles in the light of new socio-economic and political realities. Here, the Commission on Social Justice, set up by John Smith, Kinnock's successor as party leader in 1992, placed a reformulated vision of social justice at the heart of the strategic thinking that such modernisation required (for discussion see Driver and Martell, 2003, and Chapter 2 in this volume). The Commission's remit included considering the principles of social justice and their relationship with other economic and social goals and policies. It identified these principles as:

> the equal worth of all citizens, their equal right to be able to meet their basic needs, the need to spread opportunities and life chances as widely as possible, and finally the requirement that we reduce and where possible eliminate unjustified inequalities. (Commission on Social Justice, 1994:1)

Although not necessarily incompatible, this language owed little to traditional Labour Party discourse, while the Commission's report suggested that, far from being inimical to the neo-liberal values of economic efficiency, competitiveness and growth, social justice was actually a prerequisite for their effective realisation: 'There will be no solid economic success without more social justice' (Commission on Social Justice, 1994: 18). From this perspective, the way forward did not primarily lie with either an unregulated market economy or a redistributive tax and benefits system; rather, it required an investment in welfare to promote the skills and opportunities that would enable individuals to manage their own lives and compete in an increasingly globalised economy. As Driver and Martell (2003) point out, this approach sees social justice primarily in instrumental terms, as a means to economic goals rather than as a good in itself; this in turn implies that justice might be sacrificed if, in changed circumstances, it appeared to conflict with these goals (see also Burchardt and Craig, 2008). The language of the Commission also represented a decisive shift away from the idea that inequalities are an unjust product of class society and towards the New Labour idea that individuals should be given opportunities and responsibilities within such a society.

New Labour, new ideology?

These pre-existing changes in party thinking helped prepare the ground for the more overt and conscious 'rebranding' of the party that occurred once Blair became party leader in 1994, after the unexpected death of John Smith. Aimed squarely at the voters of 'middle England', this rebranding included the removal of Clause Four (discussed above), which constituted the lynchpin in a strategy of 'modernisation'. It was also epitomised by the adoption of the label 'New Labour', first used at the 1994 party conference, to signal a new beginning and a decisive break with the policies and attitudes of the past. As Chadwick and Heffernan (2003: 13) note, 'The very term "New Labour" is therefore a brand, and a key signifier of a reformed political party.'

While political differences have always partly involved struggles over the dominant language, the 'mediatisation' of politics and of government has resulted in an increasingly central role for language and discourse. The power of the media was enthusiastically embraced by New Labour's founders, and a close-knit group around Blair and Brown, including key players Peter Mandelson and Alistair Campbell, adopted a deliberate strategy for managing the presentation of their policies that owed much to business models, including promotional techniques.

As Norman Fairclough argues in *New Labour, New Language* (2000), this was the first time that a UK party treated the presentation of policies as part of the policy-making process. Fairclough also draws on Foucauldian analysis to suggest that, although this strategy of control from the centre may be regarded in one sense as inconsistent with New Labour's proclaimed policy direction of devolving power, its preoccupation with language enabled power to be ostensibly dispersed to diverse agents of government whilst maintaining control through discourse. While this point may be open to debate, it is nevertheless clear that the architects of New Labour deliberately used language to package their policies, and that a number of key linked terms gained ascendancy: of these, 'stakeholder', 'community', 'empowerment', 'choice', responsibility', 'enterprise', 'social inclusion', 'social exclusion' and 'hard-working families' are particularly important.

The new discourse supported a reconceptualisation of social justice that enabled New Labour to distinguish itself from both the harsher aspects of Conservatism and what it portrayed as out-dated 'old Labour' ideas. This 'third way' built on the Commission on Social Justice's finding that the successful pursuit of social justice requires economic efficiency, competitiveness and growth, and that individuals must be provided with the opportunity to fulfil their potential. However, when Blair identified the 'four values essential to a just society', he replaced the Commission's commitment to meeting basic needs and its critique of 'unjustifiable inequalities' with the values of 'responsibility' and 'community' (1998: 3). Although Brown tended to go less far in distancing himself from 'old Labour' ideas of equality, he too explicitly rejected what he described as 'an unrealizable equality of outcome' (2003: 135), and both leaders appeared, in the words of Mandelson (1998), to be 'intensely relaxed about people getting filthy rich'. Although Mandelson added the coda 'as long as they pay their taxes', this did not mean that the tax system should be used to promote equal outcomes; rather, New Labour argued that the prosperity gained through individual enterprise would 'trickle down' to benefit everybody, so that the interests of the individual and the wider society were the same.

In the context of this version of social justice the notion of 'stakeholding' connotes an equal concern with both the individual and the 'community'. 'Stakeholder' suggests the type of citizen who does not solely maximise short-term profits, but instead balances his or her own interests with the well-being of society as a whole, and who is a member of a community rather than an isolated individual. Such a citizen is also a 'consumer' of public services, and New Labour promised to 'empower' both the users and providers of these services by increasing 'choice' and devolving responsibilities to local levels. At the same time, individuals were also to be empowered through improved educational and training opportunities that would improve their chances in the employment market, and by welfare reforms that would combat a culture of dependence on state benefits. This meant that, while the state had an important role to play in providing the necessary conditions for success, citizens had a responsibility to embrace these opportunities, along with the responsibility to look after their own and their children's health and well-being. Welfare reforms were thereby bound up with a contractual notion of citizenship that linked rights to responsibilities, and saw paid work as both the primary responsibility of citizens and the key to ending social exclusion. Although New Labour remained committed to ending poverty, particularly child poverty, it was unconcerned with overall levels of inequality and the structural impediments to social mobility, and it rejected the idea that capitalist conditions of employment were inherently exploitative; rather, it celebrated enterprise and success, and was committed to rewarding 'hard-working families' by 'making work pay'. In thus emphasising equality of opportunity within a system of unequal rewards 'The revision to the notion of equality provided one of the most powerful rhetorical articulations of a break with the past' (Buckler and Dolowitz, 2009: 23).

Although New Labour's language was deliberately different from that of 'old Labour', Blair and Brown claimed to carry forward earlier 'moderate' strands of Labour Party thinking. Thus Blair's claim that 'The ethical basis of socialism is the only one that has stood the test of time (cited in Bevir, 2000: 277) drew on R. H. Tawney's vision of 'ethical socialism', and Brown (2003: 134) explicitly linked New Labour's version of equal opportunities to that of Antony Crosland (see Buckler and Dolowitz, 2000, 2009; Meredith, 2006). Such stress on continuity as well as change was intended to appeal to the party's traditional supporters, but conveniently downplayed the substantive break with Tawney's commitment to equality of outcomes (see Evans, 2002) and Crosland's radical views on education and the need for strong public services and redistributive taxation, not to mention his support for Clause Four.

New Labour also sought intellectual credibility from a number of contemporary writers, of whom the most important is probably Antony Giddens (1998), who argued that massive global social, scientific and economic changes had undermined the foundations of both neo-liberal and social democratic thought. This, he said, made it both possible and imperative to develop a 'third way' forward that would recast the relationship between the individual and the community by combining social democracy's commitment to social justice with insistence that rights are not unconditional, but must be bound up with responsibilities. These ideas in turn depended on a philosophical position that Giddens had set out in *Beyond Left and Right* (1994), in which he argued for a 'positive welfare' directed at fostering the 'autotelic self' (Giddens, 1994: 192): that is, 'a person able to translate potential threats into reward challenges', thereby achieving 'self-actualisation'. Since self-actualisation is a process leading to self-fulfilment, it leads to the transcendence of egotism and selfishness. The pursuit of the individual interests is therefore associated with benefits for society as a whole; self-actualised individuals will not be tempted to exploit others. The influence of these ideas was clear in Blair's vision of a just society in which 'the collective power of all [is] used for the individual good of each [so] that the individual's interest can be advanced' (Blair, 1994: 4), and Giddens's insistence on the priority to be placed on individual self-actualisation underpinned the primacy of opportunity and choice within New Labour policy. Here again, however, the architects of New Labour went further than the thinker whose ideas they claimed to use. Giddens himself has said that he would have liked New Labour to provide a more coherent defence of public institutions and public goods based on the understanding that 'A citizen is not a consumer writ large' (2008: xv), and he has expressed concern about the growth of extreme wealth and argued for a wealth tax.

Academic commentators disagree as to whether New Labour represented a new and distinctive ideology and the extent to which its ideas are internally consistent or the haphazard product of an approach based on 'pragmatism and populism' (Powell, 2000: 39) Commentators also disagree strongly in their assessment of the resulting policies, with verdicts ranging from Buckler and Dolowitz's claim that New Labour 'articulated a vision that was socially progressive, emphasizing distributive justice and reform, whilst retaining an emphasis upon individual autonomy, responsibility and self-development' (2009: 18) to Wissenburg's conclusion that 'it seems that as far as social justice is concerned, the "third way" has replaced the best part of socialism, distributive justice, by the worst part of liberalism, the survival of the fittest' (2001: 235).[1] While the chapters summarised below touch on these questions, providing a definitive account and assessment of the ideas of New Labour is beyond the scope of this book. Instead, the chapters pull New Labour's rhetoric down to earth by considering the ways that ideas translate into policy developments and outcomes and the practical effects that these can have on people's lives.

The chapters

Chapter 2, by Tim Heppell, sets the scene for later chapters. Addressing issues of social justice as these are understood within the conventional parameters of political science, it seeks to assess New Labour in its own terms. In so doing, he also opens up a major theme that is developed from other perspectives in later chapters: New Labour's promise to deliver both economic efficiency and social justice, which it discursively constructs as complementary rather than opposing goals. Heppell argues that this new discourse reflected a process of 'ideological renewal' that was driven by pragmatic considerations of electoral advantage, particularly the attempt to secure a secure electoral base in 'middle England', whose voters had consistently rejected 'old Labour' values and who were attracted by the Thatcherite language of low taxation, individual advantage, efficiency and competition, but who no longer saw the Conservatives as economically competent or shared their apparent obsession with the free market. In this context, Heppell shows how the architects of New Labour reached an accommodation with Thatcherism while also promising a fairer, more inclusive society that would create opportunities and mitigate the harsher effects of the market economy by tackling poverty, unemployment and social exclusion. While this strategy seemed successful in that the party won three consecutive elections, Heppell finds only limited success in terms of social justice, and he details the extent of continuing poverty and income inequality, which according to some measures rose under New Labour governments. He considers whether the electorally favourable climate of 1997 could have enabled the party to pursue a more radically redistributive agenda and to articulate alternative values rather than capitulating to the key tenets of Thatcherism. Although he argues that such speculation can have no factual basis, Heppell shows the problems with an electoral strategy that depended on both New Labour's apparent economic competence and its apparent commitment to social justice, while the party's leaders were willing to make 'sacrifices . . . in terms of social justice at the altar of economic efficiency'. The result was that when the economy went into crisis, New Labour's failure to deliver more substantive social justice left it with little electoral appeal.

Chapters 3–5 specifically address issues around the language and discourse of New Labour, albeit in very different ways. While discussions about political language by social scientists are usually impressionistic, Lesley Jeffries' chapter employs the tools of linguistic analysis to provide a forensic examination of the use of two key political terms – *radicalisation* and *democracy* – in five major national newspapers in

1998 and 2007. Analysing their grammatical use and emergent semantic properties, Jeffries shows that there has been a clear and measurable
shift over the period. Whereas *radicalisation* had some politically positive connotations in 1998, by 2007 its meaning had become entirely
negative and equated with Muslim fundamentalism, extremism and
often violence. In contrast, *democracy* has become increasingly used as
a general 'absolute good', whereas in 1998 it had tended to be modified, so that different kinds of democracy could be examined and compared. Jeffries concludes that because the available language constructs
as well as reflects political reality, this narrowing of political vocabulary
is likely to 'limit our ability to think critically about political events,
institutions and processes'.

While Jeffries does not see these changes as the result of conscious
political decisions, Paul Thomas's chapter focuses on a clearly deliberate shift in recent political language in the field of race relations: that
from 'multiculturalism' to 'community cohesion' in the aftermath of the
violent disturbances that occurred in a number of towns and cities in
northern England in 2001. He shows that this new language is in line
with New Labour's model of social justice, with its stress on individual
responsibility and agency, but argues that it also continues to reflect
the Labour Party's earlier commitment to diversity and racial equality.
Thomas challenges mainstream political rhetoric by drawing on interviews conducted with community youth workers in Oldham. Despite
the observed discursive shift away from earlier concerns with multiculturalism, Thomas argues that experience 'on the ground' still remains
broadly supportive of diversity whilst also bringing about significant
changes in community-level practices. He also finds that these new
practices have had a positive impact on race relations, and that they go
some way in making New Labour's commitment to inclusive citizenship
a reality.

Chapter 5, by James Avis, explicitly challenges the political discourse
of New Labour in relation to post-compulsory education and training
and, in contrast to Thomas's positive assessment, it is highly critical of
the impact of its policies. Avis employs a Marxist perspective to argue
that New Labour's rhetorical focus on opportunity, choice, inclusion
and individual agency obscures the enduring realities of structural
class-based inequalities and blames the poor for their own situation.
Avis argues that the promise of lifelong learning and personalised
learning treats education as a means of promoting individual and
national economic competitiveness, leaving little space for the view
that education and an educated citizenry are intrinsically valuable elements of a just society; rather, justice is identified with the opportunity

to compete and attain economic independence and prosperity, and the responsibility of citizens is to acquire the knowledge and skills that the market requires. From this dominant perspective, middle-class values are taken as the norm, and class is treated as 'a residual and dysfunctional phenomenon', with the critique of class reduced to complaints about privileged groups who have not achieved their position through merit and, more frequently, the condemnation of the culture of the socially excluded. Meanwhile, as Avis shows, inequalities of wealth and income remain acute and the impact of class background on educational achievement and life chances is clear, with the drive to 'personalised' learning strengthening the academic/vocational divide, and its concomitant class divisions. Avis calls for PCET research that addresses these issues and links educational practices to the wider social structures that they both reflect and reproduce; he concludes that, contrary to classical Marxist approaches, a more nuanced understanding of the perpetuation of class inequalities requires attention to the micro-exchanges and interactions in classrooms and in educational institutions and how these articulate with the macro- concerns of structural inequalities and policy.

Chapters 6–8 consider how policy shapes and informs micro-level practices and discourses in relation to various aspects of health and welfare provision. In Chapter 6, Valerie Bryson and Ruth Deery assess the rhetorical justifications for public-sector reforms against their impact in practice, focusing in particular on the National Health Service and the experiences of midwives. They find a clash within New Labour's model of social justice because this promises to support working women by providing more 'family-friendly' conditions of employment at the same time as increasing the role of market forces and stressing the importance of accountability, value for money and consumer choice in the provision of public services. Bryson and Deery argue that this clash is fundamentally about *time*: not only about the pressure on this scarce resource and its distribution between women and men, but also about the kind of time that interpersonal care and human relationships require. Here Bryson and Deery show that a focus on competition, auditing and cost effectiveness has diverted time from front-line service provision and reinforced a particular 'temporal logic' that is hostile to the provision of good-quality care, which often requires attention to 'natural' and unpredictable physical and emotional rhythms and needs that cannot appropriately be speeded up or subjected to considerations of time management. The chapter draws on two case studies of midwives to illustrate the negative effects of some recent changes, showing that 'empowerment' has meant the devolution of accountability rather than control, while stressed midwives lack the time to develop the personalised service that pregnant women have been promised. Bryson and Deery call for a redistribution of public and private time and rewards, and argue that a more inclusive model of social justice would recognise both the value of time spent caring for others and the distinct temporality that such work often requires.

Bryson and Deery's suggestion that there are tensions between New Labour's acceptance of the market economy and its promise of social justice is developed further in Chapter 7, in which Anne Chappell and Christopher Gifford also explore the power of discourse to influence policy making. Here they examine New Labour policies on disability issues to show that these have drawn both on conflicting models of disability (primarily the social versus the medical/individual model) and on conflicting models of citizenship (solidaristic versus contractarian). This has meant that disabled people have sometimes been discursively constructed as rights-bearing citizens entitled to redress against socially produced exclusion and disadvantage, and sometimes as defective individuals who should be enabled or compelled to adapt and contribute to mainstream society. Chappell and Gifford argue that New Labour's predominantly contractarian model of citizenship and justice, in which benefits are tied to responsibilities (most often participation in the labour market and 'acceptable' social behaviour), has had negative consequences for disabled people, particularly in relation to their obligation to work and the disciplining of those with mental health problems. However, they also find that other policies are framed by a more solidaristic agenda, in which the views of service users inform the development of provision and disabled people are given more control over their own lives. They argue that New Labour's failure to understand the different ways of conceptualising disability has produced inconsistent policies, providing 'a mixture of opportunity alongside continued injustices'; this in turn implies that the pursuit of more just policies requires strict attention to the discourses that frame them.

The 'rights and responsibilities' discourse based on participation in the labour force is also critiqued by Pamela Fisher (Chapter 8). Fisher argues against New Labour policy discourse within health and social care practice that tends to be based on the assumption that empowerment is uniquely bound up with economic independence and participation in the labour market. Fisher shows how policy interpretations of empowerment are articulated at the micro-level, often implicitly, in the health and social care provision for families with disabled children. The result, she argues, is that empowerment and well-being have become discursively restricted in ways that close down the potential for alternative interpretations. Drawing on the narratives of parents of disabled children, Fisher challenges the dominant view that 'empowerment' is located uniquely in the public sphere, arguing instead for the validity and importance of alternative forms of empowerment, particularly ones that recognise that individual empowerment is often embedded within relationships of interdependence. In contrast to a contractarian form of citizenship, associated with New Labour's 'rights and responsibilities' agenda, Fisher proposes that there should be a greater appreciation of diversity and that this should be central to considerations of social justice. With reference to recent work on the politics of recognition, which she links with an ethics of care, Fisher argues for greater recognition of diverse forms of empowerment, explaining, however, that these are not likely to emerge until they are also recognised and validated in the public sphere. She concludes that issues of recognition are key to social justice, as they support or impede the development of authentic forms of empowerment, patterns of respect and disrespect, and the material distribution of resources.

Criticism of the worker-citizen model of social justice recurs in Chapter 9, by Catherine McGlynn and James McAuley, which assesses New Labour's record in Northern Ireland. Securing an end to major conflict was of course an impressive achievement. However, McGlynn and McAuley argue that peace is no guarantee of social justice in itself, and that Northern Ireland has not progressed as Tony Blair and his Ministers intended. They attribute this partly to the consociational model of citizenship that was adopted in the province, whereby the interests of competing religious groups were brought forward by their leaders, and political co-operation at elite level compensated for divisions in civil society; they argue that, while this may have made progress possible, it also institutionalised existing divisions and left little scope for more informal community-level possibilities of reconciliation. More significantly for the focus of this book, McGlynn and McAuley argue that New Labour's approach has been restricted by an overly narrow conception of social justice that equates it with economic prosperity and focuses on employment as the key to social inclusion, rather than exploring the damaging effects of deep economic inequalities, bad housing and social insecurity, or the potentially inclusive role of community participation. They show that, even before the recession, the 'peace dividend' frequently produced low-quality jobs that increased the ranks of the working poor rather than ending poverty, and they argue that, although there is clearly no simple causal connection, inequality and poverty have 'played a part in the persistence of low-level spontaneous violence'. McGlynn and McAuley conclude that peace and social justice in Northern Ireland require an expanded vision of citizenship that goes beyond the workplace to recognise the value of grass-roots community activism, and that politicians must address 'structural inequalities in partnership with the communities they serve if differences are to be genuinely transcended'.

As Chapter 5 made clear, deep-seated socio-economic inequality is not confined to Northern Ireland, and class continues to structure educational and employment opportunities throughout the UK. It also structures access to legal justice, and in Chapter 10 Peter Sanderson and Hilary Sommerlad argue that this creates particular problems for people who are poor or socially excluded, who are more likely to be in trouble with the law, come into contact with state agencies or need legal protection against exploitative landlords or employers, but who are less likely to possess relevant skills or resources. In this context, Sanderson and Sommerlad argue that legal aid should be a keystone of citizenship and social justice, providing some counter to the ability of powerful groups to use the law for their own ends. New Labour's rhetorical commitment to social justice and to end social exclusion suggested that it would improve the legal aid service, which had been attenuated by previous Conservative governments. However, although Sanderson and Sommerlad welcome some of its reforms, they find that these were contradicted by New Labour's commitment to public service reform and the endorsement of neo-liberal principles that this entailed. Echoing some of the concerns expressed in Chapter 6, they report on the damaging effect of cost control and an audit culture in which intangible goals, including justice itself, are sacrificed for more measurable targets, while the dominant discourse identifies expenditure on legal aid as a problem created by 'fat cat' lawyers and irresponsible litigants rather than a right of all citizens. The result, they argue, is a residual, inadequate and stigmatised service, and they conclude by noting the irony that 'as the dominance of the neo-liberal paradigm is challenged by its manifest failure in the economic sphere, its legacy should be in part the erosion of the last legal resort of the predictable victims of that failure.'.

In the concluding chapter the editors bring the chapters together by pulling out the book's key findings in relation to five interconnected and recurrent themes: citizen-workers; stigmatisation and the construction of 'deficiency'; the delegitimisation of the private sphere; consumer choice and personalisation; and surveillance and empowerment. Their discussion shows how each of these areas articulates with and was shaped by a particular understanding of social justice that was constructed through New Labour rhetoric and policy and that was in many ways profoundly limited. However, while the New Labour understanding of social justice became hegemonic, more radical analyses continued to be developed. The book concludes with a brief survey of these alternative visions, which the editors find are in tune with many of the ideas and micro-level experiences expressed and described in the chapters.

Note

1 For a range of competing interpretations see Beech (2008), Beech and Lee (2008), Bevir (2000), Buckler (2000), Buckler and Dolowitz (2000, 2009), Chadwick and Heffernan (2003), Dolowitz (2007), Driver (2008), Finlayson (2009), Kenny (2007), Wissenburg (2001).

Bibliography

Beech, M. (2008) 'New Labour and the politics of dominance', in M. Beech and S. Lee (eds) *Ten Years of New Labour* (Basingstoke: Palgrave Macmillan).

Beech, M. and Lee, S. (eds) (2008) *Ten Years of New Labour* (Basingstoke: Palgrave Macmillan).

Bevir, M. (2000) 'New Labour: a study in ideology', *British Journal of Politics and International Relations* 2:3, 277–301.

Blair, T. (1994) *Socialism*, Fabian Tract 565, London: Fabian Society.

Blair, T. (1998) *The Third Way* (London: Fabian Society).

Brown, G. (2003) 'Equality – then and now', in A. Chadwick and R. Heffernan (eds) *The New Labour Reader* (Cambridge: Polity Press).

Buckler, S. (2000) 'Theorizing the third way: New Labour and social justice', *Journal of Political Ideologies* 5:3, 301–20.

Buckler, S. and Dolowitz, D. (2000) 'Theorizing the third way: New Labour and social justice', *Journal of Political Ideologies* 5:3, 301–20.

Buckler, S. and Dolowitz, D. (2009) 'Ideology, party identity and renewal', *Journal of Political Ideologies* 14:1, 11–30.

Burchardt, T. and Craig, G. (2008) 'Introduction', in G. Craig, T. Burchardt and D. Gordon (eds) *Social Justice and Public Policy* (Bristol: Policy Press).

Chadwick, A. and Heffernan, R. (2003) 'Introduction. The New Labour phenomenon', in A. Chadwick and R. Heffernan (eds) *The New Labour Reader* (Cambridge: Polity Press).

Commission on Social Justice (1994) *Socal Justice. Strategies for National Renewal* (London: Vintage).

Dolowitz, D. (2007) 'New Labour: the phoenix has risen', *Contemporary Politics* 13:2, 139–46.

Driver, S. (2008) 'New Labour and social policy', in M. Beech and S. Lee (eds) *Ten Years of New Labour* (Basingstoke: Palgrave).

Driver, S. and Martell, L. (2003) 'New Labour: politics after Thatcherism', in

A. Chadwick and R. Heffernan (eds) *The New Labour Reader* (Cambridge: Polity Press).

Evans, B. (2002) 'The third way', in G. Blakeley and V. Bryson (eds) *Contemporary Political Concepts: a Critical Introduction* (London: Pluto Press).

Fairclough, N. (2000) *New Labour, New Language* (London: Routledge).

Finlayson, A. (2009) 'Financialisation, financial literacy and asset-based welfare', *British Journal of Politics and International Relations* 11, 400–21.

Giddens, A. (1994) *Beyond Left and Right* (Cambridge: Polity Press).

Giddens, A. (1998) *The Third Way: The Renewal of Social* Democracy (Cambridge: Polity Press).

Giddens, A. (2008) 'Foreword' to M. Beech and S. Lee (eds) *Ten Years of New Labour* (Basingstoke: Palgrave Macmillan).

Gray, J. (2004) 'Blair's project in retrospect', *International Affairs* 80:1, 39–48.

Kenny, C. (2007) 'Does New Labour have a consistent conception of social justice?', *Politics* 27:1, 32–9.

Labour Party Manifesto 1997, http://labour-party.org.uk/manifestos/1997/1997–labour-manifesto.shtml (accessed 7 July 2009).

Lindsay, C. (2003) 'A century of labour market change, 1900 to 2000', *Labour Market Trends* March: 133–44.

Meredith, S. (2006) 'Mr Crosland's nightmare? New Labour and equality in historical perspective', *British Journal of Politics and International Relations* 8:2, 238–55.

Powell, M. (2000) 'New Labour and the third way in the British welfare state: a new and distinctive approach?' *Critical Social Policy* 20, 39–60.

Smart, C. (1996) 'Deconstructing motherhood', in E. B. Silva (ed.) *Good Enough Mothering? Feminist Perspectives on Lone Motherhood* (London: Routledge).

Walker, A. (1997) 'Introduction. The strategy of inequality', in A. Walker and C. Walker (eds) *Britain Divided: the Growth of Social Exclusion in the 1980s and 1990s* (London: Child Poverty Action Group).

Wissenburg, M. (2001) 'The "third way" and social justice', *Journal of Political Ideologies* 6:2, 231–35.

2

New Labour, social justice and electoral strategy

Tim Heppell

In their pursuit of the 'third way', New Labour under Tony Blair claimed to have combined acceptance of the market *with* the notion of an active and enabling state. What was intriguing about the third way was the manner in which it sought to move beyond the old politics of state intervention from the old left and the *laissez-faire* mentality of the new right, and claim that traditional 'opposites' could be combined into a coherent discourse (McAnulla, 2006: 138). Thus as Blair talked of 'ambition *and* compassion', 'enterprise *and* fairness' and 'rights *and* responsibilities' so New Labour placed potentially competing concepts together and claimed to have 'transcended the old ideological debates' and 'created a new electoral base and policy programme for the left' (Gamble, 2006: 300). At the heart of their new politics was the pursuit of economic efficiency *and* social justice (McAnulla, 2006: 138). As Gamble observes:

> The government adopted a social justice agenda centred around the establishment of a minimum wage, tax credits and other measures to tackle pensioner poverty and child poverty . . . This social justice agenda was combined with an emphasis on a vigorous supply side economic strategy, involving competition, promotion of the knowledge economy and entrepreneurship. (Gamble, 2006: 301)

This process of ideological renewal was a significant development which sought to challenge perceptions of the Labour Party. When referring to the notion of ideological renewal, it is important to recognise that political parties possess an 'ideological identity' tied to their history and reflecting their most deeply held beliefs (Buckler and Dolowitz, 2009: 13). The identity of the Labour Party, whether defined as old left, new left or old right, was historically framed by a social justice ideology (Hickson, 2004: 125). This had been underpinned by a statist view that social equality and wealth redistribution could be achieved through increased welfare spending, financed by progressive taxation and sustained economic expansion through Keynesian demand management (Bevir, 2005: 63). However, the modernising elites of New Labour challenged the methods that had underpinned this historical objective, arguing that adherence to such a model of social justice was no longer electorally or governmentally tenable. Ideological adaptation was deemed to be a necessary precursor to electoral success, a process which would demand that 'New' Labour dissociate themselves from the perceived negative images and policies of 'old' Labour (Buckler and Dolowitz, 2009: 11).

The New Labour project amounted to a process of ideological renewal aimed at voter mobilisation. Between 1994 and 2007 the advocates of New Labour dismissed the critiques of the increasingly marginalised left by arguing that their politics had been the 'politics of dominance' (Beech, 2008: 1). Until the onset of the economic crisis of late 2007 onwards they could argue that as an electoral strategy New Labour had been a success. Three successive election victories had been achieved, two of which justified the term landslide, and up to early 2008 Labour could claim to have usurped the Conservatives as the party of economic competence (Beech, 2008: 2–3; Lee, 2008: 189). However, as New Labour started to show the classic symptoms of governing degeneration that tend to characterise long-term administrations,[1] so the bases of New Labour's electoral and governing strategy have been questioned (Heppell, 2008: 578, 589).

This chapter examines the electoral strategy of New Labour within the context of their proclaimed pursuit of social justice. The chapter will consider three key issues. First, it will offer an appraisal of the processes of ideological renewal that culminated in New Labour and will highlight the modernisers' electoral justification for such adaptation. Second, it will provide an overview of the impact of New Labour in office and the implications of their modified model of social justice. Finally, whilst acknowledging that New Labour made some progress in terms of social justice relative to the Thatcherite inheritance, the chapter will consider the critique emanating from the left of the party. It will consider the leftist argument that the benign economic environment that appeared to persist until 2007, combined with the overwhelming parliamentary dominance of their first two terms, provided New Labour with a unique and time-specific opportunity to pursue a more radical vision of social justice.

Ideological renewal and the electoral justification for 'New' Labour

In April 1992, despite the fact that they were opposing a long-serving Conservative administration seeking re-election in the midst of an economic recession, the Labour Party under Neil Kinnock suffered a fourth successive election defeat (Shaw, 2007: 153). Those of a modernising bent saw their analysis somewhat stalled by the consolidating mentality of the new party leader, John Smith (1992–94), but it was clear what their analysis amounted to. There were a series of negative perceptions which continued to undermine the electoral appeal of the Labour Party to the middle class: they were dominated by the trade unions; they represented only the interests of the poor; Labour governments were historically incompetent; Labour in office would increase income tax; and the instincts of Labour were seen as impediments to personal ambition such that Labour was betraying the aspirations of the communities they were purporting to represent (Heath *et al.*, 2001: 101; Buckler and Dolowitz, 2009: 17).

The modernisers' concern that Labour lacked appeal to the middle class was central to their diagnosis. They argued that society was now more individualistic and middle-class as a consequence of Thatcherism, and that Labour had to break down the perception that the party was associated with holding people back or with levelling down. Such an interpretation reflected a sociological analysis of the 'new strategic paradigm' (Shaw, 1994: 59–62, 2007: 154). Central to the modernisers' analysis was a need to respond to the fact that the working class was declining as a percentage of the electorate, whilst the middle classes were expanding. Labour needed, therefore, to recognise that the era of class-driven political cleavages shaping electoral behaviour had ended. Class-configured partisan loyalties had been eroded and Labour needed to find a response to 'issue'-based voting (Mulgan, 2005: 94–5; Shaw, 2007: 153–4). Shaw argues that the courting of 'middle England' was as significant to New Labour's electoral strategy as the concept of 'old Labour' (Shaw, 2007: 155). Middle England was consumer-oriented and individualistically minded, and according to chief New Labour strategist Philip Gould was comprised of people who 'wanted higher-quality public services' but 'were strongly averse to shouldering more tax burdens' (Shaw, 2007: 155). Those defined as of middle England were actively recruited to participate in focus groups that would inform New Labour thinking. Critically, those utilised in focus group activity by New Labour were predominantly Conservative voters from 1992 who had contemplated endorsing Labour then but failed to do so and still voted Conservative. Those who then switched to New Labour in 1997 were the type of voter that New Labour were determined to retain and whose opinions they constantly sought to acquire/assuage once in office (Shaw, 2007: 155–6).

The ideological break with the past

Hay has argued that through this emphasis on courting the views of middle England New Labour set about reaching an accommodation with Thatcherism in key areas of economic policy, social policy, privatisation and trade union reform (Hay, 1997: 372–9; Hay, 1999: 77–103). Moreover, to facilitate this and to demonstrate that New Labour could create a New Britain, Blair set about proving that Labour was new. Modernisers felt that Clause IV of the Labour Party constitution, which committed them to public ownership, was a symbol of old Labour. Its continued existence was anachronistic (as Labour would not renationalise if returned to office), and it provided electoral utility for the Conservatives. It enabled the Conservatives to infer that taxation would have to rise under Labour (to finance renationalistion), and that it indicated Labour's misunderstanding of the global economy and the role of markets. Clause IV was successfully challenged and reformed by Blair. He had succeeded where Hugh Gaitskell had failed a generation earlier, and by 1995 Labour had broken with their past. New Labour possessed a new clause, which asserted their belief in a dynamic economy, the enterprise of the market and the rigour of competition (Cronin, 2004: 383–7).

Another aspect of this strategic repositioning on behalf of New Labour modernisers was their interpretation of the impact of tax as an electoral variable in the 1992 general election. New Labour strategists were convinced that the Conservatives' negative advertising campaign, following the 'shadow' Budget that John Smith[2] had presented, had been pivotal to their electoral defeat. New Labour were determined that the Conservatives would not be able to utilise the 'tax and spend' imagery for electoral gain again (Heath *et al.*, 2001: 44). Keegan observes that as Shadow Chancellor, and later as Chancellor, Gordon Brown was 'terrorised by fear of doing anything to offend middle England', who New Labour strategists felt had recoiled from Labour's 1992 shadow Budget, which the Conservatives had used to dominate the 1992 general election agenda through allegations of a 'tax bombshell' and Labour's 'double whammy' of more taxes and higher prices (Keegan, 2003: 11).

Perceptions of their vulnerability to the 'tax and spend' allegation would explain why in January 1997 Brown announced that, if elected, New Labour would adhere to the spending plans outlined by the Conservative Chancellor Kenneth Clarke for the next two years. As previous Labour administrations were deemed to have been economically incompetent, modernisers believed that stating that they were committed to the spending plans already outlined by the incumbent

Conservative administration would demonstrate their 'realism', as compared with the 'idealism/profligacy' of old Labour administrations. Through such 'prudence' they could shape electoral perceptions of them as economically (and thereby governmentally) competent. This announcement, coupled with the pledge not to increase either the basic or top rates of income tax, registered with the electorate. In 1992, 19 per cent of the electorate regarded themselves as to the left of the tax-and-spending plans that an incoming Kinnock administration planned, and 57 per cent to the right. In 1997, 31 per cent of the electorate regarded themselves as to the left of the intended taxation-and-spending plans of a future Blair administration, with only 34 per cent to the right (Hills and Stewart, 2005: 6–7).

Buckler and Dolowitz argue that evoking the rhetoric of 'old' and 'New' was central to the modernisers' ideological renewal project. (Buckler and Dolowitz, 2009: 16). They argue that the utilisation of the term 'New' allowed the modernisers to distance their Labour Party from what was perceived to 'economically inefficient' and 'insufficiently committed to individual autonomy' due to its adherence to 'structural interventions' geared towards reducing inequality. That old/New rhetoric demonstrated that New Labour would propose a model of social justice within which the state would be an enabler (New Labour) rather than an engineer (old Labour) (Buckler and Dolowitz, 2009: 17).

Towards the social justice of an 'enabling state'
New Labour was thus cloaked in electoral calculations of what was politically feasible, rather than what was ideologically desirable. For example, central to the New Labour rhetoric was the neutralisation of the perceived negatives around which the Conservative narrative could be constructed. Critically the abandonment of Clause IV and the associated shift towards the rhetoric of the state as an enabler rather than a provider or social engineer was central to limiting the tax issue. The shift provided an internal and historical comparison, as it allowed New Labour to differentiate themselves from the class-bound and sectional appeal of old Labour and from the perceived economic policy failings associated with Labour in office in the 1940s, 1960s and 1970s (McAnulla, 2006: 122). Critically it also provided an external and contemporary electoral comparison, as it provided New Labour with an alternative strategy for growth, rooted in notions of stability and investment, which could be used as a comparison with the 'boom and bust' economics associated with Thatcherism. Buckler and Dolowitz observe that in the process New Labour created for themselves the 'rhetorical space' for their discourse of 'emancipation, autonomy and choice', which were 'themes that

had been captured by the right and allied to Thatcherite free-market commitments' (Buckler and Dolowitz, 2009: 17).

The social justice dimension of their narrative did provide New Labour with electoral utility, as it allowed them to 'to position themselves against an outmoded Conservative obsession with the free market' that it could be argued had 'blunted their ability to address problems with the social fabric' and enabled New Labour to portray the Conservatives 'as socially regressive and lacking in compassion, particularly with respect to the excluded' (Buckler and Dolowitz, 2009: 24). Through this method New Labour offered a means of critiquing both their past in the shape of old Labour, portrayed as extremist, whilst also critiquing the present Conservative administration also as extreme *and* incompetent. New Labour was thus neither the Labour Party that had been rejected five years earlier under Kinnock nor was it like the Major-led Conservatives. It was as an electoral strategy known as 'triangulation' (Toynbee and Walker, 2004: 270).

The foundations for New Labour's approach of 'triangulation' had been evident in the Commission for Social Justice (CSJ) set up in December 1992, when the 'growing ascendancy of the arguments and intellectual approach favoured by the modernisers' had come to the forefront (Cronin, 2004: 341). The findings of the CSJ, which reported back in 1994, provide a crucial insight into New Labour (Annesley, 2001: 205). The CSJ identified three different futures for social justice. First, there was the deregulators' option based on the pursuit of undiluted Thatcherism within which the inequalities characterising British society would become extended and entrenched. Second, there was the levellers' future, an interpretation associated with the mentality of old Labour, for whom the primary concern was the redistribution of wealth through the state, but to the neglect of considering the means of production. The levellers' future would be rejected for its failure to recognise the importance of economic efficiency to achieving social justice (Annesley, 2001: 205). The CSJ offered a critique of a social justice agenda being pursued that was constructed 'independent' of the economy (Cronin, 2004: 341–2). The third option, the investors' future, sought to reframe the debates surrounding social provision, arguing that they could combine the ethics of community with the dynamics of a market economy, i.e. economic prosperity was the best guarantor of social justice (Driver, 2008: 50).

Therefore, whether we utilise the rhetoric of New Labour which dominated political discourse post-1994 or the language of the Third Way which gained real currency once Labour acquired office, or recognise that the trajectory towards accepting the market predated Blair and was reflected in CSJ, it is clear that the Labour Party was engaging in a process of ideological renewal as a reaction to successive election defeats. By the time New Labour sought office in May 1997 their 'centrism' appeared to represent an accommodation or endorsement of aspects of the Thatcher–Major settlement, built upon an electoral strategy predicated on a 'concordat' with middle England (Toynbee and Walker, 2001: 153). Heffernan argues that the subsequent adaptation of their ideological identity, designed to appease the preferences of key voters, amounted to a betrayal of the party's commitment to traditional social democratic politics. As such, that concordat had significant implications for the ideological identity of the Labour movement, and would shape the parameters of British politics post-1997. As Heffernan argues, this implied that New Labour was rejecting social democratic means and that their approach represented 'an illustration of a neo-liberal paradigm that characterised the contemporary socio-economic policy agenda' (Heffernan, 2001: 170).

This provides us with an initial insight into the social justice agenda of New Labour and identifies the distinction between their investors' interpretation and the rejected levellers' future of the left. It invites us to consider the distinctions between their model of social justice and a more radical left model. A more radical model for social justice would be based on the following principles. First, the notion of a *social minimum*, within which all citizens must have access to sufficient resources to enable them to meet their essential needs. Second, the promotion of *equality of opportunities* whereby the life course of each individual, notably their educational and employment opportunities, is determined by their own motivations and aptitudes as opposed to class, gender or ethnicity. Finally, and crucially, a more radical model would concentrate on equalities of outcomes through the *redistribution* of resources. This would involve state intervention to reduce income inequalities by alleviating the condition of the poorest in society (*income growth* at a higher rate for the poorest as a means of securing poverty reduction). For the left, income growth and income inequalities would be key criteria on which to evaluate the success or failure of any social justice policy strategy (Miller, 2005: 5–20).

The Blair model of social justice, configured in the 1994–97 period according to electoral calculation, rejected the more radical model of social justice advocated by the levellers' interpretation. In office, rather than being guided by the principles of a social minimum, social equality and redistribution, New Labour espoused four values that they argued were central to the creation of a 'just society': equal worth, opportunity for all, responsibility and community (Stewart, 2007: 411;

Kenny, 2007: 32–3). Such values distinguished equality of outcome from equality of opportunity and placed a lower emphasis on income inequality.

Marrying economic efficiency and social justice: New Labour in office

The above analysis clearly demonstrates the centrality of electoral strategy to the ideologically renewal that culminated in New Labour. However, after a decade of power and policy implementation guided by Third Way thinking what has been the impact of marrying social justice to economic efficiency?

Before evaluating this in detail it is worth considering how the features that underpinned the New Labour model of social justice were transmitted into policy. New Labour would narrate their model of social justice around emblematic policies such as:

- *The New Deal*. Young and long-term unemployed were to be given the choice of taking a job, a voluntary position or entering education or training within six months, or they would have their benefits withdrawn (McAnulla, 2006: 127).
- *The minimum wage*. Introduction of a national minimum wage, albeit it at a relatively modest level, was regarded as one of the early successes of New Labour in office, as it established the principle that there was a floor below which wages should not be pushed (Kelly and Gamble, 2001: 177; Robinson, 2005: 350).
- *A national child care strategy*. Investment in child care and in nursery education for three and four-year-olds and in Sure Start programmes for under-fours in areas of deprivation. The focus was on securing for parents child care that would enable them to take up employment – 'making work pay' (McAnulla, 2006: 129; Stewart, 2007: 411).
- *Cutting child poverty*. Pledge to cut child poverty by 50 per cent by 2010 through improvements in benefits, child care and work opportunities for parents (McAnulla, 2006: 127).

In addressing the central question of whether New Labour succeeded in reconciling economic efficiency with social justice, there are both positive interpretations that point to progress (Pearce and Paxton, 2005) and critical perspectives (Coates, 2009; Kenny, 2007) that say that New Labour failed to make sufficient progress, or that there was an inconsistency between their social justice rhetoric and policy choices. The positive interpretation would highlight the fact that between 1997 and

2004 there was a gradual decline in the number of households living below the unofficial poverty line, relative to when the Conservatives were in office. When the Conservatives entered office, the number of people living below half average income – which amounts to the unofficial poverty line – was 5 million; when the Conservatives left office it was 14 million (Shaw, 2007: 43). By 2004 that figure of 14 million had been reduced to 12 million, with Giddens claiming that lifting 2 million people out of poverty, including 800,000 children, should be viewed as a 'considerable' achievement, even if they failed to secure their target of 1 million children being lifted out of poverty (Giddens, 2007: 108).

In addition, Driver notes that there was a positive impact amongst the 'working poor with dependent children', who as a consequence of 'tax credits, the minimum wage and child benefit' have been the benefactors of a faster level of growth at the lower end of the income distribution scale (Driver, 2008: 56). However, the 'non-working poor' without dependent children saw their benefits increase only in line with inflation, so relative to the working poor their position did not improve as much. Moreover, New Labour policy did not reverse the decline in intergenerational mobility that has been observed since the late 1970s: the expansion in higher education appeared to be benefiting the better-off disproportionately (Blanden *et al.*, 2005). Driver also expresses concern that relative to other European countries Britain remains more unequal, with persisting differences in terms of income between ethnic communities and the lack of impact of New Labour policies designed towards reducing pension poverty (Driver, 2008: 56, 66). Blanden *et al.* (2005) suggest that New Labour policies that sought to equalise opportunities appeared to be insufficient to the task, emphasising the need for a careful evaluation of policy strategies to reduce entrenched intergenerational inequalities.

Therefore there are some worrying indicators in terms of the impact of New Labour. Toynbee and Walker have argued that inequality continued to widen under New Labour, albeit it at a slower rate than under the Conservatives, and as a consequence the gap between rich and poor was as wide as ever (Toynbee and Walker, 2005; Toynbee and Walker, 2008). Coates offers an eloquent critique of New Labour's record in terms of their marrying of economic efficiency and social justice. He concludes that New Labour had some:

> Serious shortcomings in policy on poverty and inequality . . . The total picture is bleak but clear . . . New Labour policies . . . worked less well than is often claimed . . . inequality, at best stabilised and poverty first fell and then began to once more to rise. (Coates, 2008: 3, 14, 16)

The Coates critique highlights the following limitations of the New Labour strategy. First, although poverty did decline during the first two terms, it increased again during the third term. The 2004 figure of 12.1 million defined as beneath the unofficial poverty line started to increase by 2007 up to 12.7 million. Moreover, within that child poverty increased from 3.6 million to 3.8 million (Coates, 2008: 14). Second, the New Labour strategy in terms of income differentials is questionable. Coates argues that the minimum wage had been set at too low a level, whilst both Blair and Brown showed unwillingness to curb high salaries, appearing to subscribe to 'a sort of social democratic trickle-down theory of wealth creation' (Coates, 2008: 14). Third, as Coates argues, poverty and inequality are inextricably linked. Based on this, the best that Coates can offer on the New Labour strategy is that without them inequality may well have increased, but with them it 'stabilised' at Thatcherite levels, although post-2005 the gap between rich and poor was widening again (Coates, 2008: 13–14).

Moreover, if we take income growth as a key indicator of poverty and inequality we can see the limits in terms of New Labour's impact. Table 2.1 outlines income growth according to income quintile group since 1979. Whilst it is clear that their first two terms made a significant impact in increasing the income growth levels of the poorest (2.4 per cent between 1997 and 2001; 2.6 per cent between 2001 and 2005); it is remarkable to note that overall, under Blair, New Labour had a percentage increase for the poorest of 1.8 per cent (between 1997 and 2007) that was only marginally better than that of the Major era, 1.7 per cent (between 1990 and 1997).

In addition to 'income growth' increases, it is also worth considering the Gini coefficient, as this acts as another interesting means by which

Table 2.1 Percentage increase in income growth, 1979–2007 (%)

	Income quintile group					
Government	Poorest	2	3	4	Richest	Mean
Conservatives, 1979–97	0.8	1.1	1.6	1.9	2.5	2.1
Thatcher, 1979–90	0.4	1.2	2.1	2.7	3.6	2.8
Major, 1990–97	1.7	0.9	0.6	0.5	0.7	0.8
Labour, 1997–2007	1.8	2.1	1.9	1.7	1.9	2.1
Blair I, 1997–2001	2.4	2.7	2.4	2.5	2.7	3.1
Blair II, 2001–05	2.6	2.5	2.0	1.6	1.4	1.7
Blair III, 2005–07	−1.1	0.1	0.7	0.6	1.2	1.1

Source Brewer *et al.* (2008): 22.

to observe the performance of New Labour relative to their Thatcherite inheritance. The Gini coefficient measures 'income inequality' by condensing the entire income distribution into a single number between 0 and 1. The higher the number the greater the degree of income inequality – a value of 0 corresponds to absence of inequality; a value of 1 indicates the most extreme form of inequality (Brewer *et al.*, 2008: 27). How did New Labour perform in terms of the Gini coefficient? The coefficient was at 0.33 during the final year of the Major administration (1996–97), and this figure increased slightly during the first term of New Labour, reaching 0.35 in 2000–1. That figure did start to fall during their second term of office between 2001 and 2005, although Brewer *et al.* observe that despite that decline the net effect of these changes was to leave 'income inequality effectively unchanged and at historically high levels' (Brewer *et al.*, 2008: 26–7). The most recent available indicator of income inequality shows a Gini coefficient of 0.35 for 2006–7, indicating an increase during the first part of New Labour's third term in office, matching the peak of 2000–1. After ten years of New Labour income inequality was thus at a higher coefficient figure (0.35) than the figure that they inherited from the Major administration (0.33) and the highest coefficient figure since 1961 (Brewer *et al.*, 2008: 26–7).

New Labour and social justice: a lost opportunity?

As a consequence of these worrying trends in terms of income growth and income inequality New Labour have been subject to criticism from the left, who have argued that a more radical model of social justice – the levellers' model – should have been advanced in order to provide a more extensive redistribution of wealth and to tackle inequalities. For the left there remains a sense that this may become viewed as a lost opportunity. As Stewart observes, during the early stages of New Labour's time in power there was an assumption that Blair was reluctant to pursue a more radical approach to poverty and inequality out of a fear of alienating the middle classes (Stewart, 2007: 435). However, Stewart concludes that:

> as the decade progressed it became clearer that this was not a Prime Minister unwilling to take on an unpopular policy and stick with it in face of widespread opposition. It is apparent now that that there were limits to Blair's commitment to social justice and his main priorities lay elsewhere. If his mission had been a different one – if it had led him to talk of inequality as his enemy – he might have left behind an entirely different landscape. (Stewart, 2007: 435)

Therefore, the left would argue that a more negative interpretation can be advanced which suggests that a more radical model of social justice should have been pursued. The remainder of the chapter examines the left based-critique of New Labour, and how the pursuit of social justice was constrained by their electoral strategy. It is an argument that revolves around the following three critical observations:

- There was a lack of a clear ideological *driver* or long-term strategy for the New Labour model of social justice. This is linked with the perception that the balance between social justice and economic efficiency was tilted in favour of economic efficiency, and that the self-imposed *constraints* that New Labour created by their behaviour in opposition and in the early stages of their time in office limited their capacity to make more impact in the pursuit of social justice.
- New Labour failed to adopt an *educational* role towards the electorate and shape public opinion towards the importance of social justice and the merits of redistribution.
- New Labour failed to exploit fully the positive *contexts* that they benefited from in the 1997–2005 period in terms of party political competition.

New Labour and social justice: short-term electoral gain or long-term redistributive strategy?
The central plank of the left critique of New Labour and social justice stems from the claim that New Labour's electoral strategy meant that it was working within the constraints of the Thatcherite agenda (Annesley, 2001: 213). Its resignation to the dominance of markets and the drive for economic efficiency meant that, rather than attempting to pursue a more radical model of social justice, New Labour sought merely to 'mollify' growing inequality, rather than attempting to eradicate poverty and promote equality by challenging the prevailing socio-economic framework (Annesley, 2001: 213). The 'punitive' elements that informed New Labour approaches to social policy were of particular concern to the left, who also argued that there were limits to the asset-based mentality that informed New Labour thinking (Bevir, 2005: 103; Driver, 2008: 66).The punitive elements and the notion of withdrawing of benefits would sit very uneasily with the notion of social justice, as 'the most vulnerable groups in society still need cash benefits to alleviate their poverty right now' (Bevir, 2005: 103).

Such rhetoric reflects a view from within the left that the New Labour approach lacked a clear 'long-term strategy'; rather it could be viewed as being driven by 'cost-cutting measures' designed to reassure middle England. (Annesley, 2001: 213). From their first term in office, Annesley highlights the decision to implement the cut in lone parents' benefit that had been built into the Conservative spending plans (autumn 1997) and the cutting of incapacity benefit in spring 1999. (Annesley, 2001: 213). Perhaps such positioning by New Labour was reflective of their concern that there was 'no strong constituency favouring further redistributive measures with many attributing poverty (especially amongst the unemployed) to individual failings' (Shaw, 2007: 54). Driver is also critical of the asset-based mentality that informed the New Labour approach to social justice:

> Asset-based approaches are unlikely on their own to narrow the gap in the overall distribution of wealth and income between different social groups. The focus on what individuals have to sell in the market place (their marketable assets, such as skills and educational qualifications) leaves the distribution of resources to the market . . . [however] . . . the freedom to make choices is nothing without the capacity and capability to enact upon those choices. (Driver, 2008: 66)

Bevir acknowledges the limitations to the New Labour model of social justice. He observes that to 'give skills to the poor – whether these be soft skills or not – is to do nothing to alter the fact that the market then determines the value of these skills, and it is to do nothing to change the patterns of social justice produced by the market' (Bevir, 2005: 103). Hickson expands upon the notion that market outcomes are not necessarily just. He argues that market outcomes are a consequence of promoting 'certain human attributes over others' and that there is no 'reason why the ability to compete in a market economy should be rewarded over other attributes and abilities' (Hickson, 2004: 132). Both Hickson and Bevir observe that New Labour's obsession with paid employment as the route out of social exclusion reflected their neglect of caring for children or the elderly, both of whom are valuable to the community but not rewarded within the market economy (Hickson, 2004: 132; Bevir, 2005: 103; see also Fisher's chapter in this volume).

Moreover, Shaw argues that there was a 'fundamental drag on a sustained drive against social deprivation' which was a by-product of New Labour's 'reluctance to return to a more steeply progressive tax system' (Shaw, 2007: 54). However, as was mentioned earlier, New Labour made a series of electorally strategic decisions designed to reassure their non-traditional voters that Labour could be trusted to manage the economy. New Labour strategists believed that sticking to the spending plans that the Conservatives had outlined for 1997 to 1999, and offering a commitment not to increase income tax, were pivotal to withstanding any Conservative tax and spend assault. This commitment undermined Conservative electoral strategy, and contributed towards shaping electoral perceptions of New Labour as more 'prudent' and less 'profligate' than old Labour. As such it can be argued that it contributed towards the erosion of the image of Labour as a 'tax and spend' party. However, as Driver comments, 'it did little to offer a coherent strategy' in terms of social policy (Driver, 2008: 52). Annesley refers to it as an 'unnecessary self-constraint, imposed in the pursuit of electoral popularity' (Annesley, 2001: 212); whilst Toynbee and Walker observe that the spending freeze was a significant problem as 'anti-poverty programmes are always likely to start at the pace of a glacier, so they needed to be started at once. But everything except the New Deal started two years too late' (Toynbee and Walker, 2001: 18). Ultimately, their electoral strategy superseded any redistributive strategy.

New Labour and social justice: an educational role?
New Labour strategists calculated that old Labour had made the case for a more radical pursuit of social justice and the means for redistributing wealth explicitly through increasing taxation and that old Labour had been electorally punished for their troubles. New Labour thereby sought to utilise an alternative discourse of social inclusion, as a means of presenting their attempts at redistributive policies – a method that Lister has described as 'redistribution by stealth' (Lister, 2001: 65–70). Hickson argues that New Labour decided to employ 'such language due to the fear of electoral repercussions from a more explicit endorsement of redistribution' (Hickson, 2004: 128). However, as early as 2001 Lister was implying that this might 'backfire' as an electoral strategy over the longer term as those who were being taxed by stealth began to realise that 'doing good by stealth has the disadvantage of not being seen to be doing good' (Lister, 2001: 66). This is a theme developed further by McAnulla. He suggests that central to the electoral strategy of New Labour was an appeal to the pre-existing values and prejudices of groups of voters, an approach evident when New Labour sought to placate right-leaning newspapers. This resulted in New Labour seeking to appeal to parts of the electorate who mighty not normally sympathise with Labour. There was an emphasis on 'toughness' and a desire to ensure that the presentation (through historically Conservative tabloids) was politically advantageous to New Labour. Editorials from traditional Conservative tabloids entitled 'Welfare: the crackdown' reflected New Labour's concern that such readers felt that 'many

welfare claimants are an undeserving drain on taxpayers' (McAnulla, 2006: 138).

McAnulla observes that this willingness to 'pander' to such populist instincts was an aspect of New Labour regarded as 'most regrettable' to those on the left (McAnulla, 2006: 138). Ultimately he concludes that New Labour could be open to criticism for the failure to articulate the case openly for redistributive politics and to shape public opinion to this end. On the failure to offer an educational role, it can be argued that:

> the redistributive aspects of New Labour's programme have been conducted by *stealth* rather than as a proudly proclaimed aim (e.g. minimum wage, working families' tax credit, child poverty programme) ... Consequently, it may be that New Labour is overlooking an *opportunity to appeal to its core vote, and more generally, may be passing up the chance to win people over to the virtues of redistribution.* (McAnulla, 2006: 138)

New Labour and social justice: positive political contexts
Finally, the left critique of the electoral strategy of New Labour and how it impinged upon their capacity to make more impact in terms of social justice focuses on positive contexts. Here the central argument is that New Labour overestimated the threat to them of the Conservatives (Toynbee and Walker, 2004: 271).

The Conservative Party imploded in its fourth term under Major and by the mid-1990s the key planks of the Thatcherite electoral strategy had dissolved (Heppell, 2008: 588). New Labour modernisers might wish to claim that it was their ideological metamorphosis into New Labour that propelled Labour into office, but it should be recalled that they were aided considerably by a Major administration that was considered to be administratively incompetent; the parliamentary Conservative Party was viewed as being ideologically divided; and Conservative parliamentarians were perceived to be disreputable and untrustworthy (Heppell, 2008: 585). The collapse in Conservative support and the establishment of a solid Labour Party lead occurred in the immediate aftermath of the government's humiliating expulsion from the exchange rate mechanism in September 1992. That cataclysmic policy failing, and the resulting need to increase taxation, destroyed the Conservatives' reputation for economic competence and perceptions of them as a party of low taxation (Heppell, 2008: 588). For the duration of the 1992–97 Parliament there was an expectation that they would be defeated and that Labour would win office. Between 1997 and 2005 successive leaders of the Conservative Party (William Hague, Iain Duncan Smith and Michael Howard) were constrained by the legacy of the Major era and the ideological straitjacket of Thatcherism, thus limiting the capacity of the Conservatives to chal-lenge the dominance of the Labour Party in government. Therefore the fears that New Labour had of the Conservatives were overestimated, the Conservatives were devoid of a coherent political narrative or ideo-logical identity, and their pursuit of the core-vote strategies in 2001 and 2005 were suboptimal.

On the basis of such findings the left argued that the electorate would have been receptive to 'strong' – i.e. left-tending leadership – and as such 'there was no need to shift policy in order to secure a victory in 1997' (Toynbee and Walker, 2004: 271). This argument suggests that New Labour went further right than was necessary. To suggest such a proposition, as the left has done, requires us to consider the possibility that some time between 1983 and 1994 another 'third way' could have opened up between the approaches of old Labour and the 'surrender' to Thatcherism. Could an approach built around a 'touch of union reform, sauced with some tax restraint and a cautious, but not total, rewording of Clause IV' have emerged, whereby Labour could have 'retained their idealism while it jettisoned the baggage of electoral failure'? (Toynbee and Walker, 2004: 269).

The central problem with this critique from the left of the New Labour electoral strategy of moving to the right is that it rests on a counterfac-tual claim based on faith, not evidence. Indeed, Toynbee and Walker acknowledge that the electorate demonstrated no real enthusiasm for increased taxation, public expenditure or wealth redistribution, despite their adherence to the welfare state. They therefore recognise that 'electorally' the Blair–Brown leap was indeed 'necessary', as in order 'to win national power in British elections means dealing with a southern, increasingly middle-class electorate with a limited appetite for statism or redistribution' (Toynbee and Walker, 2004: 271).

Conclusion

The left offer an interesting critique on New Labour's limited pursuit of social justice and the constraints imposed upon it by their electoral strategy. The limitation with their critique is that it is a counterfactual: an assertion that Labour could still have secured successive electoral mandates whilst pursuing a more radical form of social justice. The left cannot prove that their strategy would have been electorally successful, whereas the architects of New Labour can point the factual evidence of three successive electoral victories, the existence of a prolonged period of economic growth and the establishment of New Labour as a party of economic competence between 1997 and 2007, and some evidence of progress in terms of social justice relative to their Thatcherite inheritance. However, Lee concludes that despite their claims the New Labour version of modernised social democracy based on the Third Way philosophy seems hollow. He suggests that the strength of the Third Way was its electoral success, but it came at a price, and thus it carried with it the weakness of demanding that the Labour Party must occupy the ideological ground of their opponents (Lee, 2008: 191).

In its adherence to the market order, Lee concludes, there was little evidence of a mobilisation of a progressive mind or the sense that New Labour had won the battle of ideas (Lee, 2007: 220–5). Ultimately, the viability of the New Labour electoral strategy was dependent on evidence of economic growth and an associated electoral view of Labour as being economically competent. This was sustained by New Labour between 1997 and early 2008 (Lee, 2008: 189–90). The maintenance of economic growth also enabled New Labour to operate in an environment in which 'issues of economic management' and 'taxation' were politically neutralised, enabling them to seek to *claim* to pursue both economic efficiency and social justice, i.e. propitious economic circumstances prevented New Labour from being forced to actually choose between increasing taxation or reducing public expenditure (Gamble, 2006: 311; Bentley, 2007: 115). As early as 2001, Toynbee and Walker asked what would happen to the credibility of New Labour's electoral strategy when a choice had to be made (Toynbee and Walker, 2001: 42).

The economic collapse that coincided with Brown succeeding Blair as Labour Party leader and Prime Minister undermined New Labour's claims to economic competence, and with it the pillars upon which their electoral strategy was built. As New Labour sought a fourth successive term their dilemma was that, in their attempt to reconcile economic efficiency with social justice, critics on the left (and the Conservatives to their right) could argue that they had achieved neither. While the middle class were becoming more attracted to David Cameron and his modernised Conservative Party, which was no longer adopting the electorally alienating positions that New Labour relied upon it to hold, the working class were increasingly frustrated by the limited impact that New Labour had had on improving their conditions. Moreover the recapitalisation of the banks and the increasing of income taxation for the highest earners initiated in 2008–9 can be interpreted as signalling the 'death' of the 'economic efficiency' side of the New Labour claim. As the New Labour electoral strategy collapsed as a consequence of the economic crisis, the incumbent Brown administration faced the immensely difficult task of constructing a new post-Blair, post-Third Way strategy whilst in power.

Moreover the Coates critique of Labour's record of economic efficiency and social justice, alluded to earlier, suggests that New Labour has a limited legacy in terms of social justice. The tragedy for New Labour is the realisation that there will be few opportunities for the Labour Party to acquire power, as they did in 1997 in the midst of an economic boom, with a parliamentary majority of 179 and facing a discredited, directionless and demoralised Conservative Party. Furthermore, economic problems mean that the pursuit of the more radical model of social justice that the left have advocated may not be electorally or governmentally viable. This is an assertion which will encourage the left to argue more forcefully that New Labour missed a golden opportunity to pursue that radical vision of social justice in their first two terms; whilst New Labourites will counter-claim that such a political vision would have impeded their electoral appeal and endangered their re-election campaigns of 2001 and 2005. This debate on the legacy of New Labour and their electoral strategy – between the sacrifices made in terms of social justice at the altar of economic efficiency – will inform debate within the Labour Party in the forthcoming years.

Notes

1 It can be argued that long-serving administrations suffer from the following degenerative tendencies. First, the appropriateness of their policy objectives and their reputation for governing competence become questioned, especially in the sphere of economic management. Second, there are increasingly negative perceptions of leadership credibility and thereby electoral appeal within the governing party. Third, there is increasing evidence of ideological division and mutual suspicion within the governing party. Fourth, there are accusations of abuse of power as allegations of sleaze and corruption engulf the governing party. Fifth, the ability of the governing party to avoid culpability for past mistakes and withstand the 'time for a change' argument is significantly reduced. Sixth, they suffer from the evolution of an increasingly unified, electorally appealing, politically renewed and credible main opposition party (Heppell, 2008: 580–1).

2 Smith had proposed the restoration of a 50 per cent tax rate on incomes over £40,000 and the extension of National Insurance contributions on incomes over £22,000 (Cronin, 2004: 322).

Bibliography

Annesley, C. (2001) 'New Labour and welfare', in S. Ludlam and M. J. Smith (eds) *New Labour in Government* (Basingstoke: Macmillan).

Beech, M. (2008) 'New Labour and the politics of dominance', in M. Beech and S. Lee (eds) *Ten Years of New Labour* (Basingstoke: Palgrave).

Bentley, T. (2007) 'British politics after Tony Blair', *British Politics* 2:2, 111–17.

Bevir, M. (2005) *New Labour: A Critique* (London: Routledge).

Blanden, J., Gregg, P. and Machin, S. (2005) 'Social mobility in Britain: low and falling', *Centrepiece* (spring), http://cep.lse.ac.uk/pubs/download/CP172.pdf (accessed 29 July 2009).

Brewer, M., Muriel, A., Phillips, A. and Sibieta, L. (2008) *Poverty and Inequality in the United Kingdom, 2008* (London: Institute of Fiscal Studies).

Buckler, S. and Dolowitz, D. (2009) 'Ideology, party identity and renewal', *Journal of Political Ideologies* 14:1, 11–30.

Coates, D. (2008) '"Darling, it's entirely my fault!" Gordon Brown's legacy to Alistair and himself', *British Politics* 3:1, 3–21.

Coates, D. (2009), 'Chickens coming home to roost? New Labour at the eleventh hour', *British Politics* 4:4, 421–33.

Cronin, J. (2004) *New Labour's Pasts: The Labour Party and its Discontents* (London: Longman).

Curtice, J. (2007) 'Elections and public opinion', in A. Seldon (ed.) *Blair's Britain, 1997–2007* (Cambridge: Cambridge University Press).

Driver, S. (2008) 'New Labour and social policy', in M. Beech and S. Lee (eds) *Ten Years of New Labour* (Basingstoke: Palgrave).

Gamble, A. (2006) 'British politics after Blair', in P. Dunleavy, R. Heffernan, P. Cowley and C. Hay (eds) *Developments in British Politics* VIII (Basingstoke: Palgrave).

Giddens, A. (2007) 'New Labour: Tony Blair and after', *British Politics* 2:2, 111–17.

Hay, C. (1997), 'Blaijorims: towards a one-vision polity', *Political Quarterly* 68:4, 372–9.

Hay, C. (1999) *The Political Economy of New Labour: Labouring under False Pretences?* (Manchester: Manchester University Press).

Heath, A., Jowell, R. and Curtice, J. (2001) *The Rise of New Labour: Party Policies and Voter Choices* (Oxford: Oxford University Press).

Heffernan, R. (2001) *New Labour and Thatcherism* (Basingstoke: Palgrave).

Heppell, T. (2008) 'The degenerative tendencies of long serving governments ... 1963 ... 1996 ... 2008?', *Parliamentary Affairs* 61:4, 578–96.

Hickson, K. (2004) 'Equality', in R. Plant, M. Beech and K. Hickson (eds) *The Struggle for Labour's Soul: Understanding Labour's Political Thought since 1945* (London: Routledge).

Hills, J. and Stewart, K. (eds) (2005) *A More Equal Society? New Labour, Poverty, Inequality and Exclusion* (London: Policy Press).

Keegan, W. (2003) *The Prudence of Mr Gordon Brown* (London: Wiley).

Kelly, G. and Gamble, A. (2001), 'Labour's new economics', in S. Ludlam and M. J. Smith (eds), *New Labour in Government* (London: Macmillan).

Kenny, C. (2007), 'Does New Labour have a consistent conception of social justice?', *Politics*. 27:1, 32–9.

Lee, S. (2007) *Best for Britain? The Politics and Legacy of Gordon Brown* (Oxford: One World).

Lee, S. (2008) 'Conclusion', in M.Beech and S.Lee (eds) *Ten Years of New Labour* (Basingstoke: Palgrave).

Lister, R. (2001) 'Doing good by stealth: the politics of poverty and inequality under New Labour', *New Economy* 8:2 (June), 65–70.

McAnulla, S. (2006) *British Politics: A Critical Introduction* (London: Continuum).

Miller, D. (2005), 'What is social justice?', in N. Pearce and W. Paxton (eds) *Social Justice: Building a Fairer Britain* (London: Politicos).

Mulgan, G. (2005) 'Going with and against the grain', in N. Pearce and W. Paxton (eds) *Social Justice: Building a Fairer Britain* (London: Politicos).

Pearce, N. and Paxton, W. (eds) (2005) *Social Justice: Building a Fairer Britain* (London: Politicos).

Robinson, P. (2005) 'The economy: achieving full employment', in N. Pearce and W. Paxton (eds) *Social Justice: Building a Fairer Britain* (London: Politicos).

Shaw, E. (1994) *The Labour Party since 1979: crisis and transformation* (London: Routledge).

Shaw, E. (2007) *Losing Labour's soul? New Labour and the Blair Government, 1997–2007* (London: Routledge).

Stewart, K. (2007) 'Equality and social justice', in A. Seldon (ed.) *Blair's Britain, 1997–2007* (Cambridge: Cambridge University Press).

Toynbee, P. and Walker, D. (2001) *Did Things Get Better? An Audit of Labour's Successes and Failures* (London: Penguin Books).

Toynbee, P. and Walker, D. (2004) 'New Labour', in R. Plant, M. Beech and K. Hickson (eds) *The Struggle for Labour's Soul: Understanding Labour's Political Thought since 1945* (London: Routledge).

Toynbee, P. and Walker, D. (2005) *Better or Worse: Has Labour Delivered?* (London: Bloomsbury).

Toynbee, P. and Walker, D. (2008) *Unjust Rewards: Exposing Greed and Inequality in Britain Today* (London: Granta).

3

'Radicalisation' and 'democracy': a linguistic analysis of rhetorical change[1]

Lesley Jeffries

During the years of New Labour, and particularly whilst Tony Blair was Prime Minister (1997–2007), there was a great deal of discussion in the media about the language that was being used by the 'Blairites' as they became known. It was evident from the numbers and roles of 'special advisers' appointed that one of the main strands of Blair's strategy to gain and retain power was to control the presentation of the party and its policies very tightly. In addition, Blair appeared to emulate Thatcher's earlier successes in appropriating certain prominent keywords which seemed to sum up his political outlook. These words (such as 'stakeholding' and 'social exclusion') have been discussed very widely both in the press and in academic circles (see, for example, Fairclough, 2000: 84–93, 51–65). What is less well recognised in all such discussions is what happens to less salient, but nevertheless important, keywords which often take on specific and sometimes politically significant meanings in response to a strong ruling culture such as that found in the New Labour period.

This chapter is part of a linguistic project investigating the keywords of the New Labour era. It links micro and macro-level discussion and sets the scene for the political and sociological analyses of later chapters through a forensic examination of two of these keywords, both of which seemed to acquire particular semantic characteristics during this period. The kind of 'emergent meaning' (see Jeffries, 2003) which I am referring to here is not the Newspeak of Orwell's novel *Nineteen Eighty Four* about a totalitarian regime which has absolute control over language. Such explicit control over people's freedom to express themselves, though not unknown in human history, is at least initially easily recognised by those subjected to it, and by those outside. More invidious in some ways is the process by which those of us living in a 'free' society may find ourselves using words differently as a result of a strong political climate. This, of course, is fundamentally the same process by which words change meaning generally, and it is partly for this reason that politically driven changes are potentially so powerful, since they operate beneath the radar of language users' conscious choices.

The processes by which words take on specific meanings and may influence popular views of politically sensitive issues is one of the focuses of Critical Discourse Analysis (e.g. Fairclough, 1989) and Critical Stylistics (e.g. Jeffries, 2010b). That the language we use may not only *reflect* but also *construct* the social meanings that affect our lives has been observed throughout the history of modern linguistics, not least in the famous Sapir–Whorf hypothesis (see Sapir, 1929; Whorf, 1956). The extreme form of this hypothesis, which claims that some form of stable language system is in complete control of our every waking thought, has been moderated in recent years,[2] now proposing simply that most discourse, and specific linguistic texts in particular, have the capacity to influence our thinking towards certain viewpoints. The mechanisms by which this may happen require further study (though see Jeffries, 2010b, for some discussion of this process), but the fact that texts create meaning rather than simply reflecting some kind of independent 'reality' is not in dispute.

The two words under the spotlight in this chapter, *radicalisation* and *democracy*,[3] were chosen for similar reasons, though as we shall see they also illustrate different issues of meaning change. Impressionistically, both words seemed to have taken on an evaluative meaning in recent years, and I wanted to see whether there was evidence for this impression. In the case of *radicalisation*, and its related forms (*radical, radicalise*, etc.),[4] during the period under investigation it lost its recent (twentieth-century) history as a word which has positive connotations for certain political outlooks (socialist and other left-leaning groups), and seemed to take on an undifferentiated negative evaluation, in response to the increasingly polarised world after the attacks of 11 September 2001 on the United States. In the case of *democracy* the reverse was true, as it seemed to have become ever more an 'absolute good'. Although of course it has not been exactly 'bad' in living memory, under New Labour it seemed to become less of a negotiated meaning with interesting facets and more of a self-evident and universal absolute like *virtue* or *goodness*.

These, then, were the hypotheses underlying this chapter, which investigates the specific meaning and use of the words *radicalisation* and *democracy* in the British press at the beginning and towards the end of the New Labour era. After a brief discussion of underlying theoretical premises and methodology, the chapter demonstrates that there is indeed evidence for changes in the use of these two words. It therefore documents a shift in political vocabulary that may limit our ability to think critically about political events, institutions and processes.

Theoretical background

Structuralism

I will not dwell here on the general linguistic issues that are raised by this research. However, it is worth taking a little space to introduce one or two of them, since they may have wider relevance for political thinking in general. Much of linguistic thought since the early twentieth century has been influenced by structuralism (de Saussure, 1966), which made explicit one of the basic assumptions about language that many people share, which is that it is rather like a 'code'. Like a code, then, it has a set of items (sounds, words, etc.) which are combined into larger units (sounds into words, words into clauses, etc.) and the relationship between these items and the world they refer to is completely arbitrary. Another aspect of structuralist thinking sees the code (the core of language) as an internally structured system where all the units in the system are partly defined by other units. Thus the precise meaning of the word *stool*, which includes the information that it has 'no back-rest', is influenced by the related words *chair*, *sofa*, etc., which do. If no seat ever used by human beings had back-rests, this information would be redundant and not be part of the meaning of the word *stool*.

The problem of the extreme view of language-as-system is that it leaves no room to explain the process by which language changes, as it evidently does. The internal structure of the code, then, must have some ability to be flexible in response to new uses of words, leading to new and different relationships between the items in the system. Whilst this mechanism is still not well understood, the micro-investigation of local and time-limited word meanings is one way to demonstrate the mutual reliance that links the code and its evolution.

Previous studies of this kind include Jeffries (2003), where I investigated the meaning of the word *water* during the Yorkshire water shortage of 1995. The study demonstrated that the word took on many of the characteristics of a (countable, portable and valuable) commodity during the period investigated, rather than those of a natural resource. A study of the nature of political apology focused on Blair's 'apology' for the Iraq war (Jeffries, 2007a) used similar techniques of investigation, though it focused on a speech act (apology) rather than a word meaning. A number of studies (see Jeffries, 2007b, 2010a) have used similar techniques to investigate the contextual construction of opposites in texts as diverse as poetry and women's magazines.

Keywords and linguistics

In 1976 Raymond Williams published a book called *Keywords* which purported to capture the language of the post-war period and explain some of its keys terms. Williams, a cultural historian, wrote mini-essays on each of the words that he chose, explaining the particular meaning and significance of terms such as *underprivileged* and *hegemony* with illustrations from his experience and knowledge of the world. The sub-title of the book was *A Vocabulary of Culture and Society*. Whilst it is a very readable book, and of historical significance itself over thirty years later,[5] there was nothing in the text which explained why Williams chose those particular words, nor did it explain how he came to the conclusions he did about their use and meaning, beyond introspection by an admittedly well educated mind.

The development of linguistics as a discipline in the twentieth century was partly a reaction to this kind of study, and attempted to appropriate the techniques and rigour of the social and natural sciences to apply to questions of language and meaning. The field known as corpus linguistics has developed from humble beginnings but is now aided by the power and scope of computer technology and enables linguists to find and consider many thousands of examples of any word or structure within the ever larger corpora which are available to the researcher. In recent times the disciplines of stylistics and critical discourse analysis,[6] which are concerned with the language of texts and their effect in usage, have also embraced corpus-based techniques as a way of identifying patterns of usage in addition to the individual usage that they have traditionally been concerned with.

One of the consequences of increased computing power is that new questions can be asked, and answered, about the nature of texts. One of these is to discover which words are more frequent in a particular text (or set of texts) than in the language in general.[7] The term 'keywords' is used for these frequent items and this reflects something of what Williams was getting at in a less systematic way – the words which somehow capture the zeitgeist of the times. This larger task, to discover the keywords (in this sense) of the New Labour years, is under way. This involves collecting all news articles from the major national newspapers from the period 1998–2007 into a corpus which will produce a list of the keywords of this significant period.[8] This chapter reports on part of that work and describes a detailed investigation into two of the words which seem key to the period because they appear to have acquired positive or negative connotations in that particular political climate.

There are a range of theoretical issues about text and meaning which we have no space to address here, but which are of interest to those engaged in examining the ideology of texts. These include the question of whether, and to what extent, texts can 'have' meaning or whether all linguistic meaning is somehow negotiated between producer and receiver. The short answer, from a stylistician, is that I do believe that texts have some meaning in themselves, but that the related question of to what extent readers (and hearers) are bound to (1) understand, (2) accept and (3) be influenced by such meaning is much more difficult to answer. However, progress in stylistics is beginning to provide some explanation of the way in which we read and understand literary texts, including fictional worlds we can know nothing about personally, and it is likely that in time we will be able to apply such models of reading to non-fiction texts in order to explain the power of language to influence people ideologically.

Methodology: the study of two keywords

In order to assess the meaning and usage of individual word forms, it is necessary to find a set of examples in context and consider each one for linguistic features which cannot be automatically found by computational methods. This qualitative type of study is time-consuming, and the focus of this search for examples was therefore narrowed from the whole corpus of news articles throughout the period 1998–2007 to compare the occurrences of the two keywords in all articles from five newspapers (*Daily Mail*, *Guardian*, *Independent*, *Sun*, *Times*) during just two months: June 1998 and June 2007. This focus was used to make it possible to compare similar periods from the start and the end of the New Labour period to maximise any differences.

The method used for this sub-set of the corpus was as follows:

- Extract all occurrences of words with context (concordances).
- Examine all occurrences for their semantic prosody (regular collocation).
- Examine all occurrences for their grammatical properties.
- Examine all occurrences for their semantic properties.[9]

The usefulness of concordancing software in such studies is to enable the researcher to pull out a list of examples of the same (or similar) words, with enough context to demonstrate how the word is being used in each case. This allows the grammatical and semantic context to be compared for all cases, and for any patterns of occurrence to be found relatively easily. The basis of these comparisons will be explained below, with as few assumptions about linguistic knowledge as possible, so that readers from a range of backgrounds may follow the argument. Here is an example of a concordance for the word *democracy*:

- The renewal of **democracy** should bring great benefits.
- When John Major won the 1992 election he spoke of a property-owning **democracy** in which wealth would be 'cascading down the generations'.
- Good architects, like good artists, are primarily concerned with the language of form, while good urbanists must have an equal commitment to the things that erode such language: compromise, **democracy**, pluralism, entrepreneurial skills and patience.
- The necessary reform of the role of the military will not be brought about by exposing a few officers to lessons in human rights and **democracy**.

'Semantic prosody' (Louw, 1993) refers to the kinds of words that a keyword tends to occur with, and how that affects our perception of the meaning of the keyword itself. This does not change the denotation (referential) meaning of a word, but alters the way we feel about it. The connotations of a word like *monumental*, which superficially seems to mean only 'huge' or 'enormous', may include a slightly negative semantic prosody drawn from its tendency to occur alongside negative words like *mistake* or *error* so that when it is used in a poem, for example Larkin's *monumental slithering*, to refer to violin playing, we tend to interpret this to mean that the poet does not like the music.[10] We will see below some of the semantic prosodies of our two keywords.

The grammatical properties of the keywords, which are both nouns, include the following:

- What modifies the noun? (e.g. adjectives and determiners)
- What grammatical role does the noun play in the larger structure? (e.g. is it an Actor or a Goal? etc.)

We will see below that how a noun is used may affect its meaning. Thus, for example, the indefinite article (*a/an*) modifying the noun *democracy* makes it into a countable noun (*a democracy*) rather than a mass noun (*democracy* in general) and this has significance for the way we read the word.

The semantic properties of the keywords are more specific to the particular words, as can be seen from the following questions, which were asked in relation to the examples in the data set:

- Is the verbal origin of *radicalisation* evident in the context?
- Is *democracy* presented as a single, unified concept?
- Are they measurable?

- What metaphors are used?
- Are opposites (or synonyms) being constructed?

Whether or not it is clear that *radicalisation* derives from an activity (verb) of radicalising could be important in the way that we see the word, since consciousness of its dynamic nature reminds us that someone or something is responsible for the process, and that people are the targets of the process too. The question of whether we see *democracy* as a single, unified and undifferentiated concept, rather than a complex and contested one is also important for the way in which voters relate to their political system. Whether democracy is something that you can have more or less of is also significant in the way that we see it, and the linguistic context of the word can answer such questions. We may also derive some understanding of how the texts are using the keywords if we look at any oppositions that they seem to enter into in context. The results below, then, reflect a comparison of part of the available data – from June of 1998 and June of 2007 – and are aimed at discovering whether there is any discernible difference between the two years in the contextual meaning of these words.

Radicalisation: results

This section reports on the findings for the word *radicalisation* in June of 2007 and June of 1998. The more recent results are presented first, since they will naturally be more familiar to the reader. The changes since 1998 will be more evident once the recent usage has been made explicit. This word, being a noun derived from a verb, was expected to 'package up' a whole set of processes without making explicit the participants involved or their relationships. It was also anticipated that the connotations of this word would be largely negative, though it is known to have had a more benign meaning in the past.

Clearly, one of the major world events during the years of New Labour was the attack on the World Trade Center in New York in 2001. This was a watershed which raised many questions about the relationship between West and East, and focused the eyes of the West on the possible causes of the extremism that led to such terrorist activities. Whilst many column inches of newsprint have been expended since then on debating the issues that were raised by 9/11, there is nevertheless an impression that a single cause was quickly identified, labelled and then given the name of *radicalisation*, with no further need to remind the reader that this arose from Islamic fundamentalism.

The first question that was asked in relation to *radicalisation* was the extent to which by 2007 the nominalisation of the verb *to radicalise* had become so complete that the result was a name for a process which did not mention the Actor (who did the radicalising) or the Goal (who was radicalised), but rather assumed that the reader would automatically know the answers to these questions, so intrinsic had they become to the ongoing story of Islamic fundamentalism by the end of the period. Nominalisation occurs when a verb (e.g. *transform*) is presented in noun form (e.g. *transformation*) and as a result the Actor is usually missing and the Goal too in many cases. So *She transformed the room* becomes *It was a transformation*, losing both *She* (Actor) and *the room* (Goal), though you may also have a version where the Goal is retained: The *transformation of the room*. In the case of the recent developments of the meaning of *radicalisation*, the loss of the Actor could be significant, as its inclusion would force the writer to draw some conclusions about who/what is responsible (e.g. *Poverty radicalised the young Muslim*). The elision of the Goal, most normally some version of *Muslim* or *Arab* when it occurs, is indicative of the fact that we no longer see *radicalisation* as connected with anything other than Islam. Thus the Goal of the radicalisation process can safely be omitted by a writer in the full knowledge that the reader can fill in the gap from her/his background knowledge. This ellipsis of course reinforces the effect by automatically associating the two – radicalisation and Islam.

The results from 2007 were, as expected, as follows:

- Goals were mainly young, mainly Muslim and sometimes omitted.
- Actors were mainly absent.
- Determiners were mainly definite articles (*the*).

Here are some of the examples which demonstrate these features:

- the **radicalisation** *of* Arab youth
- the **radicalisation** *of* young men and women
- in more extremism, **radicalisation** *of* Muslim students
- the **radicalisation** *of* Palestinian society.
- to the **radicalisation** *of* the anti-G8 scene.
- the **radicalisation** *of* parts of the Muslim community.
- the **radicalisation** *of* the British people
- the **radicalisation** *of* Russia's Muslims

Notice that although the main collocation of the keyword is with variations on Islam, there remain occasional uses which are not associated with this big story, so that we have, for example, *the radicalisation of the anti-G8 scene*. Note that, unlike earlier uses of the word, this other usage is evaluatively negative, and is likely to be interpreted on analogy with popular ideas of Islamic radicalisation as a form of extremism connected with violence or terrorism. Notice that in all the examples above the Goal is included (in a prepositional phrase, usually beginning with the preposition *of*), though if they were omitted the assumption would be that it referred to Islamic radicalisation. Occasionally, the Actors are included, but usually in rather general ways:

- The **radicalisation** *of* students *by* Islamist groups on campus

The Actor here, *Islamist groups on campus*, is not specific and, like the term *radicalisation* itself, is not really available for scrutiny, being instead shorthand for a threat which is not examined in any detail.

In all the cases above, the definite article (*the*) gives a sense of there being a specific referent – *the radicalisation* – which assumes that the reader knows what is being referred to. This assumption of background knowledge, even in its absence, has the effect of reifying the process, and a reader without the requisite knowledge will therefore assume they at least *should* have known about this evidently well recognised process that is clearly assumed by the writer. A similar level of assumption is made by the very many examples where the determiner is a possessive form, which places the Goal in modifying position before the keyword:

- His radicalisation
- his brother's long process of radicalisation.
- modern Islam's radicalisation

Note that in the first and second examples here there is an assumption that the reader will know what kind of radicalisation is involved, though the second does also acknowledge that it is a process, rather than a product (*long process of* . . .). Despite the inclusion of the Goals, and this recognition of process, there remains an absence of explanation about what is involved in the 'package' that is the referent of the noun *radicalisation*. There appears to be an assumption that we all know what it means, and this is reflected in the relatively common 'bald' uses of the term with no Actor or Goal in sight:

- a sign of radicalisation
- in danger of radicalisation.
- the 'fight against radicalisation and extremism'.

An inevitable aspect of language change in the modern world and particularly in media texts is the use of 'shorthand' to encompass rather complex and changing concepts. This is often an innocent question of economy of space or time, rather than a wilful or even unconscious manipulation of ideology. However, in the case of the *radicalisation* usage, there is so much acreage of newsprint expended on the problem of Islamic fundamentalism that the usual excuses of space and time do not seem to apply. Rather, there is a relatively widespread ideological viewpoint which is adopted by all the news media and which is reflected in an unquestioning use of terms like *radicalisation* to describe the process by which (mainly) young Muslim men in Britain and elsewhere have been persuaded to become suicide bombers.

The final example above, like others, assumes an equivalence between *radicalisation* and *extremism*, which does not recognise their earlier differences, with *radicalism* having had in the past at least some potentially positive evaluation and being ideas-led, whereas *extremism* has probably always been connotatively negative and associated with terrorism. A similar example (below) shows how the two are equated by the structure of 'apposition' whereby two noun phrases are used in the same grammatical role and as a result are assumed to have the same referent (as in *Mr Brown, The Prime Minister* or *Mrs Bun, the baker*):

- The failure to engage and address the needs of modern Islam could result in more extremism, **radicalisation** of Muslim students

I chose to examine the use of radicalisation in the later period (2007) first, as it is likely to seem more familiar, and possibly therefore unsurprising, to the reader. The usage of the keyword in the 1998 data, by comparison, demonstrates that what seems familiar to us now is nevertheless a recent development.

In the 1998 data we find no possessive adjectives (*his radicalisation*), and indeed the keyword is generally attached to words denoting groups of people such as *society* or *community* rather than individuals. We also find not only definite articles modifying the keyword (i.e. *the radicalisation*) as though it were a known phenomenon, but also some indefinite articles (*a radicalisation*):

- Over the past two weeks, thanks to the Decane offensive and the refugee crisis, there has been **a radicalisation** of Kosovo society at almost all levels.
- The deep aftershocks resulted in **a new radicalisation** of the nationalist community, which in turn led to a record Sinn Fein vote in the 1997 general election

Note that the seeds of the more recent negative connotation are already evident here, though as we shall see they were not universal at that time. Also, the use of the keyword in 1998 was not almost exclusively in relation to Islam, as it was in the 2007 data, but was used of other troubled areas of the world such as Kosovo and Ireland too.

Other differences in the 1998 data are that there are more evident Actors (i.e. the causes of the radicalisation) than in 2007, and the emphasis seems to be more on radicalisation as a process, rather than a product:

- The strongest stimulus to the **radicalisation** of the Macedonian Albanians will be a constant pressure-cooker of revolt and suppression in Kosovo.
- The three victims were buried yesterday in their home village, Dura, in a sea of green flags, showing allegiance to the radical Islamic movement Hamas – a vivid gauge of the steady **radicalisation** of the West Bank in the year since the collapse of the peace process.

Note that the evidence of *radicalisation* as a process in the first example is the phrase *strongest stimulus to* and the fact that it refers to the future (*will be*). In the second case, the adjective *steady* which modifies the keyword is an indicator that this is a drawn-out process.

As indicated above, there is also evidence that in 1998 the word *radicalisation* was not yet seen as fully negative, as is indicated in the following examples:

- The politicisation of the cartoon? The **radicalisation** of American mainstream movies? A lovely idea if it were true, but it isn't.
- The VW Lupo: a **radicalisation** of the SEAT Arosa which comes with the customary Volkswagen trimmings
- The English have always considered themselves as subjects, subordinate to the Establishment, rather than citizens. What happened this decade changed all that. It is still continuing, with the re-**radicalisation** of students, a formerly active body which had been dormant for 30 years.

An example found in other 1997 data[11] referred to *the radicalisation of the Women's Institute* (WI) and this adds to the impression that the word has not always been linked with violence and terrorism and other negatively valued concepts, since the WI connotes peaceful activity and civic engagement rather than suicide bombing. The very fact that this example may make us smile now is evidence of how far the word is now associated with terrorist violence. In the examples above we find evidence of its positive connotations in the adjective *lovely* used in relation to the idea of radicalisation of American cinema, in a car company using the keyword to promote its products (unthinkable in 2009?) and an implicitly positive reference to the *re-radicalisation* of students in opposition to the clearly negative description of them as *dormant*.

To summarise, the findings of this study in relation to the word *radicalisation* are that in the period under consideration (i.e. between 1998 and 2007) the word has changed usage in the British press from a relatively neutral word denoting significant and dramatic change (both good and bad), usually involving politicisation, to an extremely negative word associated almost entirely with Islamic fundamentalism which also denotes significant politicisation, and usually also connotes violence. There is also a change from recognition of the process and the players involved in this process to an almost complete reification of the concept of radicalisation where the Actors and Goals are taken for granted.

Democracy: results

This section reports on the findings of this study in relation to the word *democracy*. It begins with the earlier data and traces its changes to the present in chronological order.

The data show that one of the most noticeable features of the word *democracy* in 1998 is its tendency to be modified in some way, leading to the impression that *democracy* was a contested and debated word at that time, with a plethora of types of democracy being put forward for scrutiny:

- the Tories' conversion to '**Scottish democracy**'
- in most **enlightened democracies**
- a **modern democracy** with a market economy
- a **property-owning democracy**
- in a **liberal democracy**
- **popular democracy**

Whilst not all the above are recognisable politically defined terms that politics scholars would recognise, they represent what the press was referring to at the time, so that *Scottish democracy* refers to the idea of devolution and *modern democracy* is defined in context as having a market economy, and so on. The point to be made here, though, is the general one, that *democracy* was not a given; its meaning was being negotiated in public through the press.

In 2007 there are also examples of modified *democracy*:

- We have transformed ourselves . . . into an inventive and fairly rich **social democracy**.
- the Polish gay community learned to hide under communist rule and is continuing to hide in the **new democracy**.
- Gordon Brown wants to encourage a '**home-owning democracy**'.

- Our leaders might be keen to impose **Western democracy** on oil-rich nations in the Middle East,
- to create a **'world-class democracy'**
- Finding out what goes on in **open democracies**?

Apart from *social democracy* and *home-owning democracy*, which are similar to those of the earlier period and indicate that democracy may take different forms, the modifiers in 2007 are less concerned with the internal workings of what is meant by *democracy* and more inclined to position *democracy* in opposition to other forms of governance. So the *new democracy* in Poland is implicitly opposed to communism and *Western democracy* is opposed to the monarchies and sheikdoms of the Middle Eastern nations. Similarly, the contrast implicit in *open democracy* is not with 'closed' democracy but with totalitarian states, and *world-class democracy* does not indicate different forms but different standards of a single concept which can be executed either well or badly. The modifiers in this later period each appear to highlight one of the features of a singular concept of democracy, rather than indicating that democracy may have different forms.

Whilst there are some significant differences in the use of *democracy* in the two sets of data, the metaphors are similar and all conceptualise it as a natural organism:

- Local democracy is dying on its feet (1998)
- Other cancers in our democracy threaten more obviously (1998)
- There can be few issues more central to the health of a democracy. (1998)
- Equally, we believe our democracy would be healthier if churchmen spoke out more often on issues of principle and morality (2007)
- one of the world's youngest democracies is being ravaged by widespread gang violence (2007)

These personifications of democracy are interesting because they demonstrate a continuity between the two periods in conceptualising democracy as a naturally occurring phenomenon which may be subject to disasters or disease only partly treatable by those with the knowledge and power to do so. Note that the extension of this metaphor implies that age and death would be the natural end of the process, though this is not explicitly mentioned in the data.

On the other hand, the regular collocates of the keyword show some difference in their rhetorical force between the two periods. In 1998 the keyword turns up in a number of two-part lists:

- **peace and democracy** and that violence is genuinely being given up for good (1998)

- principles of **non-violence and democracy** (1998)
- **human rights and democracy** (1998)

The significance of this is that there is a tendency to associate democracy with peace or absence of violence and with human rights. Two-part lists are usually taken to be genuine lists (see Jeffries, 2010b) which either equate (as in this case) or occasionally contrast related concepts. In 2007, by contrast, the keyword is found in a three-part list:

- the principles of **freedom, democracy and justice** around the globe. (2007)

As many commentators have pointed out (see, for example, Atkinson, 1984; Jeffries, 2010b), the three-part list is a symbolic, rather than a 'real' list. In other words, it implies that the list comprehensively covers the field that it relates to, rather than actually doing so. The phrase quoted above, then, is intended to represent all that is good in Western political systems by the conjoining of the keyword we are considering here with two other unquestioned concepts, *justice* and *freedom*, lending more support to the notion that over the period in question *democracy* has also become one of the foundational axioms of our time. Note also that the *lack* of mention of peace and non-violence may be significant too. The use of even a negated form like non-violence or a positive term like peace, which is strongly associated with its opposite, war, can summon up the opposite for the reader[12], and may thus be a term which is more commonly avoided in relation to *democracy* in these troubled times when there appears to be an absolutism about the right way (Western democracy) and the wrong way (Islamic fundamentalism) to organise human affairs.

Democracy in 1998 is described as having qualities as well as being of different kinds:

- leaving our **democracy** less stable and a weak government inevitable
- a need for more **democracy**
- Pakistan's **democracy** is a corrupt shambles

Here we see that *democracy* was considered more of a neutral organisational tool which could be effective or ineffective (*less stable* and *weak; a corrupt shambles*). In 1998 too it is a mass noun referring to an abstract concept which can be owned (*our democracy; Pakistan's democracy*) and quantified (*more democracy*). This, then, is a substance, like air, sugar or goodness, which may be measured, but not in units, and which may be good or bad, like the concept of government itself or politics.

Contrast the use in 2007 of the countable version, where individual countries are seen as embodying the idea of democracy:

- India is **a democracy**.
- we still have the nerve to sell ourselves as a **democracy** to the world.

This use of the indefinite article (*a*) identifies *democracy* at least partly as a concrete identifiable item which is coterminous with a nation or state. It does not completely eclipse the mass noun usage in 2007, however, though the latter is significantly more positive in its evaluative connotations than in 1998 and is presented as an undifferentiated (unmeasurable) and automatically positive ideal:

- He said: 'Whoever voted to get rid of **democracy**?'
- Mr Blair challenged African leaders to embrace **democracy** in return for increased investment.
- On the contrary, **democracy** demands that minorities must receive protection,

The final aspect of the behaviour of the word *democracy* in this data which I will discuss here is the construction of its opposite in context. Though out of context we may consider the opposite of *democracy* to be *dictatorship* or *autocracy*, one of the findings of work in Critical Discourse Analysis (Davies, 2008; Jeffries, 2010a) is that texts often construct local oppositions by structural means. In 1998 an opposition is created between the contemporary values and practices of democracy (at that time a free-market economy and its effects on social justice arising from Thatcherism) with different types of democracy such as that in Scandinavia:

- Deregulation applies to money, but not to you. As business and capital shrug off the remaining constraints of the post-war years, so the individual is confined to an ever-narrowing corridor of acceptable behaviour, at work, home, even in bed. In contrast to previous conformist social systems – like Scandinavian social *democracy* – there is no trade-off between shrinking personal liberty and economic security. The constraints on the person exist beside a financial system which believes that it is neither possible nor desirable to offer economic security and that those who fail to be competitive must be downsized.

By contrast, the opposites of *democracy* in 2007 tend to assume an undifferentiated concept which as a whole is opposed to other ideologies:

- When did **democracy** end and **racism** start?
- proof that **democracy** and **Islam** can coexist and a future member of the European Union

These two examples demonstrate a link between the two keywords that I have investigated in this chapter. Not only has *radicalisation* become the embodiment of all that is perceived to be bad about Islam but *democracy* is now represented linguistically as the shining and undifferentiated light that can counter the darkness of terrorism and extremist ideology. Note that the final example above argues precisely against this notion, apparently claiming that Islam is not anti-democratic and democracy not anti-Islam. However, the very fact that there appears to be a need to express this view is evidence of the dominant ideology that these are indeed opposites. The structure used here is one that typically juxtaposes conventional opposites to demonstrate that, despite their opposite natures, they are not mutually exclusive. Thus we may commonly find clauses like *good and evil can coexist in the same community*, which illuminates an interesting logical conclusion of the democracy/ Islam opposition example above. Coexistence between *good* and *evil* does not mean that they are necessarily reconciled, and it is not the same as co-operation. Whether the writer intended the same to apply to democracy and Islam is not clear, but it may well be the reader's conclusion.

Conclusion

This chapter has provided a detailed analysis of the use of two words which are commonly used in discussing world affairs and politics. These words, like others we could also study, have been shown to have changed the emphasis of their meaning in subtle ways which can be demonstrated only by the kind of corpus-based study that is reported here. The subtlety, however, belies the importance of how such words often package up ideologies that may become too easily accepted or assimilated by the reading (and voting) public if they go unquestioned. Here we have seen that both words started out at the beginning of the New Labour period as having the potential for both positive and negative evaluations, *radicalisation* as the ideas-based force for social and political change or reform and *democracy*, though positively evaluated as a whole, was seen as having variable quality.

By the end of Blair's time in office these two words had polarised, with *radicalisation* being almost synonymous with extremism and associated almost invariably with Islam. *Democracy* during the same period had moved to the extreme of positive evaluation, with no sense that the term covered a range of different practices which could be quantified or measured for their effectiveness. Most significantly of all, perhaps, the two words, which in 1998 would never have been seen as connected by their oppositeness, by 2007 were beginning to be juxtaposed in precisely this way.

By 2009 the scandal of MPs' expenses was tearing at the heart of the Westminster Parliament, leading to calls for widespread reform of the type of democracy which governs the UK. This may mean that the days of this Blairite keyword as one of the absolutes of social understanding are numbered. What will happen to *radicalisation* is less clear, though Obama's dismantling of some of the pillars of Bush's policies may also lead to the revision of this word in due course.

The chapter has shown that language does not exist as an independent entity but is constituted and transformed according to the rules of changing discursive contexts. This means that language can actively contribute to the construction of a 'reality' rather than just passively describing it. In this chapter the discursive reconfiguring of *radicalisation* and *democracy* has been considered within a political context in which *terrorism* has been constructed as a major threat and the centre ground of British politics has shifted sharply to the right. It is important to recognise that linguistic changes, although ideologically significant, are not necessarily consciously constructed. However, the power of such meanings to influence and persuade is undoubted and further research into the precise mechanisms by which we are affected by texts is required. The fact that politicians and media commentators will continue to produce ideologically slanted meanings leads to the conclusion that the need to educate citizens to be critical readers and independent thinkers[13] is pressing if they are to be truly 'empowered' members of a society where social justice means something real. Subsequent chapters in this volume address the discursive shaping of terms such as 'empowerment', 'social cohesion', 'disability', 'time', 'well-being' and 'class' since 1997. While their focus is social scientific rather than linguistic, their consideration of how these terms have been construed within (and have contributed to) a particular understanding of social justice is strengthened by the evidence of this chapter.

Notes

1 This chapter employs some technical terms, which are explained in the glossary.
2 In fact there is some evidence that Whorf did not see 'his' hypothesis in this extreme way. See O'Halloran (1997) for discussion of this point.
3 Note that I am using italic font to indicate when words are being referred to as linguistic items rather than being used for their own meaning in context. This is a common convention in linguistic work.

4 There may well be different results if the different forms of the word are investigated separately. Because of its prominence in recent events I have focused here on *radicalisation*.

5 Indeed, some linguists have been testing Williams's ideas recently. See, for example, Durant (2006).

6 See, for example, Fairclough (1989, 1992) and Fowler (1991, 1996) for critical discourse analysis and Leech and Short (1981, 2007), Short (1996) and Leech (2008) for stylistics.

7 Note that the question of what exactly is meant by 'the language in general' is a taxing one, and is solved in practical terms by the use of a 'reference corpus' which is usually made up of a broader range of texts than those under consideration or may be constructed specifically to provide certain points of contrast such as those between written and spoken or fictional and non-fictional texts.

8 A University of Huddersfield-funded corpus project investigating the keywords of the New Labour period in the British press will begin to report its findings in 2010. The corpus used was constructed from the holdings of ProQuest, and accessed through Metalib.

9 For this qualitative analysis I considered all occurrences of the two keywords within the periods under comparison. There were approximately 300 examples of *democracy* in each period, and rather fewer (less than 100) examples of *radicalisation*. No counter-examples have been ignored here, so patterns are variable, and indicate tendencies rather than absolute changes in usage and thus in meaning.

10 See Jeffries (1993) for a discussion of this example in the poem 'Broadcast', first published in *The Listener* in 1962.

11 From Hughes-Hallett (1997).

12 Nahajec (2009) and Jeffries (2010b) discuss this capacity for negation to suggest the positive scenario to readers.

13 This, indeed, is one of the explicit aims of the founders of critical discourse analysis. See, for example, Fairclough (1992).

Glossary of terms

Actor The role given to the person (or animal) that initiates a material action. Often the grammatical subject, but not always.

collocates The words that occur regularly with other words. See *collocation*.

collocation the co-occurrence of words in context. Sometimes used only to refer to those words which regularly co-occur.

concordance A set of examples of a word taken from a corpus of texts, and laid out to show the context in which that word occurs. Usually electronically produced these days.

connotation The associations a word has, such as that it is pejorative (e.g. *leer*) or that it is usually used when speaking to children (e.g. *choo-choo*). See also *denotation*.

countable nouns Nouns which refer to individual units which may be enumerated (e.g. *trees*), rather than a mass substance or phenomenon (e.g. *nature*). They usually have a plural form (e.g. *book–books*).

critical discourse analysis (CDA) The study of language in context to discover the naturalised (commonsense) ideologies which are embedded in texts. Often, but not only, having an explicit left-leaning political agenda.

denotation The intended referent, and thus the popular notion of the meaning of a word or words. See *connotation*.

determiners Words which pre-modify nouns, and include articles (*the, a*), possessive adjectives (*my, his*, etc.) and demonstratives (*this, these, that* and *those*).

Goal The role assigned to the intended recipient of a material action. Often the grammatical object, but not always.

keywords Used in two ways here. Firstly, the significant words of a political or historical period. Secondly, the words which occur more commonly in a corpus of texts that would be expected. The intention here is to link these two meanings of the term.

mass nouns Nouns which refer to mass substances or phenomena (e.g. air, love) that cannot be counted and thus have no plural form.

nominalisation The process of changing a verb to a noun (e.g. *transform–transformation*) and also the product of that process (*transformation*).

referent The item or phenomenon that a word refers to. A link between language and the world.

semantic prosody The result of regular collocation which may 'infect' a word with its usual collocational flavour, particularly when that is an evaluative flavour.

Bibliography

Atkinson, M. (1984) *Our Masters' Voices: The Language and Body Language of Politics* (London: Routledge).

Davies, M. (2008) 'Oppositions in News Discourse:the Ideological Construction of "Us" and "Them" in the British Press', unpublished Ph.D. thesis, University of Huddersfield.

Fairclough, N. (1989) *Language and Power* (London: Longman).

Fairclough, N. (ed.) (1992) *Critical Language Awareness* (London: Longman).

Fairclough, N. (2000) *New Labour, New Language?* (London: Routledge).

Fowler, R. (1991) *Language in the News: Discourse and Ideology in the Press* (London: Routledge).

Fowler, R. (1996) 'On critical linguistics', in C. Caldas-Coulthard and M. Coulthard (eds) *Texts and Practices* (London: Routledge).

Durant, A. (2006) 'Raymond Williams's keywords: investigating meanings "offered, felt for, tested, confirmed, asserted, qualified, changed"', *Critical Quarterly* 48:4, 1–26.

Hughes-Hallett, L. (1997) 'The history of our mothers and grandmothers', *Sunday Times*, 15 June.

Jeffries, L. (1993) *The Language of Twentieth Century Poetry* (Basingstoke: Palgrave Macmillan).

Jeffries, L. (2003) 'Not a drop to drink: emerging meanings in local newspaper reporting of the 1995 water crisis in Yorkshire', *Text* 23:4, 513–38.

Jeffries, L. (2007a) 'Journalistic constructions of Blair's "apology" for the intelligence leading to the Iraq war', in Sally Johnson and Astrid Ensslin (eds) *Language in the Media: Representations, Identities, Ideologies* (London: Continuum).

Jeffries, L. (2007b) *Textual Construction of the Female Body: A Critical Discourse Approach* (Basingstoke: Palgrave Macmillan).

Jeffries, L. (2010a) *Opposition in Discourse* (London: Continuum).

Jeffries, L. (2010b) *Critical Stylistics: the power of English* (Basingstoke: Palgrave Macmillan).

Leech, G. (2008) *Language in Literature: Style and Foregrounding* (London: Longman).

Leech, G. and Short, M. (1981, 2007) *Style in Fiction* (London: Longman).

Louw, B. (1993) 'Irony in the text or insincerity in the writer? The diagnostic potential of semantic prosodies', in M. Baker, G. Francis and E. Tognini-Bonelli (eds) *Text and Technology: In Honour of John Sinclair* (Amsterdam: Benjamins).

Nahajec, L. (2009) 'Negation and the creation of meaning in poetry', *Language and Literature* 18:2, 109–27.

O'Halloran, K. A. (1997) 'Why Whorf has been misconstrued in stylistics and critical linguistics', *Language and Literature* 6:3, 163–80.

Sapir, E. (1929): 'The status of linguistics as a science', in E. Sapir, *Culture, Language and Personality*, ed. D. G. Mandelbaum (Berkeley, CA: University of California Press, 1958).

Saussure, Ferdinand de (1966) *Course in General Linguistics*, ed. Charles Bally and Albert Sechehaye, in collaboration with Albert Riedlinger, trans. Wade Baskin (New York: McGraw-Hill).

Short, M. (1996) *Exploring the Language of Poems, Plays and Prose* (London: Longman).

Whorf, B. L. (1956): *Language, Thought and Reality*, ed. J. B. Carroll (Cambridge, MA: MIT Press).

Williams, R. (1976) *Keywords* (Harmondsworth: Penguin).

4

Multiculturalism and the emergence of community cohesion

Paul Thomas

Issues around multiculturalism, race relations and race equality throw this book's concern with the shifting language and 'reality' of New Labour policy into particularly sharp relief. Since the 1950s there have been a series of shifts in dominant political discourse from 'assimilation' to 'multiculturalism' and 'racial equality', with a further shift during New Labour's time in office. Here the 2001 disturbances in various towns and cities in the north of England mark a watershed. In the aftermath of those violent events a genuinely new term, 'community cohesion', was advanced by the government both as an explanation for the disturbances themselves (Cantle, 2001) and as a source of changed priorities around race relations and racial equality (Home Office, 2005, 2007; DCLG, 2007b).

After briefly introducing key terms, the chapter focuses on the most recent discursive shift, from 'multiculturalism' to 'community cohesion', and considers whether this heralded genuine policy changes or simply a change in rhetoric. In contrast to those critics who see the focus on community cohesion as a step backwards, a break with past Labour Party commitments to diversity and racial equality, the chapter finds that the changed language and priorities of community cohesion continued to reflect these, although they were now expressed in terms of New Labour's model of social justice, with its stress on individual responsibility and agency. This means that the apparently new approach was actually built on substantial continuity with past policy and its acceptance of the reality and importance of ethnic diversity. The chapter also draws on a study of community youth workers in Oldham, Greater Manchester, to show that at ground level the effects of the focus on community cohesion can be highly positive. It therefore concludes that, rather than representing a denial of diversity, community cohesion is an attempt, largely consistent with wider New Labour approaches to social justice, to make 'race relations' and ethnic diversity part of a wider, inclusive and coherent citizenship.

Key terms and approaches

The post-war labour shortages that drove the recruitment of labour from the Caribbean and the Indian subcontinent were conceptualised according to the 'the immigrant–host' model (see Patterson, 1965). From this broadly functionalist perspective, the 'host' society was understood as based on consensus. The 'immigrant' group, viewed as temporarily disrupting societal consensus, was expected to adapt to the way of life of the 'host' society, gradually relinquishing their separate cultures, languages and customs. This process of assimilation demanded a significantly higher degree of effort and flexibility on the part of immigrants than the relatively minor adjustments expected of the 'host' society. Any claim of specific needs was viewed with suspicion and education policy of the early 1960s aimed to disperse immigrant children across schools to encourage the use of English (Solomos, 2003). The unintended result of this 'colour-blind' approach for many non-White immigrants was unchecked racial prejudice and discrimination, with 'sticking together' an understandable survival strategy. In this context, there were growing calls for a strengthening of the weak anti-discrimination laws and for 'multiculturalism': the official recognition that communities have different cultural and linguistic needs and interests, that these should be acknowledged and accepted by policy makers, and that ethnic or cultural groups can coexist provided that they respect each other as equals. Although anti-racist critics saw progress as too slow, the Labour governments of 1964–70 and 1974–79 responded positively to these arguments, and in 1966 the then Home Secretary, Roy Jenkins, marked the official move towards 'multiculturalism', defining this 'not as a flattening process of assimilationism but as equal opportunity, accompanied by cultural diversity in an atmosphere of mutual tolerance' (cited in Sivanandan, 2005: 1).

This move was followed by the progressive strengthening of anti-discrimination laws, culminating in the 1976 Race Relations Act and the establishment of the Commission for Racial Equality (CRE) to police it. This acceptance of the need to counter and outlaw racial discrimination was a decisive turning point in Britain, but also one that sidetracked the concern to promote good race relations Although this policy shift was accompanied by the rise of far-right groups like the National Front in the 1970s, these met mass opposition from the Anti-Nazi League and Rock against Racism; involvement in such anti-racist activity was a formative political experience for a number of the (mostly White) New Labour MPs who came to Westminster in 1997.

Whilst well meaning, early policy moves towards multiculturalism could seem largely rhetorical, and were seen by critics as hopelessly naive and liberal in their assumption that racism was purely based on personal ignorance of other cultures. The graphic evidence of the systematic racial discrimination and police harassment faced by ethnic minority Britons provided by the 1981 urban disturbances (Scarman, 1981) led policy makers towards more substantive change, with a decisive move towards stronger 'anti-racist' or political multiculturalist policies. Such approaches were pioneered by Labour-dominated local authorities, such as the Greater London Council of Ken Livingstone, and centred on firm targets to increase the employment and involvement of marginalised non-White groups, 'ethnic data monitoring' to ensure that genuine progress was being made, and a focus on anti-racist training and education based on the key principle that White-dominated countries like Britain were racist and had to face up to the legacy of colonialism and slavery in the shaping of unequal social structures.

Subsequently, the key assumptions of such policies became mainstream at all levels of government and society as part of 'equal opportunities' strategies that focused on ethnic and gender 'equality', rather than the more traditional class concerns of the Labour movement. In 1997 the arrival of many New Labour MPs with clear track records of progressive activity against racism raised hopes of enhanced social justice for ethnic minority communities. These hopes seemed justified in New Labour's early years, with the establishment of the Stephen Lawrence inquiry, following the unprovoked racial murder of the Black teenager in south-east London by five White young men who had evaded prosecution. This was bolstered by the subsequent acceptance of Lord Macpherson's (1999) findings of 'institutional racism', which suggested that the operation of public organisations like the police systematically failed to address the legitimate needs and concerns of ethnic minority communities, and by enhanced action against racial harassment. Alongside this, the infamous 'primary purpose' immigration rule (requiring foreign nationals married to British citizens to prove that the primary purpose of their marriage was not to obtain residence rights) was dropped in 1997, and in 2000 the Race Relations Amendment Act was passed. This Act introduced the potentially groundbreaking Equality Impact Assessments for all public bodies, requiring them to demonstrate that they are actively combating racism and promoting equality of opportunity and good race relations in all areas of their employment practices and service provision (Unison 2000); the implications of this are still unfolding.

The 2001 disturbances as a political watershed

The violent urban disturbances in Oldham, Burnley and Bradford in the north of England during the summer of 2001 were the most serious outbreaks of disorder in Britain since the widespread inner-city disturbances of the early 1980s. The disturbances all involved young men of Asian origin (Pakistani and Bangladeshi) in conflict with the police, and with White young men to a lesser extent. The most serious disturbances were in Bradford, where 326 police officers were injured and damage to property was estimated at over £8 million. In total, over 400 people were arrested for their part in the various disturbances, with many eventually receiving substantial, and arguably harsh (Burnett, 2004), prison sentences. The governmental response was to swiftly establish an 'independent' inquiry panel, which reported in December 2001 (Cantle, 2001), alongside an 'official' governmental endorsement (Denham, 2001) of the key themes and concerns. Both documents proposed 'community cohesion' as a concept to analyse the disturbances and to map future policy directions. Whilst not actually using the term 'community cohesion', reports of local inquiry panels in the affected areas mirrored this new approach, with their focus on 'parallel lives' (Ritchie, 2001; Clarke, 2001).

None of these reports focused in detail on the actual events of the disturbances, seeing them instead as symptomatic of much wider and deeper problems with the state of ethnic relations nationally. This was in stark contrast to the forensic examination of the events of the previous 'watershed' 1981 urban disturbances in Brixton, south London (Scarman, 1981), and suggests that analysis of the 2001 riots provided an opportunity for policy makers to advance a new dialogue already under way (CFMEB, 2000). Because this new perspective suggested that the 2001 disturbances could have happened in numerous British towns and cities, it ignored the 'flashpoints' (King and Waddington, 2004) that escalated tensions in to violence. It also seriously downplayed specific and important causal factors for the disturbances, such as far-right racist political agitation (Bagguley and Hussain, 2008) and local policing, including the misrepresentation of racial crime data (Ray and Smith, 2002); both these factors had been significant in previous, race-related urban disturbances in Britain (Solomos, 2003).

Ignoring these local specificities, community cohesion was rapidly deployed as the new priority for 'race relations', with guidance given to all local authorities to 'promote' cohesion, and to measure it through regular qualitative surveys, with a steady growth in posi- tive attitudes towards diversity and national identity expected over time (LGA, 2002; DCLG, 2007b). Experimental activity to generate 'evidence-based practice' was funded in a number of locations (Home Office, 2003), and community cohesion confirmed as a central prior- ity for national race equality strategies (Home Office, 2005, 2007), with the implication that all types of public funding to voluntary and community organisations should demand the 'promotion of cohesion'. Since September 2007 all British schools have had a duty to promote cohesion, despite wider governmental policies of 'parental choice' and an expansion of the faith school sector that arguably work against this (Cantle, 2005).

The '7/7' London bombings by Islamist extremists in July 2005, and subsequent further terrorist plots, have added further urgency to this focus on cohesion and 'integration' (DCLG, 2007b), with many of the measures originally proposed in 2001 (Cantle, 2001), such as English language tests for all new migrants, more focus on 'Britishness' and greater policy engagement with young people and women within Muslim communities, activated in their wake. This policy direction, along with persistent attempts by politicians to discuss 'Britishness' and to attack multiculturalism (Phillips, 2005), suggests that the model of multiculturalism dominant for several decades had been abandoned by New Labour (Kundnani, 2002). If so, community cohesion represents the end of recognising and celebrating ethnic difference. To assess whether this is true, the following sections examine the key themes and concerns of community cohesion and investigate the impact of the new approaches at community level.

Community cohesion: key themes and concerns

'Community cohesion' had no pedigree as a term within British political debates prior to its deployment after the 2001 disturbances (Flint and Robinson, 2008). Actual definitions of the term itself were surprisingly brief in these governmental reports (Cantle, 2001), leading to consider- able academic analysis and argument over its true meaning (Kundnani, 2001; Kalra, 2002; McGhee, 2003; Alexander, 2004; Thomas, 2007). Much of this academic debate has failed to draw on any empirical evidence as to how community cohesion is actually understood and put into practice, something that this chapter, and the more detailed research that it draws upon (Thomas, 2006, 2007), aim to rectify.

A number of key themes can be detected within the community

cohesion and 'parallel lives' discourse developed by the various reports and taken up as governmental policy. They can be summarised as:

- Ethnic segregation is real and growing, and is causal to tension and mutual fear.
- Community and individual 'agency' play a significant role in accepting and deepening this segregation.
- The problematic nature of over-developed 'bonding' social capital in the absence of forms of 'bridging' contact.
- The negative, unintended, consequences of past 'race relations' policy approaches and the need to reorientate them.

The latter three themes are based on the first, with its core premise that growing ethnic physical and cultural segregation is producing a situation of 'parallel lives', with little social interaction between communities, and a clear lack of 'shared values' or concern with commonality. This focus is highly contested, as much of the empirical data suggest that ethnic segregation is slowly breaking down, while so-called 'White flight' is more about the drift of older and more prosperous communities towards suburban and rural areas than a deliberate rejection of mixed neighbourhoods (Finney and Simpson, 2009). Nevertheless, ethnic segregation is significant in many of Britain's towns and cities, especially in the ex-industrial areas witnessing disturbances in 2001.

Individual and institutionalised racism, such as the reality of racial harassment (Modood *et al.*, 1997) and Oldham Local Authority's past policy of allocating Asian and White tenants to different housing areas, clearly helped to create ethnic segregation (Kundnani, 2001). However, the suggestion in official discourse is that the 'agency' (Greener, 2002) of individuals within all communities has played a role in accepting and deepening this segregation, as shown by their housing and schooling decisions. This is highlighted by the focus on both White flight (Cantle, 2001) and ethnic minority congregation (CRE, 2001). This reflects a consistent focus on 'agency' across New Labour social policy (Greener, 2002; Levitas, 2005), part of the 'Third Way' belief that government alone cannot guarantee social change in an era of rapid global economic and social change. According to this model of social justice, rights are always accompanied by responsibilities, so that individuals must both strive to improve their individual situation and share responsibility for improving the community (Giddens, 1998). Here there is a clear communitarian suggestion that past policy approaches have focused on the rights of different ethnic groups without stressing the necessary and balancing shared responsibilities we all have to build an open and cohesive community (Etzioni, 1995; Cantle, 2001).

In New Labour thinking these concerns became allied to the problematisation of 'bonding' social capital (Putnam, 2000; McGhee, 2003). This drew on the influential model developed by the US academic Robert Putnam (2000), who argued that strengthening 'social capital' (his term for networks and links) could both combat social inequality and address a perceived deficit in cohesive trust within and between communities. He argued that there are two distinct types of social capital: 'bonding' social capital refers to the social ties that link people in homogeneous communities; 'bridging' social capital is built through voluntary associations, ties and common interests *between* communities that are heterogeneous in terms of ethnicity, religion and/or socio-economic status. In terms of social cohesion, 'bridging' social capital is generally considered more helpful, as it prevents the entrenchment of 'bonded' monocultural communities that have little interest in other ethnic communities and minimal contact with them.

In the wake of the 2001 disturbances there was a perceived urgent need to develop avenues for meaningful 'bridging' social capital which would enable dialogue and relationships across ethnic divides, so facilitating the development of shared values and priorities. Official responses were underpinned by the belief that although 'multiculturalist' policy approaches to 'race relations' over the past twenty-five years had achieved notable progress in tackling racial inequality (Modood *et al.*, 1997) they had also had unintended negative consequences. In particular, these policies were thought to have deepened and solidified the divides between different ethnic communities. This post-2001 official analysis saw policies flowing from the 1981 disturbances as having privileged essentialised, separate ethnic communities, and their 'community leaders', through funding for ethnic-specific facilities and organisations. Post-1981 policies also focused on 'ethnic data', with the inclusion of an ethnicity question in the 1991 census, and the use of such data to identify areas of the economy and society where non-White ethnic minorities were underrepresented, or doing less well than average, with the clear implication that this 'ethnic penalty' is due to individual and institutional White racism (Modood *et al.*, 1997; Solomos, 2003).

Arguably, ensuring 'equality' in terms of educational and employment outcomes, and in community facilities, for each separate ethnic group took priority over common needs and identities, including over multiracial movements against racism (Sivanadan, 2005). By 2001 many policy makers felt that although 'multiculturalism' represented a genuine attempt at remedying profound ethnic inequalities, and accommodating difference, it had actually accepted and deepened ethnic segregation through focusing on the separate needs of each essentialised ethnic group whilst neglecting common forms of identity and the inter-ethnic contact and dialogue which can develop it (Bhavnani, 2001). From this perspective, community cohesion could be seen as a necessary and overdue correction to the problems of past policy approaches, replacing the past focus on difference with a focus on commonality (Cantle, 2001; 2005). The explicit criticism of 'multi-culturalism' for perpetuating, or even partially causing, ethnic segregation, demanded that it should be sidelined as a policy approach, and its juxtaposition with integration (Phillips, 2005) seemed to suggest that it had been abandoned in favour of New Labour's focus on cohesion.

The 'death of multiculturalism'?

The initial reaction of anti-racist commentators to the new policy approach was that it indeed represented 'the death of multiculturalism' (Kundnani, 2002). This perception was strengthened by the political pronouncements, including those of the then Home Secretary, David Blunkett, that accompanied the new policy launch, and that seemed to focus very partially on the agency of ethnic minority communities in creating segregation (Travis, 2001) rather than on racism. These comments, made just a few months after the 9/11 attacks on New York of 2001, helped to set a tone for long-running public debate focused on the apparent 'refusal' of some ethnic minority communities to 'become British' (Goodhart, 2004), with the suggestion here being that the 2001 disturbances represented a refusal by Muslim communities to integrate, encouraged by multiculturalism. The idea that multiculturalism is dead is supported by a reading of some sections of the key reports, with their associated demand that Asian communities show 'a universal acceptance of the English language' and 'develop a greater acceptance of, and engagement with, the principal national institutions' (Cantle, 2001: 19).

For some critics of the new policy, the disturbances represented frustration by Asian young people at their inability to access mainstream citizenship because of racism and social exclusion, rather than symbolising a lack of interest in being British (Kundnani, 2007). The disturbances occurred in areas where the dominant textile industries and their associated trade unions which had provided some forms of 'bridging' social capital (Kundnani, 2001) between Asian and White workers had disappeared. This disappearance, and the failure to develop viable post-industrial economies locally is clearly relevant to the subsequent lack of 'bridging' social capital, while within many of the White and Asian communities experiencing post-industrial social exclusion as 'losers' in a rapidly globalising economy, inward-looking and defensive forms of 'neighbourhood nationalism' (Back, 1996) are developing. Such monocultural community identity is strongest amongst those who have been most damaged by economic change (May, 1999), and critics blamed New Labour's wholehearted endorsement of neo-liberal economic orthodoxies for the social exclusion and associated alternative cultures and identities slowly developing in such areas (Byrne, 1999).

From such critical perspectives, the community cohesion discourse is a racialised narrative that blames the victims of racism for their own situation, conveniently avoiding focus on the structural causes of this segregation and alienation (Alexander, 2004; Burnett, 2004). Indeed, the very reality of 'segregation', a central tenet of the community cohesion analysis, has been questioned in a situation where all publicly educated British young people experience the same educational curriculum and, increasingly, the same mass-media-based youth culture (Kalra, 2002). Community cohesion, critics have suggested, has portrayed the symptom of ethnic segregation as the cause of inequality and alienation amongst non-White ethnic minorities. The subsequent questioning of the continued use of Asian-community languages, the linking of this with Muslim community educational under-achievement (Ritchie, 2001), the questioning of future minority-language translation of public documents, and an initial move towards ending public funding for community groups serving specific ethnic communities unless they clearly promote cross-community contact (DCLG, 2007b) all suggested to some a move away from multiculturalism and back to the discredited policy of assimilationism (Kundnani, 2007). Such criticisms of the apparent assumptions and priorities of community cohesion make it all the more important that empirical data on how cohesion are actually understood and operationalised is presented and discussed.

Field research evidence: context

This chapter draws on empirical evidence from research carried out in Oldham amongst youth workers working with marginalised young people from the town's different communities. The aim was to explore what they understood community cohesion to mean and represent, and how, if it at all, it has altered their work with young people. Youth workers are mainly employed by local authorities, but there is also a very significant range of independent, voluntary-sector youth work organisations. Thirty youth workers, of ethnically mixed backgrounds and at levels of responsibility within both types of organisations, took part in in-depth, semi-structured, one-to-one interviews. In this context, the White male researcher was acutely aware of the need to not 'take for granted' essentialised notions of ethnic identity, and the importance of both 'working with and against' categories of 'race' and ethnicity (Gunaratnam, 2003). In all cases, respondents nominated a pseudonym by which they are identified. Youth workers were chosen as a focus for a number of reasons. The reports on the 2001 disturbances highlighted not only that more youth work provision was needed for the sort of young people involved in this racial tension and violence (Cantle, 2001; Denham, 2001), but also that the pre-2001 youth work provision in Oldham was not adequate, so contributing to youth aliena-tion (Ritchie, 2001). Clearly, interpretations of policy and changes to it are always situated and contingent, but by focusing on such a key group of welfare professionals working in Oldham, one of Britain's most ethnically segregated and tense towns, the aim was to shed light on the reality of community cohesion, and its implications in practice for multiculturalism.

At the time of the 2001 disturbances Oldham was the thirty-eighth most deprived of 354 local authorities in England (Cantle, 2006), with three electoral wards amongst the 1 per cent most deprived in England. Once the 'cotton-spinning capital of the world', Oldham's unemployment rate is more than twice the national average (Cantle, 2006) with low wage rates for many of those in work. Problems are particularly acute for the White working class, and for the Pakistani and Bangladeshi communities. With almost 50 per cent of the town's Asian population aged twenty-five years old or under, the 13 per cent ethnic minority section of Oldham's population overall becomes 23 per cent of its under-twenty-five-year old population, with the non-White element of its under-eighteen-year-old population forecast to rise to 40 per cent by 2021(Oldham MBC, 2006). Racial tension between ethnically segregated housing areas of Oldham is a reality, and local racial attack statistics have consistently been the highest in the Greater Manchester area. The reporting of the 'fact' that Whites formed a (slight) majority of the victims of Oldham's reported incidents (out of step with virtually every other area nationally) is seen a key trigger of the 2001 distur-bances (Ray and Smith, 2002). Much racial crime and conflict locally, as nationally, involves young people, and research with young people in Oldham shortly after the 2001 disturbances (Thomas, 2003) showed high levels of mutual fear and suspicion, and common experiences of racially aggravated violence.

Field research evidence: findings

Detailed findings are discussed elsewhere (Thomas, 2006, 2007) but can be summarised as follows. Community cohesion had clear understanding and support from youth workers in Oldham, who highlighted significant changes in the assumptions, priorities and methods of their professional practice as a result. This new post-2001 policy of community cohesion was understood as distinctly different, and better, than previous approaches. There was a clear consensus that community cohesion meant the promotion and facilitation by youth workers of 'meaningful direct contact' amongst young people of different ethnic backgrounds:

> Building relationships, friendships, and knowing what other cultures, other religions are doing and why, and understanding each other. (Asad, male, Bangladeshi origin)

Bringing young people together across ethnic divides has become the fundamental cohesion priority for youth work agencies in Oldham. Youth clubs and projects serving different communities have been linked up (including areas of the same ethnic background with conflicts over 'territory') and given the responsibility of devising a number of shared events, trips and festivals, so that young people of different backgrounds have the chance to build dialogue and relationships. Town-wide events, such as parties for Christmas and the Muslim Eid festival are held, at which delegations of young people from every youth project come together for shared activities and discussions. This may seem very normal, routine work with young people, but in the context of an ethnically segregated, tense town such work is risky and innovative. The risk is illustrated by this account of a residential trip involving White and Asian youth groups:

> We went for an Indian meal on the first night we took them to Whitby . . . and one of the White lads said, 'God, if people on Thorndale knew what we're doing now, we'd get leathered' [beaten up], and that was just going to a restaurant. (Johnson, White-origin male)

Given this racialised reality, a key principle of the new community cohesion work is that activities bringing young people together are about fun, using sports and arts, rather than discussions and conferences about racism and problems. This is a deliberate attempt to portray ethnic diversity as normal and positive, with common youth identities of all being from the same town with common interests and the same desire for fun and new experiences. The aim here is that, rather than make young people formally talk about diversity and racism, dialogue develops informally through friendship, talking at a time when they feel comfortable. This is illustrated by an account from an annual residential trip where delegations from every high school in Oldham (including young people with disabilities) take part in activities organised by the youth workers with the aim of encouraging mixing:

> One of the Muslim young women was praying at night, so the other girls watched her pray and asked her really interesting questions about it. The fact was that it was done at one o'clock in the morning, and they really should have been in bed, but I didn't stop it because it was a really interesting dialogue going on. (Mary, White-origin female)

These new approaches are seen by youth workers as in clear contrast to the past, when different areas and communities had no contact or joint activities at all and each kept to its own area, with insularity and separation the result. This past policy approach included the 'norm' that young people were served by youth workers from the 'same' ethnic background (usually the same geographical community), with it being 'inappropriate' to have workers of a different background working with ethnic minority young people. Community cohesion in Oldham has meant a total reversal of this, with youth workers being deliberately encouraged to work with young people of a different background, in order to encourage dialogue and questioning, and to have a diversity of positive role models. This has included a Pakistani-origin youth worker moving to an all-White social housing area seen as a target for the far-right British National Party:

> I've never had a problem here working as a Black worker . . . yes, people, have taken me very well. (Qummar, Pakistani-origin male)

Working with a different community in a situation of segregation and racism (Ritchie, 2001) has obviously been challenging for youth workers, with some initial hostility, but all supported this new policy direction, believing that it is vital to provide young people with what may be their first chance to get to know and debate with an adult from a different ethnic background. This is all seen as in clear contrast to the pre-2001 policy norms, which youth workers in Oldham understood as 'anti-racism'. Youth workers understood 'anti-racism' as meaning that they should only work with young people of the same ethnic background, that there was nothing to be gained from bringing young people together, and that youth work projects on racism should involve quite formal lesson-type approaches which told young people that racism is wrong, punishing any behaviour or comments seen as 'racist'.

This, and the negative reaction youth workers reported often receiving from White young people in response to these approaches, echoes other previous studies on the down side of 'anti-racism' as it has often been understood and practised at ground level (MacDonald, 1989; CRE, 1999):

> It's [anti-racism] not respectful, it's not effective, and I actually think it is damaging as well. (Alex, dual-heritage-background female)

Such anti-racist educational approaches were well intentioned but have often led to resentment from White working-class young people, who responded to the stress on ethnic identity with the feeling that they were being marginalised and ignored by policies that saw non-White ethnic minorities as having greater needs and priorities whilst the culture, language and behaviour of White communities were judged negatively (Hewitt, 2005).

Discussion: multiculturalism alive and well?

This empirical case-study evidence sheds significant light on the key community cohesion themes and concerns discussed above. The community cohesion analysis of deep and problematic ethnic segregation, and of considerable 'agency' in perpetuating that division, was accepted by the respondents, confirming that community cohesion is focused on bringing different ethnic communities together in search of dialogue and common identities. However, this need not mean that multiculturalism is dead, and that there has been a lurch back towards assimilationism. In contrast to some unhelpful political pronouncements (Travis, 2001; Phillips, 2005), the empirical evidence suggests that, as it is being actually understood and practised, community cohesion represents a new and refocused form of multiculturalism, not a rejection of it. The key issue here is community cohesion's acceptance of the reality of ethnic diversity, with youth work in Oldham focusing on negotiation, accommodation and dialogue between those differences, rather than attempting to deny or undermine them (Thomas, 2006, 2007). Not only does the community cohesion activity with young people focus on negotiation of their different experiences and understandings, but it works with and accepts their continued need for separate facilities and identity. This continued need for locally based youth provision representing specific ethnic backgrounds and identities here runs alongside, and is a vital component of, the activities that bring young people together with others of a different ethnic background, as shown by this example from a young women's drama project:

It had to be both, it had to be work with their own community and the opportunity to integrate and mix with others. (Deborah, White-origin female)

In working in this way, and so ensuring that the 'meaningful direct contact' between young people of different ethnic backgrounds in the name of community cohesion only occurs after preparation work with, and agreement from, young people of each ethnic background, youth workers in Oldham are practising what could be termed 'transversal politics' (Yuval-Davis, 1997). This approach stresses the multidimensionality and context-dependent nature of identity, which is seen as constructed around the intersections of ethnicity, gender, religion and culture. Rather than asserting a model of cohesion that emphasises allegiance to so-called British values, Yuval-Davis suggests instead an arguably more self-confident and flexible approach of 'rooting and shifting' of individual attitudes and assumptions. This can take place during 'direct contact', when attitudes to 'others' can be reconsidered and amended because one's own identity is *not* being threatened or put under unwanted scrutiny. This view appears to be consistent with the informal, fun element of the youth work conducted on 'neutral territory' that was observed for this research. Whilst working with diversity, the implicit expectation is that, over time, these differing identities will soften and become more accommodating of difference.

These community cohesion approaches support the thesis of 'contact theory', the belief that in a reality of stark ethnic segregation and conflict contact must take place in groups, be chosen voluntarily and be sustained over time to have a meaningful impact on mutual prejudices and fears. Unsurprisingly, many of these lessons for towns like Oldham come from Northern Ireland (Hewstone *et al.*, 2007). Critics of community cohesion suggest that 'voluntary' activities like these youth work examples, and parallel 'twinning' activities between schools with different ethnic populations, were prioritised because New Labour lacked the political will to tackle the fundamental segregation issues of housing and school allocation (Kalra, 2002). However, the evidence from attempts to force the creation of 'socially (i.e. class) mixed' housing areas is negative, with much more positive evidence from initiatives promoting voluntary contact and co-operation between social (rented, low-income) and owner-occupied (middle-income) housing areas (Robinson, 2005).

This empirical evidence stresses the importance of continued ethnic-specific community agencies and facilities that can work with and prepare specific ethnic (coterminus with geographic in Oldham) communities for community cohesion approaches, and the acceptance of the reality of diversity within those approaches. For that reason, the clumsy understanding of community cohesion by some local authorities resulting in withdrawal of funding for community organisations serving one ethnic/religious group only was badly misguided (Bourne, 2007).This unhelpful direction stemmed from recommendations of the Commission on Cohesion and Integration (DCLG, 2007b), and has since been reversed. However, more significant contradictions were presented by the government's 'Preventing Violent Extremism' (PVE) initiative. As an education-based 'hearts and minds' element of the 'CONTEST' counter-terrorism response to the 7/7 London bombings of July 2005 and to subsequent Islamist bomb plots, this programme had positive aspects, but also major problems. Foremost here is the reality that the initial phase of the programme worked almost exclusively with Muslim young people (Thomas, 2008). This focus on one community and identity only, and public funding of activity with them, is in flat contradiction to the priority of community cohesion, and the associated analysis that sees singular identities, and the progression towards violent and antagonistic forms of those identities for small minorities, as a direct result of segregation, and of the policy privileging of such separate ethnic identities. Such an approach risks hardening separate Muslim identities whilst further fuelling the White sense of 'unfairness' (Hewitt, 2005) at another public funding stream concerned with ethnic minorities only. Alongside this is a lack of focus in PVE on extremism in other communities, such as the significant growth in support for the British National Party, some of whose members have recent track records of political violence (Thomas, 2009).

Notwithstanding that contradiction, the community cohesion acceptance of diversity whilst focusing on the need for commonality, rather than being counter to the Labour government's wider race equality measures (Back *et al.*, 2002), was actually quite consistent. Here, an overarching 'human rights' framework is being developed that recognises diversity of all kinds, but which also insisted on universal adherence to 'core' values whereby religious/ethnic 'identity' cannot be allowed to supersede fundamental individual rights. In an increasingly complex and 'hybrid' (Hall, 2000) Britain, community cohesion is part of attempts to create 'cooler', decentred and intersectional forms of identity, rather than (inevitably conflictual) 'hot' forms of identity (McGhee, 2006). Here, progress towards genuine 'multiculturalism' can be made only if all forms of identity are given weight and respect, with the rights and access to equality of gay and lesbian people, or women of all ethnic backgrounds being just as valid and important as the rights and equality of ethnic minority 'communities'. This suggests that all backgrounds and identities need to be willing to adapt assumptions and behaviour, and that the Labour government was being quite consistent in amalgamating the separate equality bodies like the CRE and Equal Right Commission into the over-arching CEHR to reflect the reality of multiple identities and experiences. However, this demands genuine consistency from the government, with New Labour's focus on 'consulting' faith-based Mosque federations such as the Muslim Council of Britain as 'representatives' of the Muslim 'community' difficult to justify when there are hundreds of Muslim-faith elected councillors, MPs and magistrates around Britain who are well equipped to comment on situations relating to Pakistani and Bangladeshi communities. This suggests that the community cohesion journey from the group-rights focus on a 'community of communities' (CFMEB, 2000) to a multiple-identity-based citizenship is far from complete (McGhee, 2006).

Arguably the most problematic result of the prioritisation of community cohesion has been the downplaying of language associated with 'race' and racial equality. Alongside the attacks on multiculturalism, this has led some critics to detect a downplaying of concern with racism itself, as was echoed by some respondents in the field research:

> It's [community cohesion] put race equality on the back burner, because in this town you see the term 'cohesion' bandied around all over the place, but as soon as you mention race equality it's like saying, 'No, you're going back five years, no, you're going back ten years' . . . but you can't realistically ignore race equality . . . it's not divided on cohesion grounds, it's divided on racial grounds. (Imran, Pakistani-origin male)

The racial equality policy measures outlined above suggest otherwise. Critics have characterised community cohesion as a racialised agenda that enables government to talk about 'problematic' ethnic minority communities without naming them, as shown by 'slippages' in language (Worley, 2005), but arguably such slippages represent genuine governmental ambiguity over the extent to which experience can be explained by 'race' and ethnicity. The clear focus on the disadvantage of some ethnic minority communities in New Labour's social exclusion agenda (SEU, 1999) demonstrates a continued awareness of ethnicity as a factor, but the reality of very different educational experiences for different non-White communities (Modood *et al.*, 1997) suggests that class is as relevant as 'race' here. Indeed, the over-attention given to ethnicity and educational achievement may well have obscured the very serious disadvantage faced by White working-class boys in a policy context that has privileged 'race' over class (Runnymede Trust, 2009).

The ambivalence shown by many research respondents in Oldham over whether community cohesion should be focused on 'race' or on wider 'social' and economic cohesion reflects that reality.

Conclusion

With the introduction of the new policy concept of 'community cohesion' the 2001 disturbances proved to be a turning point in New Labour policy approaches to 'race relations'. For some, this renewed focus on commonality, rather than the continued prioritisation of essentialised ethnic difference, inevitably represented the 'death of multiculturalism' (Kundnani, 2002). However, the empirical evidence from grass-roots activity in Oldham discussed in this chapter suggests that the allegation of a move back towards assimilationism is misplaced. Rather than denying or opposing ethnic difference, community cohesion youth work in Oldham accepts diversity and is engaged in negotiating dialogue and contact between that difference through enjoyable and informal forms of youth activity that enable relationship building and prejudice/fear reduction without existing community identities or assumptions being overtly challenged or disrespected. The fact that this community cohesion activity accepts both diversity itself and the need for specific ethnic groups to have distinct identities and facilities within the process suggests that it represents continuity with previous forms of 'multiculturalism' (Solomos, 2003).

Additionally, this community cohesion-based youth work in Oldham has been concerned with 'difference' on the basis of class, territory, dis/ability and sexuality, suggesting that the multiculturalism being accepted and worked with here is a more complex form of 'critical multiculturalism' (May, 1999) that considers the variety of influences on individual identity, rather than privileging essentialised forms of ethnic identity (Bhavnani, 2001).This is consistent with wider New Labour approaches, with ethnicity seen as only one of a number of important creators of experience (SEU, 1999). In this way, community cohesion, and the way it is practised by youth workers in Oldham, represents not the 'death of multiculturalism' but the rejection of one form of it, 'anti-racism', in favour of a more complex and holistic multiculturalism that is attempting to operationalise understandings of citizenship and social justice based on the reality of complex multiple identities, including shared ones that cut across ethnic and religious divides. Arguably, this creates the possible conditions for multi-racial alliances for social justice, something much needed in an increasingly unequal, neo-liberal economic reality.

73

Bibliography

Alexander, C. (2004) 'Imagining the Asian gang: ethnicity, masculinity and youth after the riots', *Critical Social Policy* 24:4, 526–49.

Back, L. (1996) *New Ethnicities and Urban Culture* (London: UCL Press).

Back, L., Keith, M., Khan, A., Shukra, K. and Solomos, J. (2002) 'New Labour's white heart: politics, multiculturalism and the return of assimilationism', *Political Quarterly* 73:4, 445–54.

Bagguley, P. and Hussain, Y. (2008) *Riotous Citizens?* (Aldershot: Ashgate).

Bhavnani, R. (2001) *Rethinking Interventions in Racism* (Stoke on Trent: Trentham Books).

Bourne, J. (2007) *In Defence of Multiculturalism*, IRR Briefing Paper 2 (London: IRR).

Burnett, J. (2004) 'Community, cohesion and the state', *Race and Class* 45:3, 1–18.

Byrne, D. (1999) *Social Exclusion* (Oxford: Blackwell).

Cantle, T. (2001) *Community Cohesion: A Report of the Independent Review Team* (London: Home Office).

Cantle, T. (2005) *Community Cohesion: A new Framework for Race Relations* (Basingstoke; Palgrave).

Cantle, T. (2006) *Challenging Local Communities to Change Oldham* (Coventry: Institute of Community Cohesion).

CFMEB, Commission on the Future of Multi-ethnic Britain (2000) *The Parekh Report* (London: Runnymede Trust).

Clarke, T. (2001) *Burnley Task Force Report on the Disturbances in June 2001* (Burnley: Burnley Borough Council).

CRE, Commission for Racial Equality (1999) *Open Talk, Open Minds* (London: CRE).

CRE (2001) *A Place for Us All: Learning from Bradford, Oldham and Burnley* (London: CRE).

DCLG, Department for Communities and Local Government (2007a) *Preventing Violent Extremism: Winning Hearts and Minds* (London: DCLG).

DCLG (2007b) *Commission on Integration and Cohesion: Our Shared Future* (London: DCLG).

Denham, J. (2001) *Building Cohesive Communities: A Report of the Inter-departmental Group on Public Order and Community Cohesion* (London: Home Office).

Etzioni, A. (1995) *The Spirit of Community: Rights, Responsibilities and the Communitarian Agenda* (London: Fontana).

Finney, N. and Simpson, L. (2009) *Sleepwalking to Segregation? Challenging Myths about Race and Migration* (Bristol: Policy Press).

Flint, J. and Robinson, D., eds (2008) *Community Cohesion in Crisis?* (Bristol: Policy Press).

Giddens, A. (1998) *The Third Way: The Renewal of Social Democracy* (Cambridge: Polity Press).

Goodhart, D. (2004) 'Discomfort of strangers', *Guardian*, 24 and 25 February.

Greener, I. (2002) 'Agency, social theory and social policy', *Critical Social Policy* 22:4, 688–705.

Gunaratnam, Y. (2003) *Researching 'Race' and Ethnicity* (London: Sage).

Hall, S. (2000) 'Conclusion. The multicultural question', in B. Hesse (ed.) *Un/Settled Multiculturalisms* (London: Zed Books).

Hewitt, R. (2005) *White Backlash: The Politics of Multiculturalism* (Cambridge: Cambridge University Press).

Hewstone, M., Tausch, N., Hughes, J. and Cairns, E. (2007) 'Prejudice, intergroup contact and identity: do neighbourhoods matter?', in M. Wetherell, M. Lafleche and R. Berkley (eds) *Identity, Ethnic Diversity and Community Cohesion* (London: Sage).

Home Office (2003) *Community Cohesion Pathfinder Programme: The First Six Months* (London: Home Office).

Home Office (2005) *Improving Opportunity, Strengthening Society: The Government's Strategy to increase Race Equality and Community Cohesion* (London: Home Office).

Home Office (2007) *Improving Opportunity, Strengthening Society: A Two-year Review* (London: Home Office).

Kalra, V. S. (2002) 'Extended view: riots, race and reports: Denham, Cantle, Oldham and Burnley inquiries', *Sage Race Relations Abstracts* 27:4, 20–30.

King, M. and Waddington, D. (2004) 'Coping with disorder? The changing relationship between police public order strategy and practice – a critical analysis of the Burnley riot', *Policing and Society* 14:2, 118–37.

Kundnani, A. (2001) 'From Oldham to Bradford: the violence of the violated', in *The Three Faces of British Racism* (London: Institute of Race Relations).

Kundnani, A. (2002) *The Death of Multiculturalism* (London: Institute of Race Relations), www.irr.org.uk/2002/april/ak000001.html (accessed 24 June 2009).

Kundnani, A. (2007) *The End of Tolerance? Racism in Twenty-first-century Britain* (London: Pluto).

Levitas, R. (2005) *The Inclusive Society?* 2nd edn (Basingstoke: Palgrave).

LGA, Local Government Association (2002) *Guidance on Community Cohesion* (London: LGA).

Macdonald, I. (1989) *Murder in the Playground: the Report of the Macdonald Inquiry* (Manchester: Longsight Press).

Macpherson, W. (1999) *The Stephen Lawrence Inquiry: Report of an Inquiry by Sir William Macpherson of Cluny* (Cm 4262) (London: Stationery Office).

McGhee, D.(2003) 'Moving to "our" common ground: a critical examination of community cohesion discourse in twenty-first-century Britain', *Sociological Review* 51:3, 366–404.

McGhee, D. (2006) 'The new Commission for Equality and Human Rights: building community cohesion and revitalising citizenship in contemporary Britain', *Ethnopolitics* 5:2, 145–66.

May, S. (1999) 'Critical multiculturalism and cultural difference: avoiding essentialism', in S. May (ed.), *Critical Multiculturalism* (London: Falmer).

Modood, T., Berthoud, R., Lakey, J., Nazroo, J., Smith, P., Virdee, S. and Beishon, S. (1997) *Ethnic Minorities in Britain: Diversity and Disadvantage* (London: PSI).

Oldham Metropolitan Borough Council (2006) *Population Forecasts for Oldham: Children and Young People* (Oldham: OMBC).

Patterson, S. (1965) *Dark Strangers* (Harmondsworth: Penguin).

Phillips, T. (2005) *After 7/7: Sleepwalking to Segregation*, speech given to the Manchester Council for Community Relations, 25 September.

Putnam, R. (2000) *Bowling Alone: The Collapse and Revival of American Community* (London: Touchstone).

Ray, L. and Smith, D. (2002) *Racist Offending, Policing and Community Conflict*, paper presented to the British Sociological Association annual conference, University of York.

Ritchie, D. (2001) *Oldham Independent Review: One Oldham, One Future* (Manchester: Government Office for the Northwest).

Robinson, D. (2005) 'The search for community cohesion: key themes and dominant concepts of the public policy agenda', *Urban Studies* 42:8, 1411–27.

Runneymede Trust (2009) *Who Cares about the White Working Class?* (London: Runneymede Trust).

Scarman, Lord (1981) *A Report into the Brixton Disturbances of 11–12th April 1981* (London: Home Office).

SEU, Social Exclusion Unit (1999) *Bridging the Gap: New Opportunities for 16–18 year olds* (London: SEU).

Sivanandan, A. (2005) *Its Anti-racism that was failed, not Multiculturalism that failed* (London: Institute of Race Relations), www.irr.org.uk/2005/october/ak000021.html (accessed 24 June 2009).

Solomos, J. (2003) *Race and Racism in Britain*, 3rd edn (Basingstoke: Palgrave).

Thomas, P. (2003) 'Young people, community cohesion, and the role of youth work in building social capital', *Youth and Policy* 81, 21–43.

Thomas, P. (2006) 'The impact of "community cohesion" on youth work: a case study from Oldham', *Youth and Policy* 93: 41–60.

Thomas, P. (2007) 'Moving on from "anti-racism"? Understandings of community cohesion held by youth workers', *Journal of Social Policy* 36:3, 435–55.

Thomas, P. (2008) *Evaluation of the Kirklees Preventing Violent Extremism pathfinder: issues and lessons from the first year* (Huddersfield: University of Huddersfield).

Thomas, P. (2009) 'Between two stools? The government's Preventing Violent Extremism agenda', *Political Quarterly* 80:2, 282–91.

Travis, A. (2001) 'Blunkett in race row over culture tests', *Guardian*, 10 December.

Unison (2000) *Race Relations Amendment Act 2000: A Guide for Branches*, www.unison.org.uk/acrobat/14207.pdf (accessed 24 June 2009).

Worley, C. (2005) '"It's not about race, it's about the community": New Labour and community cohesion', *Critical Social Policy* 25:4, 483–96.

Yuval-Davis, N. (1997) 'Ethnicity, gender relations and multiculturalism', in T. Modood and P. Werbner (eds) *Debating Cultural Hybridity* (London: Zed Books).

5

Class and individualisation within post-compulsory education and training

James Avis

This chapter explores questions of class in post compulsory education and training (PCET)[1] in England and relates these to wider questions of social justice and citizenship. While at first sight the presence of class within PCET is blindingly obvious (one need only enter a college of further education to become aware of markers of class distinction), the chapter argues that the logic of much New Labour policy has been to play down the significance of class as a structural phenomenon, while PCET research tends to downplay the 'making' of class though educational processes.

The chapter shows that New Labour's policies in the area have been underpinned by a particular understanding of social relations, citizenship and economy that treats equality of opportunity as a central aspect of social justice. This understanding draws on earlier models of social democracy, but has reworked these to emphasise the pursuit of economic competitiveness as a collective and individual good. Consequently the citizen is rhetorically constructed as one who bears the responsibility for developing themselves through lifelong learning in order to contribute towards this goal. New Labour's emphasis upon the individual, allied to a consensual understanding of social relations that sees everyone benefiting from the pursuit of competitive advantage, sidelines the analysis of structural inequalities and rules out the possibility that the economic interests of different classes might at times conflict. From this New Labour perspective, social justice means both that individuals are provided with opportunities to succeed and that they are responsible for using these opportunities to further their own careers; this is seen as a source of collective prosperity, but underlying hierarchies and structural inequalities remain unexamined.

This chapter addresses these issues from a broadly Marxist position. The first section considers the broader policy context of PCET, exploring the discourses of class and competition that characterised New

Labour thinking and linking these to evidence of class inequalities. The second section focuses specifically on how class has been conceived within education policy and New Labour thinking. The concluding section comments on existing ethnographic work and its relationship to class formation, arguing for a more nuanced approach that takes account of the micro everyday experiences within PCET that articulate with structural divisions, thereby contributing to the perpetuation of class inequalities.

Policy context: competition and class

New Labour's consensual image of a society in which all can benefit from a culture of learning and in which high level skills and competition are key to individual and collective prosperity is clear in official documents from 1997. Thus in 1998 *The Learning Age* stated that:

> Our vision of the learning age is about more than employment. The development of learning will help to build a united society, assist in the creation of personal independence, and encourage our creativity and innovation . . .
>
> For individuals:
> - learning offers excitement and the opportunity for discovery . . . It helps all of us to improve our chances of getting a job and getting on . . .
>
> For businesses:
> - learning helps them to be more successful by adding value and keeping them up-to-date . . .
>
> For communities:
> - learning contributes to social cohesion and fosters a sense of belonging, responsibility and identity . . .
>
> For the nation:
> - learning is essential to a strong economy and an inclusive society. In offering a way out of dependency and low expectation . . . (DfEE, 1998: 10–11)

Nine years later, *World Class Skills: Implementing the Leitch Review of Skills* reported that:

> [Leitch] demonstrated why skills are so important to the UK's continuing prosperity.
>
> For adults, better skills and economically valuable qualifications are a route to achieving better jobs, career progression and higher incomes to support their families. Better skills are the key to greater social mobility, ensuring that individuals can get on because of their talent and hard work, and not just because of background.
>
> For employers, a more highly-skilled workforce is a route to achieving

higher productivity and, in private sector, greater competitiveness and profitability.
For communities, better skills can create an escape route from generations of low ambition, and low achievement. (DIUS, 2007: 6)

The assumption that education plays a pivotal role in the development of national competitiveness is central to such statements. The aim is to create a learning culture for all. The outcome of such a culture, it is claimed, will be a successful economy, a society marked by social cohesion and inclusion, which will lead to patterns of social and occupational mobility that match the individual's potential and talent. In other words the development of a learning culture will lead to a fairer and more just society. As the *New Opportunities* White Paper (Cabinet Office, 2009) states:

This is an economy in which the knowledge and skills of people are now the most important resource as well as our best chance of social progress. The countries which succeed will be those which make the most of the talents and potential of all their citizens. So if we make the right decisions in the downturn and continue to invest in skills and people, we can provide better jobs, wages and prospects for our citizens in the years to come. This means stepping up our efforts to unlock the talents of every child and young person from their earliest years, and supporting adults right through their working lives, so that we can build a more prosperous economy and a stronger, fairer society. (Cabinet Office, 2009: 3–4)

Such statements equate equality with equality of opportunity rather than outcomes, and rest on a model of citizenship and social justice that locates these atomistically, in the provision of opportunity and the individual's responsibility to develop themselves for their own benefit as well as that of society. It assumes a consensual model of society that marginalises structural relations and patterns of social antagonism, and sets opportunity at the individual level, with the state ensuring the absence of discrimination.

The new rhetoric of class
When class is considered in New Labour's discursive rhetoric, it has been marshalled in two ways, either as a gloss for disadvantage and those cultures that devalue education, or as a critique of the elitism of privileged groups. In the case of the former, the goal is to enculture the socially excluded to develop dispositions or forms of subjectivity that enable educational engagement and success. An early manifestation of this is expressed in the Fryer Report:

In our country today, far too many people are still locked in a culture which regards lifelong learning as either unnecessary, unappealing, uninteresting or unavailable ... to change this culture will require action on many fronts, over an extended period, winning people to new ways of working, new priorities and a new sense of what is seen as normal and largely unremarkable. (Fryer Report, 1999: 8)

The need to create a new culture of learning in which the learner takes responsibility for their own development is similarly found in *World Class Skills:*

We must create a new culture of learning at all stages of a person's career and skills development. Too many people, even in today's environment of high employment and rising skills levels, are left behind. (DIUS, 2007: 22)

The second stance on class represents a more submerged theme within New Labour's policy discourse, presenting itself as a critique of unwarranted and undeserved privilege (see Lawton, 2005). John Prescott (2000), the then Deputy Prime Minister, and Gordon Brown (2000), then Chancellor of the Exchequer and subsequently Prime Minister, criticised the elitism of Oxbridge for failing to support meritocratic principles (see also Brown, 2007b). This critique was directed at the prejudices of those placed in privileged positions rather than at the structural relations of class. Here class becomes reworked as cultural elitism rather than a facet of structural relations. There is an affinity between this critique, with its Fabian echoes, and that forwarded by a managerialist or technocratic middle class of the traditional upper/ middle class founded on the elitism of the older professions and the more prestigious universities (Lawton, 2005; and see Apple, 2001).

The critiques of privilege and of the culture of the socially excluded came together in the critique of the complacency of welfare professionals forwarded by a particular current within New Labour, which has been aligned with a managerialist fraction of the middle class. This critique reflects meritocratic notions in which class inequalities are not seen as a consequence of systemic or structural features of society. Rather, these are said to derive either from discriminatory practices by traditional élites out of kilter with the thrust of modern society or from the cultural deficits of those unwilling to avail themselves of the opportunities provided. In these discussions class is treated as a residual and dysfunctional phenomenon, something more akin to that found in a previous age, which has no place in a vibrant knowledge society (Beck, 1992; Giddens, 1998). Class comes to be seen as the antithesis of a modern progressive society, atavistic and out of step with society's preferred 'direction of travel' and its related model of social justice.

This model involves both rights and responsibilities. Thus in 2007 the then Prime Minister, Gordon Brown stated:

> The Britain I believe in is a Britain of fairness and opportunity for all. Every British citizen with every chance to make the most of themselves – every community fair to every citizen – *if you work hard, you're better off. If you save, you're rewarded. If you play by the rules, we'll stand by you.* These are for me the best of British values: responsibilities required in return for rights; fairness not just for some but all who earn it. (Brown, 2007a, my emphasis)

The middle-class model

Brown's model of justice expresses a version of meritocracy together with an implicit critique of unwarranted privilege (Brown, 2007b). The paradox is that class is smuggled into the discourse, present in the 'othering' of particular sections of the working class as well as the upper class who possess significant inherited wealth. This rests alongside the constitution of the middle class as the 'particular universal class':

> That is to say, although it was in fact a particular class with a specific history, nonetheless it has become the class around which an increasing range of practices are regarded as universally 'normal', 'good' and 'appropriate'. (Savage, 2003: 536)

The consequence of these shifts is that the middle class whilst being normalised is rendered unremarkable, unnoticeable and, in this sense, invisible. As a result of such processes it became constituted, in Savage's terms, as the paradigmatic class. Thus class becomes smuggled into a policy discourse that construed itself as having moved beyond class. In this instance class represents an ideological configuration built upon a model of the neo-liberal, professional, managerial, individualised, middle-class subject – one for whom notions of rights and responsibilities as well as individual development rests comfortably.

The subject of this paradigmatic class aligns with neo-liberalism, stressing individualism and competition. Brown's emphasis on rights and responsibilities echoed neo-liberal themes, and for all its concern with fairness and justice, capitalist relations were left unquestioned and securely in place, as were the resulting patterns of inequality. Here there is an affinity with the 'third way' of Antony Giddens, which implied a shift in the relationship between capitalism and class (Giddens, 2000) with the knowledge or information society marking an epochal change. As with the earlier discussion, there is the suggestion that class is an atavistic concept, belonging to a previous epoch.

The ideological significance of such arguments is apparent and is reflected in the constitution of the middle-class subject. Yet it is important not to homogenise the middle class and to recognise that such constructions lean towards a particular fraction, embodied in state policy with individualisation being framed by the state. Olssen comments:

> The shift from classical liberalism to neo-liberalism . . . involved a change in subject position from 'homo economicus' . . . to 'manipulatable man', who is created by the state and who is continually encouraged to be 'perpetually responsive'. It is not that the conception of the self-interested subject is replaced or done away with . . . but that in an age of universal welfare the perceived possibilities of slothful indolence create necessities for new forms of vigilance, surveillance, performance appraisal and of forms of control generally. In this new model, the state has taken it upon itself to keep all up to the mark. (Olssen, 2003: 199–200)

A fraction of the middle class assumes this mantle. Commenting on the regulative apparatus of neo-liberalism, Walkerdine *et al.* write:

> The two classes are not simply the bearers of differing amounts of power and cultural capital, but the regulative apparatuses of particular modes of government at different historical moments produce different kinds of subject, and power is implicated not in the possession of capital but in the actual self-formation of the subject. (2001: 142)

Walkerdine *et al.* remind us that the regulative apparatus of the state, despite protestations otherwise, constitutes the middle and working-class subject differently. The former is normalised as the neo-liberal subject, with the latter being the other who lacks these desired attributes and who needs to acquire the appropriate dispositions for success in the knowledge society. The sidelining of class serves a key ideological function, as does the uncritical acceptance of capitalism.

Class, inequality and state policy

Paradoxically, in a conjuncture in which class inequalities have deepened, they have become increasingly marginalised in state policy (Feinstein, *et al.*, 2007). Part of the reason for this lies in the way in which recent economic changes are understood. Here the arguments of Beck (1992, 1999) and Giddens (1998, 2000) are significant. Whilst it is overstated to imply these authors work with notions of classlessness, nevertheless their arguments imply that class has far less salience in the current conjuncture. Beck (1999) goes so far as to suggest that class has become a 'Zombie category'. Older understandings of class are thought to be increasingly irrelevant, as there is limited scope for class in detraditionalised societies. Similarly, if working-class communities are deemed to be emblematic of class, their decomposition can be seen as a marker of the decline of its significance.

At the same time, social democratic policy, as expressed by New Labour, has been reconfigured. For Giddens, the pursuit of redistribution is far less salient than the 'redistribution of possibilities':

> Recent discussion has . . . shifted the emphasis towards the 'redistribution of possibilities'. The cultivation of human potential should as far as possible replace after the event 'redistribution'. (Giddens, 1998: 100–1)

This is indicative of an emphasis upon individualisation and detraditionalisation, as well as a rupture with conceptualisations of collective class-based cultures. Although in state publications in 2009 the language of class reappeared (Cabinet Office, 2009; Government Equalities Office, 2009) it was set within the social investment state, orientated towards a redistribution of possibilities by encouraging *individuals* to take advantage of further and higher education rather than by seeking to address structural inequalities of class.

Within such a context class relations are marked by continuity as well as change. In terms of education, this means that learners are placed within a socio-economic structure that serves to reproduce not only inequality but also the privileges of those already advantaged. The historical relationship between class and educational achievement remains in place, with those drawn from higher social classes overachieving, being more likely to attend élite universities (Blanden *et al.*, 2005; Reay, *et al.*, 2005; Blanden and Machin, 2007). It is important to recognise that class is necessarily raced, gendered and aged, as well as set in particularly spatial locations. Thus, for example, Preston's (2003) work can be related to the racialisation of a particular section of the white working class with Skeggs's (1997, 2004) exploring a section of white working-class women. Similar analyses have explored processes relating to the black and Asian working class (Archer, 2003; Shain, 2006; Archer and Francis, 2007).

The patterning of inequality is further reflected in the distribution of income and wealth. In 1976 the wealthiest 5 per cent owned 38 per cent of marketable wealth; by 2003 this had increased to 40 per cent (National Statistics Online, 2006) [2] Sennett, commenting on the remuneration of top executives, notes:

> massive compensation of top executives, a widening gap between wages at the top and the bottom of corporations, the stagnation of the middle layers of income relative to those of the elite. Winner-takes-all competition generates extreme material inequality. (Sennett, 2006: 54)

Such inequality is legitimated by the requirement to recruit top executives able to add value to the organisation, even if only minutely, to gain competitive advantage. The consequence is that such remuneration becomes legitimated as a requirement for success within a globalised economic system. State intervention to ameliorate such inequalities is seen as antithetical to long term competitiveness. In late 2008 the banking crisis led to some re-evaluation of this stance. Bankers have been criticised for taking large salaries and bonuses at a time when their banks face insolvency. There is an affinity here with New Labour's critique of an unaccountable élite engaged in unfair and unjustifiable activities. Yet such caveats need to be set within a social formation intent on developing its competitiveness in a global economic system, thereby legitimating salaries that can apparently secure this aspiration.

Over the last three decades there has been a continuing and deepening polarity in the distribution of income and wealth (Allen and Ainley, 2007; Hills, Sefton and Stuart, 2009). While by 2009 the economic crisis may have led to the 'appearance' that wealth was more equally distributed as a result of the declining value of investment and property portfolios of the wealthy, the reality was that the downward valuation of investments and property had not altered the trend towards growing disparities of wealth (see Elliott and Curtis, 2009). These inequalities are set within a context in which the middle class faces increasing insecurity in what has been described as the hour-glass economy, so that middle-class parents place a premium upon the educational success of their children (Thompson and Lawson, 2006). Yet this is placed in a context in which young people's life chances are highly structured by social class, race and gender. Walkerdine et al., in their study of girls, remind us:

> Our data show that class location designated on the basis of parents' occupation and importantly, educational credentials, is the most efficient predictor of life chances in the lives of girls and their families. (2001: 58)

This situation is compounded by a decline in the rate of intergenerational mobility (Blanden et al., 2005; Thompson and Lawson, 2006; Fabian commission, 2006: 14).

Education policy and PCET
As the preceding section has shown, the PCET policy context is one in which issues of class have been appropriated in a very particular way. However, class remains an important feature of social relations, exercising a profound impact upon the life chances of young people, albeit mediated by race and gender. In a conjuncture characterised by

a decline in social mobility and an increase in insecurity faced by what Allen and Ainley (2007) refer to as the insecure working/middle class, the class structure has been subject to recomposition. Perhaps the error has been to tie class relations to a very particular historical moment and therefore to ignore the dynamic and processual nature of these. Such relations are always in the process of being reshaped and re-formed.

This section links changing discourses of class to consideration of changes affecting 14–19 education, as well as New Labour's focus on 'personalisation' of educational provisions. It would be overstated to straightforwardly associate the interest in personalisation with individualisation and the formation of the neo-liberal bourgeois subject. Savage (2000) reminds us that in an earlier period the working-class male subject was shaped by forms of individualism that emphasised personal autonomy and control over the labour process. Savage's argument refers to the collective and historical formation of working-class communities as well as the autonomy and control that craft workers exercised over the labour process, suggesting there is no necessary contradiction between individualism and collectivity. The point is that individualism and allied processes of personalisation cannot straightforwardly be applied to a particular class disposition. It is important to recognise that personalisation will be accented differently and discursively shaped in relation to variously classed, and we could add, raced and gendered subjects. The normalisation of a particular construction of the middle-class subject serves to 'other' differently positioned subjects, sitting alongside related differentiations. This is reflected not only in curriculum and institutional divisions but also in processes of personalisation and individual action planning.

The emphasis on personalisation was heralded in New Labour's five-year strategy:

> The central characteristic of such a new system will be personalisation – so that the system fits to the individual rather than the individual having to fit the system . . . and as young people begin to train for work, a system that recognises individual aptitudes and provides as many tailored paths to employment as there are people and jobs. (DfES, 2004: 4; see also Blair, 2004; DfES, 2004)

Gordon Brown shares a similar commitment to personalisation, stating: 'Education available to all – not one size fits all but responding to individual needs. This is the future for our public services. Accessible to all, personal to you. Not just a basic standard but the best quality tailored to your needs.' And repeating a Blairite theme, 'Education is my passion.' (Brown, 2007b) The 2006 White Paper on Further Education echoed these concerns, anticipating the focus on a demand-led system subsequently expressed in the Leitch Review (2006) and *World Class Skills* (DIUS, 2007 and see Cabinet Office 2009):

> A system which focuses on employability and aims to support the future success of young people and adults will be one which responds more and more sharply to the needs and demands of its customers – learners and employers. (DfES, 2006a: 34)

14–19 education and skills states:

> A tailored 14–19 phase must mean that young people can pursue their aspirations, choose learning that is tailored to meet their needs and through study and hard work qualify themselves to achieve their aims. (DfES, 2005: 23)

The focus on personalisation and learner need was unevenly accented. This has been reflected in the development of vocational pathways in the new diplomas for 14–19 year olds (DfES, 2006a, b), directed towards those who are or may become disaffected from education. It was hoped that by addressing the vocational interests of these young people, initially at the age of 14, they would be able to retain a foothold in education (Higham and Yeoman, 2007). Whilst this may occur in the case of vocational diplomas, the hierarchical structure of English education means that it is unlikely that any more than a very small proportion of these young people will access tough-entry universities (Brown and Lauder, 2006).

There are moves to raise to 18 the age at which young people must remain in compulsory education. The proposal being that:

- All young people should participate in education or training until their eighteenth birthday;
- Participation could be at school, in a college, in work-based learning, or in accredited training provided by an employer;
- In order to count as participating, young people would be required to work towards accredited qualifications; and
- Participation should be full time for young people not in employment for a significant part of the week, and part time for those working more than 20 hours a week. (DfES, 2007: 19)

This extension of formal education is marked by differentiating between types of learners that mirror tripartite divisions that have historically been a feature of English education (Allen and Ainley, 2007). There is a resonance in these proposals with the Youth Training Schemes of the 1970s, which emphasised compliance and acceptance of a transient youth labour market (Moos, 1979).

Under the guise of personalisation and emphasis on a demand-led system the vocational–academic divide, with its concomitant class divisions, is being reproduced. Similarly PCET's tripartite structure and divisions between the academic, technical and vocational are on-goingly constituted (Brown, 2006). These divisions are in part reflected in the contrast between an inclusive stance towards those disaffected with education, for whom the diplomas are developed, and one towards the academically orientated. For the latter group the focus is on GCE A levels that offer greater differentiation and 'stretch' learners. Brine (2006) points to similar differentiations in European Union policy documents. *14–19 Education and Skills* called for 'greater stretch and challenge' (DfES, 2005: 63) as well as for increased differentiation at A level so that universities will be able to choose between 'the highest performing candidates' (DfES, 2005: 63). It was anticipated that A* grades would be awarded from 2010 (Meikle, 2007).

While this élitist and exclusionary focus appears to sit uneasily with and in contradiction to New Labour's commitment to social justice, it reflected New Labour's focus on individual opportunities and respon-sibilities and its neglect of underlying class formations. These educa-tional processes are indicative of a tripartism which coincides with a curriculum offering differentiated forms of knowledge, 'delivering' learners to qualitatively different labour markets and classed futures. For those allocated to lower level vocational courses the likely route is towards semi- and low-skilled work, with educative experiences aimed at developing the dispositions required for waged labour. These processes are linked to class formation, albeit that these are lived at an individual level. Such processes contribute towards the formation of class relations as well as to practices of social control, serving an important ideological function. Personalisation and individualisation shifts the focus away from systemic and structural processes to those set at the individual level. Consequently, the individual is held culpable and responsible for their educational and work based trajectories. This represents a truncated and limited model of social justice, one rooted within the social investment state, which minimises the significance of structural relations.

PCET research and class

Early ethnographic studies of PCET were concerned with class repro-duction, that is, with how class inequalities continue to be perpetuated and reinforced within further education. Such approaches are associ-ated with theoretical difficulties (Avis, 2009) and, despite attempts to recognise complexity through acknowledging intersectionality (the interrelationship between class, race and gender) (Anthias, 2005), there remain a number of difficulties. These are associated with determinism, the neglect of struggle and, in particular, a detailed analysis of pedagogic/classroom practices (see Giroux, 1984). Such approaches not only took for granted the labour market positions for which young people were being prepared, but also appeared to work with a direct relationship between education, curriculum and class destinies (Bowles and Gintis, 1976).

This led to a tendency to downplay educational experience at the expense of class reproduction, which was seen to arise in a direct manner, as exemplified in the 'correspondence principle'. This is a sociological perspective that maintains that educational institutions reinforce social class by preparing children and young people for employment that is congruent with the present social standing of their families. Similarly, the notion of 'interpellation' (Althusser, 1972) has been applied to demonstrate how students are positioned as particular classed subjects (Althusser, 1972). To be 'interpellated' is to identify oneself in a particular way. A young person in an educational context that positions him or her as future 'worker' is likely to internalise their identity thus. Both the correspondence principle and 'interpellation', however, tend to lead to a neglect of the micro-relationships and experiences within education that contribute to the perpetuation of class inequalities.

Currently it is possible to draw a distinction between sociological analyses, concerned with the relationship between class, gender and race, and those orientated towards pedagogic processes in PCET. Inevitably, and in some of the best work, there is an overlap between these two currents (Ball et al., 2000). Yet policy, and in particular state research funding, has placed a premium on pedagogy through its preoccupation with the development of learning culture(s) deemed suited to the twenty-first century. Although such cultures derive from participatory and collective learning processes, they are ultimately played out at the individual level (see Biesta and James, 2007). There are two points to be made. First, in relation to educational processes and individualisation, Savage reminds us:

Class is effaced in new modes of individualization, by the very people – mainly in professional and managerial occupations – whose actions help reproduce class inequality more intensely. But class cannot be completely effaced. Class creeps back, surreptitiously, into various cultural forms, though often in oblique ways. (Savage, 2000: 156)

These notions encourage analyses to explore not only the way 'class creeps back' but also the manner in which this contributes towards the 'making' of class in individualised forms as refracted through learning culture. The second point to note is the way in which:

> the 'individualisation' of contemporary societies is not something which simply happens; it is also something actively encouraged by governments persuaded that the market is the only mechanism by which collective decisions can and should be taken over the allocation of resources in a complex situation. (Gilbert, 2007: 52–3)

Warren and Webb note:

> If personal dispositions are, in part, actively constructed through state action, and the social conditions of choice are complicit with relations of power, what is the role of research in PCET? Is a focus on learner experience and their accounts of their 'choices' adequate to understand processes at play that constitute these conditions of choice? At a time when globalised forces are producing localised effects in terms of economic restructuring and educational reform, is largely localised educational research focus enough? (2007: 10)

This is the wider context in which PCET research takes place and the terrain on which new forms of personalisation and action planning operate, necessitating a politics and analysis that link localised relations to the wider social formation. In other words we need to link educational practices to those of wider society in order to interrogate these in relation to the formation of class based inequalities that necessitate a relational understanding of society.

Warren and Webb (2007) suggest when Bourdieu's notion of habitus (i.e. dispositions acquired through previous cultural experience) is marshalled, it serves to alerts us to cultural processes that bear upon the dispositions carried into education. However, this can be at the expense of the allied conceptualisation of 'field' (i.e. the structural relations surrounding, in this instance, the 'field' of post-compulsory education). In other words early processes in the formation of habitus are highlighted, which inform the dispositions brought into education. The consequence is to push explanatory accounts further and further back into an individual's biography so that family, childhood socialisation and early schooling become manifest in the habitus and dispositions carried into PCET. Certainly, these are strongly articulated with patterns of inequality being pivotal in the formation of classed, raced and gendered subjects and inform current educational experiences. However, it is also important to consider on-going processes that are connected to the 'making' of class. We need to be attentive to the specificity of such processes within PCET, especially those that mark a break with class origins as well as those that conspire to form the middle class subject.

When thinking about PCET the foregrounding of class processes could be construed as 'tinkering around the edges' (Reay *et al.*, 2007). For many young people their educative experiences in PCET may hold relatively little significance when set against the rest of their lives. It is important to see the 'making' of class as an active process rather than merely acting in continuance with the trajectory of other social relations and locales. PCET becomes a site of class struggle in which processes of resistance, rupture and formation arise unevenly. Yet these processes are necessarily contained within the wider structural relations in which education is located. Thus the 'making' of class has to be considered relationally, and it is because of this that we need to operate with a politicised and expansive understanding of practice. The 'making' of class is a cultural process in which distinctions and forms of 'othering' are constructed. Up to now little attention has been paid to the cultural practices and experiences within education and how these relate to wider societal structures. The micro and everyday practices related to the formation of class in PCET need to be articulated to those in wider society. A politicised practice seeking to interrupt these processes cannot remain located solely in education and needs to move beyond the classroom and institutional context to wider society.

There are a number of tensions in the preceding discussion, foremost that I could be accused of playing down the significance of recent work exploring class-based processes in PCET. So for example, work rooted in Bourdieu's notions of field and habitus is centrally concerned with the articulation of structure and agency and the playing out of class in educational and classroom processes (Colley, 2006; Morrison, 2007; Warren and Webb, 2007). Yet I believe that the 'making' of class within PCET could be more directly addressed.

It is here that notions of 'othering', hierarchicalisation and differentiation play a part. These are explored within Kehily and Pattman's (2006) study relating to academic sixth-formers who constituted themselves as middle-class *subjects-in-the-making* by pathologising working-class dropouts. Other research (Skeggs, 1997, 2004; Walkerdine *et al.*, 2001) focusing on the psychological costs of educational engagement also points towards the 'making' of class. Psychological costs manifested in a sense of 'inadequacy', of not being good enough and the resulting anxiety reflects classed processes. Skeggs (1997, 2004) illustrates this in her study of working-class women. Similarly, Walkerdine *et al.* (2001) illustrate the way in which such processes affect not only working-class but also middle-class girls, whereby anxiety and a sense of inadequacy become accented in a particular manner, being articulated with class formation. These processes may become mapped on to divisions within and across educational institutions (Grubb, 2006) whereby learners 'choose' a particular course on the basis of their assumed capabilities. Bathmaker has explored this in her study of General National Vocational Qualification (GNVQ) students who felt they were not good enough to study A levels, and has noted similar effects within a differentiated higher education system (Avis *et al.*, 2002). Reay *et al.* (2007) also point towards the 'making' of class in their discussion of working class students. These students engage differentially with higher education, with those located in tough-entry institutions holding qualitatively different orientations from those in colleges of further education or new universities. In this instance differentiated class-based formative processes can be discerned that anticipate varied class trajectories. Working-class students placed in tough-entry universities follow trajectories that anticipate the 'making' of middle-class subjects, whereas those following a higher education route in further education face qualitatively different class destinies. Whilst the previous discussion may simplify these processes, it serves to illustrate and raise questions about the 'making' of class.

Educational experiences cannot be fully thought through without considering the wider socio-economic context within which learners are placed, and the relational context of education. That is to say educational processes taking place within PCET need to be considered in relation to those arising within schools, sixth-form colleges, universities, and so on. If we wish to challenge the perpetuation of class inequalities, we need to operate at different levels – the classroom, the institution as well as the wider socio-economic context. This calls for a politicised practice that extends beyond the classroom and that seeks to interrupt wider patterns of inequality. Such a practice necessitates an engagement with those social movements committed to progressive change – in other words the pursuit of non-reformist reform that moves beyond cultures of resistance.

In the current conjuncture in which neo-liberalism has become hegemonic, with New Labour accepting uncritically the tenets of capitalism, it becomes difficult to identify such movements. Yet the contradictions that beset not only the policies of New Labour but also the economic context contain progressive possibilities. Countervailing currents are present amongst radical educators and those orientated towards widening participation. Similar currents also exist amongst young people, parents and those faced with the contradictory outcomes of education –

its 'broken promises' (Finn, 1987). Paradoxically the 'hollowing out' of class structure in the 'hourglass' economy undermines the complacency of a middle-class fraction, replacing it with a sense of risk and insecurity. Here lies a possibility for the development of progressive alliances. Progressive tendencies exist within the traditional organisations of the working class – the trade unions and elements within the Labour Party (Cruddas, 2006; Thompson and Lawson, 2006; *Renewal*, 2007; Hill, 2007).

Towards a conclusion

This chapter has examined the construction of class in New Labour policy discourse as well as related social theory. In such accounts class was viewed as an atavistic concept, though this is belied by the material inequalities that crisscross society. Later sections of the chapter sought to recentre class formation as a pivotal focus for analysis of PCET. There is a tension between analyses that address the 'making' of class and the structural relations of class within wider society. An interest in interrupting such processes in PCET can only take us so far, with localised interventions necessarily having to be set alongside those in wider society. There is a conundrum. In a class-based society we cannot escape processes of class formation and will be positioned in relation to these. Whilst those working in education may struggle for participatory parity[3] for their learners as well as the development of criticality, this remains set within a class society. This leads to the need for an expansive and politicised practice that engages with wider movements that are struggling for social justice that moves beyond a focus on cultures of resistance.

Notes

1 PCET is used in a fluid way, being associated with colleges of further education, institutions bearing some resemblance to community colleges in the United States and technical and further education colleges (TAFE) in Australia. Further education (FE) colleges deliver vocational and technical education but also play an important role in 16–19 education, latterly in provision for 14–19 year olds and also in adult education. Further education colleges are diverse institutions whose provision can range from basic skills to degree-level work.

2 Analysis of income and wealth distribution is notoriously difficult. Dorling *et al.* suggest: 'analysis of income data between 2003 and 2005 indicates that areas with the highest average incomes experienced the greatest increases, in both absolute and relative terms, while some areas with the

lowest average incomes experienced declining incomes, increasing polarisation' (2007: xiii). Babb *et al.* similarly commented: 'there is evidence . . . based on the Family Resources Survey (FRS), but also from data from tax returns, that there has indeed been much more rapid growth in the top one per cent of incomes than for the rest of the distribution. The reasons for this growth are not yet well understood, but possible explanations include changes in the nature of executive remuneration and the dynamic effects of the cut in top rates of tax over the 1980s on capital accumulation' (2004: 44).

3 Participatory parity 'requires social arrangements that permit all (adult) members of society to interact with one another as peers. For participatory parity to be possible . . . two conditions must be satisfied. First, the distribution of material resources must be such as to ensure participant's independence and "voice" . . . The second condition requires that institutionalised patterns of cultural value express equal respect for all and ensure equal opportunities of achieving social esteem' (Fraser, 2003: 36).

Bibliography

Allen, M., and Ainley, P. (2007) *Education make you fick, innit?* (London: Tuffnell Press).

Althusser, L. (1972) 'Ideology and ideological state apparatuses', in B. R. Cosin (ed.) *Education: Structure and Society* (Harmondsworth: Penguin).

Anthias, F. (2005) 'Social stratification and social inequality: models of intersectionality and identity' in F. Devine, M. Savage, J. Scott and R. Crompton (eds) *Rethinking Class* (London: Palgrave).

Apple, M. (2001) *Educating the 'Right' Way* (London: RoutledgeFalmer).

Archer, L. (2003) *Race, Masculinity and Schooling* (Maidenhead: Open University Press).

Archer, L., and Francis, B. (2007) *Understanding Minority Ethnic Achievement: Race, Gender, Class and Success* (London: Routledge).

Avis, J. (2009) *Education, Policy and Social Justice: Learning and Skills*, rev. edn (London: Continuum).

Avis, J., Bathmaker, A-M., and Parsons, J. (2002) 'Communities of practice and the construction of learners in post-compulsory education and training', *Journal of Vocational Education and Training* 54:1, 27–50.

Babb, P., Martin, J., and Haezewindt, P., eds (2004) *Focus on Social Inequalities* (London: Stationery Office).

Ball, S. J., Maguire, M., and Macrae, S. (2000) *Choice: Pathways and Transitions post-16* (London: RoutledgeFalmer).

Beck, U. (1992) *The Risk Society* (London: Sage).

Beck, U. (1999) *World Risk Society* (Cambridge: Polity Press).

Biesta, G., and James, D., eds (2007) *Improving Learning Cultures in Further Education* (London: Routledge).

Blair, T. (2004) *My Passion to Transform Education is Undimmed*, Fabian lecture, Institute of education, London, 7 July, www.fabian-society.org.uk/press_office/ (accessed December 2004).

Blanden, J., Gregg, P., and Machin, S. (2005) *Intergenerational Mobility in Europe and North America* (London: Centre for Economic Performance, London School of Economics).

Blanden, J., and Machin, S. (2007) *Recent Changes in Intergenerational Mobility in Britain*, Putney: Sutton Trust, www.suttontrust.com (accessed 13 December 2007).

Bowles, H., and Gintis, S. (1976) *Schooling in Capitalist America* (New York: Basic Books).

Brine, J. (2006) 'Locating the learner within EU policy', in C. Leathwood and B. Francis (eds) *Gender and Lifelong Learning* (London: Routledge).

Brown, G. (2000) 'My vision of a fairer Britain for everyone', *Times*, 3 June.

Brown, G. (2007a) 'Speech to the nation', 11 May (London: London's Imagination Gallery).

Brown, G. (2007b) 'Strength to change Britain', speech to the Labour Party Conference, www.labour.org.uk/conference/brown-speech (accessed 26 September 2007).

Brown, P. (2006) 'The opportunity trap', in H. Lauder, P. Brown, J-A. Dillabough and A. H. Halsey (eds) *Education, Globalisation and Social Change* (Oxford: Oxford University Press).

Brown, P., and Lauder, H. (2006) 'Globalization, knowledge and the myth of the magnet economy', in H. Lauder, P. Brown, J-A. Dillabough and A. H. Halsey (eds) *Education, Globalisation and Social Change* (Oxford: Oxford University Press).

Cabinet Office (2009) *New Opportunities: Fair Chances for the Future*, Cm 7533 (Norwich: Stationery Office).

Colley, H. (2006) 'Learning to labour with feeling: class, gender and emotion in childcare education and training', *Contemporary Issues in Early Childhood* 17:1, 15–29.

Cruddas, J. (2006) Neo-liberal Labour, *Renewal* 14:1, 34–41.

DfEE (1998) *The Learning Age: a Renaissance for a new Britain*, Cm 3790 (London: Stationery Office).

DfES (2004) *Five-year Strategy for Children and Learners*, Cm 6272 (London: DfES).

DfES (2005) *14–19 Education and Skills* (London: DfES).

DfES (2006a) *Further Education: Raising Skills, Improving Life Chances*, Cm 6768 (London: Stationery Office).

DfES (2006b) *14–19 Education and Skills: Gateway Guidance* (Annesley: DfES).

DfES (2007) *Raising Expectations: Staying in Education and Training post-16*, Cm 7065 (Norwich: Stationery Office).

DIUS (2007) *World-class Skills: Implementing the Leitch Review of Skills in England*, Cm 7181 (Norwich: Stationery Office).

Dorling, D., Rigby, J., Wheeler, B., Ballas, D., Thomas, B., Fahmy, E., Gordon, D., and Lupton, R. (2007) *Poverty, Wealth and Place in Britain, 1968 to 2005* (Bristol: Policy Press).

Educational Review (2007) *Transforming Learning Cultures in Further Education*, special issue, 59: 4.

Elliott, L., and Curtis, P (2009) 'Divided Britain: gap between rich and poor widest since '60s', *Guardian*, 8 May.

Fabian Commission (2006) Narrowing the Gap: the Fabian Commission on Life Chances and Child Poverty (London: Fabian Society).

Feinstein, L., Hearn, B., and Renton, Z., with Abrahams, C., and MacLeod, M. (2007) *Reducing Inequalities, Realising the Talents of all* (London: National Children's Bureau).

Finn, D. (1987) *Training without Jobs* (London: Macmillan).

Fraser, N. (2003) 'Social justice in the age of identity politics: redistribution, recognition, and participation', in N. Fraser and A. Honneth, *Redistribution or Recognition?* (London: Verso).

Fryer Report (1999) *Creating Learning Cultures: Next Steps in Achieving the Learning Age*, second report of the National Advisory Group for Continuing Education and Life Long Learning, www.lifelonglearning.co.uk/nagcell2/index.htm (accessed 7 June 2008).

Giddens, A. (1998) *The Third Way: The Renewal of Social Democracy* (Oxford: Polity Press).

Giddens, A. (2000) The Third Way *and its Critics* (Oxford: Polity Press).

Gilbert, J. (2007) 'The complexity of the social', *Soundings*, 41–53.

Giroux, H. A. (1984) *Theory and Resistance in Education* (London: Heinemann).

Government Equalities Office (2009) *A Fairer Future: the Equality Bill and other Action to make Equality a Reality* (London: Equalities Office).

Grubb, W. N. (2006) 'Vocationalism and differentiation of tertiary education: lessons from US community colleges', *Journal of Further and Higher Education* 30:1, 27–44.

Higham, J., and Yeoman, D. (2007) 'Working through Vocationalism again: Emerging Conceptions in the 14–19 Curriculum', paper presented to BERA annual conference, Institute of Education, London, 5–8 September.

Hill, D. (2007) 'Vacating the Battlefield: Class War from above, Neoliberal Capitalist Globalisation and the Flight from Class Analysis in Revisionist Left Analyses such as that of Michael W. Apple', paper presented to BERA annual conference, Institute of Education, London, 5–8 September.

Hills, J., Sefton, T., and Stewart, K. (2009) *Poverty, Inequality and Policy since 1997.* (York: Joseph Rowntree Foundation, www.jrf.org.uk (accessed 29 June 2009).

Kehily, M., and Pattman, R. (2006) 'Middle-class struggle? Identity. work and leisure among sixth-formers in the UK', *British Journal of Sociology of Education*, 27:1, 37–52.

Lawton, D. (2005) *Education and the Labour Party Ideologies, 1900–2001 and Beyond* (London: RoutledgeFalmer).

Leitch Review of Skills (2006) *Prosperity for All in the Global Economy: World Class Skills*, final report (Norwich: HMSO).

Meikle, J. (2007) 'Comprehensives falter as top grade gap widens', *Guardian*, 17 August.

Moos, M. (1979) 'Government youth training policy and its impact on further education', occasional stencilled paper (Birmingham: CCCS, University of Birmingham).

Morrison, A. (2007) 'A Case Study of Learners on an AVCE in Travel and Tourism at a College of FHE in the West Midlands', Ed.D. thesis, Open University.

National Statistics Online (2006) *Share of the Wealth*, www.statistics.gov.uk/cci/nugget_print.asp?ID=2 (accessed 28 August 2007).

Olssen M. (2003) 'Structuralism, post-structuralism, neo-liberalism: assessing Foucault's legacy', *Journal of Education Policy* 18:2, 189–202.

Prescott, J. (2000) 'The battle is still on to deliver opportunity for the many', *Independent on Sunday*, 4 June.

Preston, J. (2003) 'White trash vocationalism? Formations of class and race in an Essex further education college', *Widening Participation and Lifelong Learning* 5:2, 6–17.

Reay, D., Crozier, G., Clayton, J., Colliander, L., and Grinstead, J. (2007) 'Fitting in or Standing out: Working-class Students in Higher Education', paper presented to BERA annual conference, Institute of Education, London, 5–8 September.

Reay, D., David, M. E., and Ball, S. (2005) *Degrees of Choice: Social Class, Race and Gender in Higher Education* (London: Trentham Books).

Renewal (2007) issue on social democracy,15:2–3.

Savage, M. (2000) *Class Analyses and Social Transformation* (Buckingham: Open University Press).

Savage, M. (2003) 'A new class paradigm', *British Journal of Sociology of Education* 24:4, 535–41.

Sennett, R. (2006) *The Culture of the New Capitalism* (New Haven CT: Yale University Press).

Shain, F. (2006) *The Schooling and Identity of Asian Girls* (Stoke on Trent: Trentham).

Skeggs, B. (1997) *Formation of Class and Gender* (London: Sage).

Skeggs, B. (2004) *Class, Self, Culture* (London: Routledge).

Thompson, P., and Lawson, N. (2006) 'Putting class back into British politics', *Renewal* 14:1, 1–7.

Walkerdine, V., Lucey, H., and Melody, J. (2001) *Growing up Girl* (London: Palgrave).

Warren, S., and Webb, S. (2007) 'Challenging lifelong learning policy discourse: where is structure in agency in narrative-based research?', *Studies in the Education of Adults*, 39:1, 5–21.

Acknowledgements

A version of this chapter appeared as 'Class, economism, individualisation and post-compulsory education and training', *Journal for Critical Education Policy Studies* 6:2 (December 2008), www.jceps.com/?pageID=article&articleID=130.

6

Social justice and time: the impact of public-sector reform on the work of midwives in the National Health Service

Valerie Bryson and Ruth Deery

At the time of the 1997 general election, New Labour's model of social justice included an unprecedented commitment to address the needs of women and promote gender equality. This commitment was bound up with a promise to develop 'family-friendly' working practices to support working women; some Labour women believed that these changes would also encourage a more equitable division of time within the home. These positions implied that a just distribution of scarce resources involves the distribution of time as well as material goods and services, and by 2009 New Labour governments had intervened in the labour market to deliver a series of reforms around maternity, paternity and parental leave provision, flexible employment and maximum working hours.

At the same time, New Labour was also committed to principles of accountability, value for money and consumer choice in the provision of public services, seeing these too as principles of social justice. The pursuit of these principles involved increasingly elaborate attempts to quantify the outputs, evaluate the performance and set targets for public-sector providers while also achieving 'efficiency savings' in staffing levels.

This chapter finds that these two sets of commitments frequently pointed in contradictory directions, as the time-consuming requirements of constant monitoring and the effects of increasingly tight staffing levels clashed with the promise of flexible working; in many cases they also ran counter to the provision of good-quality services. The chapter begins by standing back from immediate policy debates to consider underlying theories of social justice in relation to time and gender equality and to relate these to New Labour policies. This section also explores some other ways of thinking about time and temporal justice, including the claims that women and men relate to time in different ways, and that 'women's time' is often forced to conform to the inappropriate demands of 'men's time'.[1] The second section builds on this to consider whether public service reforms strengthened a kind of 'temporal logic' that countered New Labour's rhetorical commitment to work–life balance and that was particularly hostile to the caring work that is mainly provided by women. The third section assesses this expectation in the light of two research studies: an action research study that explored midwives' support needs and a comparative ethnography, funded by the Health Foundation, that explored midwife-led care and obstetric culture on three sites. Both studies took place in the north of England, and they indicate that although there appear to have been some women-friendly changes, these were countered by the 'time is money' rationality of public-sector reforms. The chapter concludes that New Labour's stated commitment to gender equality and good maternity services was undermined by failure to recognise either the value of time spent caring for others or the distinct temporality that such work often involves. The chapter also concludes that the increased marginalisation of 'women's time' is having detrimental effects on society as a whole.

Social justice and time: New Labour and beyond

The labour movement in Britain has a long history of campaigning around working hours, while Karl Marx's theory of surplus value was essentially a theory about time – that is, the appropriation of workers' time as the source of profit for capitalist employers. Today, concern about the damaging effects of long working hours is widely articulated, and the Trades Union Congress's 'It's about time' campaign aims to put long hours and work–life balance at the top of the workplace agenda.

In contrast, most mainstream theories of social justice have focused on issues around freedom and the distribution of material resources, and have had little to say about how time should be valued and how leisure time should be distributed. Meanwhile, New Labour not only loosened its links with trade unions and jettisoned any residual elements of Marxist thought, it also shifted away from the traditional social democratic concern with equality of outcomes and the need for state intervention to secure this. Instead, it focused on equality of opportunity and stressed individual and community responsibilities. This limited the role of the state to that of enabler rather than social engineer and saw the market economy in a generally positive light. As Steve Buckler and David Dolowitz have argued (2000), the resulting 'social liberalism' had strong affinities with some of the ideas of John Rawls, whose *A Theory of Justice* (1971) is probably the most influential recent work on social justice (but see also Marcel Wissenburg, 2001 for a more critical assessment of the New Labour–Rawls relationship).

According to Rawls, justice requires the maximisation of equal basic liberties, while social and economic inequalities can be just only if there is genuine equality of opportunity and if the inequalities benefit the least advantaged (most usually by providing incentives to wealth creation and hence promoting general prosperity). Although *A Theory of Justice* ignores time-related issues, Rawls's later *Justice as Fairness* briefly discussed leisure time as a 'primary good' whose distribution should be governed by principles of justice. Here Rawls argued that if someone chooses to go surfing rather than work a standard day (which he suggested might be eight hours), they cannot expect to have their needs met by other people (2001: 60, 179); although he did not argue that leisure has to be equally distributed, his just society therefore allows no place for either the idle rich or the work-shy welfare claimant.

This seems clearly in line with New Labour's stress on getting people off benefits and into paid employment, which it saw as both the key responsibility of all adult able-bodied citizens and the primary source of social integration. Such an approach falls far short of the more radical model proposed by Tony Fitzpatrick, who argues that access to 'meaningful time' is a basic human right that cannot be realised without a radical challenge to capitalist society. He contests Rawls's notion of a 'standard' working day and draws on Marx to argue that the apparently free choices available to citizens today are based on a limited capitalist concept of freedom; this requires 'a willing submission to the economic laws of private exchange', and is the only kind of temporal freedom available in societies in which 'Social time revolves around market imperatives that are made to resemble physical absolutes' and in which leisure is primarily time for consumption (2004: 206 and 202).

Gender, justice and time
Fitzpatrick does not explore the implications of his analysis for gender relations, while Rawls had very little to say about the social and economic inequalities between women and men and completely ignored inequalities within the family. Rawls also equated leisure time with time left over from paid employment, ignoring the time needed for work within the home, such as cooking, cleaning and caring for children, and the contributions that citizens can make through unpaid activities in their communities. However, in *Justice, Gender and the Family* (1990) the feminist writer Susan Okin extended his underlying principles to both gender and domestic time. She argued that 'Until there is justice within the family, women will not be able to gain equality in politics, at

work, or in any other sphere' and that the distribution of time spent on unpaid labour within the family is a central issue of justice, both in itself and because of its consequences (Okin, 1990: 4). Okin therefore advocated state subsidies for child care and much more flexible patterns of employment to facilitate the more equal division of both paid work and care between the sexes.

By the early 1990s some prominent women in the Labour Party were reaching similar conclusions, arguing not only that gender equality needed to be prioritised but that the redistribution of time between the sexes was central to this. Harriet Harman argued in *The Century Gap* (1993) that the workplace must be transformed to enable men as well as women to balance their domestic and employment responsibilities, thereby redistributing both domestic and paid work between the sexes. When Harman was first elected to the House of Commons in 1982 she was one of only ten Labour women members; after the 1997 general election the number had dramatically risen to 101, and included many women who identified themselves as feminists (Childs, 2004). Of the women appointed to Labour Cabinets, not only Harman but also Patricia Hewitt and Ruth Kelly had a track record of concern with working hours and the implications for gender equality (see Coote *et al.*, 1990; Harman, 1993; Hewitt, 1993; Kelly, 2000).

In 1997 the Labour Party as a whole was officially committed to gender equality, and its manifesto proclaimed that 'The clock should not be turned back. As many women who want to work should be able to do so. More equal relationships between men and women have transformed our lives.' More tangibly, the manifesto promised to develop a national child-care strategy and to develop more 'family-friendly' working practices; in particular, it stated that 'we support the right of employees not to be forced to work more than forty-eight hours a week; to an annual holiday entitlement; and to limited unpaid parental leave.' (Labour Party manifesto, 1997). Labour governments have since introduced some limited but significant measures designed to help mothers (and, to a lesser extent, fathers) balance the competing demands of family and workplace. These developments appear to be linked to women's increased political presence (Childs, 2004), and in 2009 Labour women MPs resisted a retreat from 'family-friendly' policies in the economic downturn (Woolf, 2009).

While New Labour's recognition that workers may have other legitimate demands on their time goes some way to address feminist concerns, it falls far short of more genuinely radical analysis. As Nancy Fraser has argued, this would involve a redistribution of leisure time. She argues that the principles of a just society based on gender equity would include leisure-time equality based on the 'universal caregiver' model of time use. In contrast to both the 'universal breadwinner' model, which expects all citizens to behave like male workers (and provides state support for caring responsibilities to make this possible), and the 'caregiver parity' model (which supports those who care in the home by providing allowances for carers or making part-time work an easier option) this 'universal caregiver' model would expect and enable *all* citizens to combine earning and caring as well as participating in community and political activity; far from expecting women to adjust to existing male patterns, this would 'make women's current life-patterns the norm for everyone'. This model is of course very radical; indeed, as Fraser says, in 'effectively dismantling the gendered opposition between breadwinning and caregiving' it would also effectively dismantle the entire gender order (Fraser, 2000: 25, 27).

'Women's time' and 'men's time'

Like much other recent feminist work, Fraser's approach also dismantles the distinction between public and private rights and obligations that underpins most Western political thought, and it runs counter to New Labour's focus on paid work. This narrow focus has been criticised by a number of feminists (see for example Levitas, 2001; Lister, 2003), and their ideas have fed into an increasingly influential discourse of 'work–life balance' in which time acquires a new currency, so that '[i]n a sense, there has been a shift from the demands for a "family wage" to "family time"' (Williams, 2001: 473). As Fiona Williams has argued, this move also supports a shift in ethical thinking that enables the rational calculations of individual advantage involved in an ethic of paid work to be balanced by a care-based ethics that recognises human interdependence and values the qualities of 'attentiveness, responsibility, competence and responsiveness' that good care requires (Williams, 2001: 477, drawing on Tronto, 1993; see also Fisher's chapter in this volume).

These qualities require a flexible approach to time that often requires attention to 'natural' physical and emotional temporal rhythms and needs that cannot appropriately be automated or subjected to considerations of 'time management', and that are often necessarily slow and in the present. This means that the 'problem of time' goes beyond the distribution of hours available for paid and unpaid work and leisure, and involves our relationship with time itself.

Many writers now argue that the ways in which we experience and understand time are culturally variable, rather than either innate or a straightforward reflection of the natural world (see in particular Adam,

1995; Thompson, 1969, and the overview in Bryson, 2007). From around the fifteenth century, Western societies saw a general shift away from the natural, cyclical, task-oriented time associated with agricultural economies and towards the commodified, linear, clock time of capitalism and factory production, in which time could be bought and sold as a quantifiable commodity and the hours and pace of wage labourers were standardised according to the needs of the mechanical production process and the maximisation of profit. However, while commodified clock time has become hegemonic, other 'time cultures' persist: our bodies have their own temporal needs and rhythms; we experience time subjectively (it often appears to speed up or slow down); and past, present and future constantly interact as we plan, predict, remember, hope and fear. As indicated above, caring for others can also involve distinct temporal rhythms, and Karen Davies (1994) has coined the useful concept of 'process time' to describe the plural, relational and context-linked nature of the time that caring for others involves.

Gender roles in most Western societies are increasingly fluid and variable, with many women in traditional male occupations and many men caring for others; we also all necessarily inhabit more than one 'time culture'. Nevertheless, time-use studies consistently find that women continue to spend more time in providing unpaid care and domestic work, while men spend longer hours in paid employment (for a critical discussion of these studies see Bryson, 2008); within the workplace, caring professions remain dominated by women. This gender division of labour makes it meaningful to describe the time culture associated with care as 'women's time', in contrast to the 'men's time' that structures paid employment. This description also links the subordination of relational/caring time to the economic rationality of clock time to the more general privileging of men's experiences and needs in our society.

Such considerations mean that, while New Labour's commitment to flexible and 'family-friendly' working conditions is welcome, it does not address the deeper problems that arise when the temporal rhythms involved in caring for and interacting with other people are required to slot into a predetermined and rigid time frame. In terms of family time, this means, for example, that parents have to rush children through dressing and breakfast so as to be seen to arrive at work on time, rather than letting them choose what to wear and butter their own toast. In employment, it similarly means that a community midwife may have to rush through morning visits to new mothers, rather than discussing their needs and anxieties, in order to be 'on time' for an afternoon clinic.

Although by 2009 the economic recession had led to short-time hours for some employees, the fear of redundancy had increased the disciplinary effects of timekeeping on many others. Particular difficulties were faced by members of the caring professions, who were increasingly expected to be more 'productive' and 'cost-efficient' in their work (see Deery, 2008). As discussed in the next section, the general difficulty of allocating care according to the clock rather than immediate need was exacerbated by public service reforms and an increased stress on 'efficiency targets' that were quite unable to capture the intangible processes and relationships that good care involves, and that at times seemed to prioritise the processes of record keeping and quality assurance over the care work itself.

The impact of public-sector reforms

This section provides a brief outline of New Labour's approach to the public sector and the temporal impact of this, before focusing on the National Health Service (NHS). This sets the scene for the next section, which focuses on maternity services.

New Labour consistently asserted its support for the welfare state. It particularly stressed the importance of education and the National Health Service, and it significantly expanded funding in these areas. It also presented itself as the party of welfare reform, arguing that a modern welfare state should embrace the principle of consumer-led choice, that the private sector can work in partnership with public providers, that business principles can improve the efficiency of services, and that the success of welfare provision should be measured by outputs rather than by the amount of money the government provides. In many ways this discourse built on the New Public Management approach of the Thatcher years, which saw 'market forces as an unlimited good' (Edemariam, 2009) and stressed value for money, efficiency and performance management (Dopson, 2009; Drewry, 2005); it also incorporated John Major's focus on the rights of citizen consumers. However, as Martin Powell has noted, its roots can also be found in the 1994 report from the Commission on Social Justice (which had been set up in 1992 by John Smith, the then Labour Party leader), which saw social justice and economic efficiency as 'two sides of the same coin' (quoted in Powell, 2000: 43). Such thinking justified the devolution of financial responsibilities from central and local government to those who deliver services, so that, for example, school governors and head teachers were given greater control over their budgets, while most NHS funding was devolved to local Primary Care Trusts (PCTs) through the Strategic Health Authorities (SHAs).

While this devolution might seem to empower local providers and front-line staff, New Labour also insisted on the importance of establishing national standards against which performance could be measured, so that 'as powers were devolved within the public sector, and local managers "set free" to conduct their new enterprises, so control would be exercised through the measurement of outputs and the regulation of standards in accordance with prescribed norms' (Rustin, 2008: 47). In other words, there was a shift from governing to governance, whereby the government retreated from direct provision of services but attempted to retain control through a 'series of mechanisms via which multiple and interacting varieties of stakeholders are regulated, audited, held accountable and asked to work to defined standards' (Cooper, 2008: 34). As Hannah Cook has observed, the result was often a form of 'empowerment' that transferred responsibilities rather than power and that, with its emphasis on value for money, required that workers 'who have been used to judging their actions by a code of professional ethics must learn to think in new ways' (Cook, 2002: 175).

These 'new ways' of thinking required of public-sector workers included being constantly aware of the requirements of external auditors and public perceptions of their performance, often assessed through league tables that ranged from mortality rates and waiting times in hospitals through examination results and 'added value' in schools to the number of arrests made by police officers. These measures were designed to improve 'outputs' by enforcing national standards and ensuring accountability to service users and taxpayers as well as the government. However, many public-sector workers and academics argue that the proliferation of targets and monitoring systems has become counterproductive, and that many workers feel increasingly submerged by an ever-present 'audit culture' that involves a plethora of ever-moving targets and performance indicators and a mountain of paperwork, impenetrable bureaucracy and obscure jargon that gets between them and the job. Such an organisational system trains staff to clinically manage and measure aspects of their work, but does not provide time and space to reflect upon and develop their practice (Deery, 2005, 2008).

Combined with the ever-present threat of being exposed as a 'failing' organisation, constant monitoring can have a highly detrimental effect on staff morale (see Ball *et al.*, 2002; Hughes *et al.*, 2002; Deery, 2005). As Cooper says:

> Everyone who works in the public sector, lives in the same household as a public-sector worker, or who has children of school age, lives in the

shadow of the anxious, inspectorial culture that promises to visit the shame of failure upon us . . . Governments have not wished to trust professionals, and thus they have opted to control them. (Cooper, 2008: 39)

Temporal implications

Time is obviously a finite resource. Although auditing processes may sometimes help workers use it more effectively, these processes themselves are highly time-consuming, and can divert resources and hours from front-line service provision. Targets can also be counterproductive: for example, the Police Federation of England and Wales complained that government targets for rates of arrests, cautions and on-the-spot fines diverted police time from the investigation of serious crime to relatively trivial offences (BBC News Channel, 15 May 2007). The damaging effects of the audit culture were also clear in a 2008 study led by Sue White of children's social care. White found that although the 'computerised recording, performance management and data-sharing system' was 'much lauded by government and senior managers as a valuable and time-saving tool for social workers and, ultimately, the multi-agency safeguarding system', its effects in practice were highly negative. Not only did social workers report spending between 60 per cent and 80 per cent of their time at the computer screen, but the system also imposed 'onerous workflows and forms [that] compound difficulties in meeting government-imposed timescales and targets' and often bore 'no relationship to protecting a child' (White, 2008). White and her research team were therefore unsurprised that monitoring practices had failed to prevent the death in 2007 of 'Baby P' in the London borough of Haringey, where the child had been seen by twenty-eight different social workers, doctors and police officers and where children's services had been awarded a three-star rating by inspectors.

These examples highlight the extent to which a culture dominated by quantitative targets and audits can consume the time of already over-stretched workers. As White says, 'Good skills of analysis and complex judgments require time, dialogue and sufficient knowledge of the child in question and their family'; the problem was not that Baby P's records were incomplete, but that no one had such time and knowledge. More fundamentally, most front-line public service workers are interacting with other people, while the whole 'time is money' rationality of the auditing and monitoring system reaffirms the priorities of a dominant time culture that is unable to see that '[n]ot all time is money. Not all human relationships are exclusively governed by the rationalised time of the clock' (Adam, 1995: 94). As indicated in the first section of this chapter, the result is that members of caring professions have been torn between the conflicting demands of two time cultures, while the widespread subordination of 'women's time' has had negative effects on both their ability to do their work and their own job satisfaction.

Seventy per cent of jobs in education, health and public administration are held by women (Opportunity Now, 2008) who, as mentioned earlier, continue to do most of the unpaid domestic and caring work within the home. The pressures on the public-sector work force are therefore particularly acute, as workers are caught between the conflicting demands of accountability, their wish to do the best for those who use their services and their own need to balance their workplace and domestic responsibilities. Although, as indicated earlier, New Labour took measures to ease this conflict by providing parents with greater rights to family-related leave and flexible employment, the effects of these were countered by the ever-increasing demands of workplace practices and a general culture of long working hours that is unlikely to be seriously challenged by any mainstream political party at a time of recession and job insecurity.

NHS reforms

These conflicts are particularly clear in the case of the National Health Service. New Labour at first appeared to recognise some of the pitfalls of the Thatcherite New Public Management approach, and its 1997 manifesto promised to 'restore the NHS as a public service working co-operatively for patients, not a commercial business driven by competition' and to end the internal market that the Conservatives had introduced into health-care provision (Labour Party Manifesto, 1997). However, the continued separation of providers and purchasers of health care meant that the internal market continued, while New Labour governments actively promoted the 'perceived benefits of stimulating competition between a range of health care providers, public and private' (Crinson, 2005: 511). Pro-market arguments were bound up with its increased emphasis on expanding patient choice and a commitment to 'personalised' health care.

The result was a series of major organisational changes intended to free local providers from government control and provide financial incentives for improved performance, combined with an increased use of league tables, audit trails and performance indicators intended to measure performance and thereby enable patients to make informed choices about their treatment. At the same time, Cook has shown how changes in management structure involved delegating budgetary responsibilities to front-line staff such as nurses, who were thereby 'conscripted into the day-to-day implicit rationing decisions which have dominated public services in an era of retrenchment. Whenever they change an incontinent patient the question of cost must now enter their calculations'. She adds that such 'empowerment' meant 'the decentralisation of responsibility and a concomitant centralisation of power. For front-line health workers it has meant worsening conditions of work, increased workloads, and loss of control' (Cook, 2002: 174, 175).

By 2009 most NHS provision was via local Primary Care Trusts. These were established in 1998 and by 2005 formally controlled 80 per cent of the NHS budget. Although they are responsible for commissioning services from primary and secondary care providers for the populations they serve, the bulk of their budget has been allocated centrally to meet national targets set by the Department of Health, leaving them with little scope to set their own priorities in accordance with their perception of local needs (Crinson, 2005).The Clinical Negligence Scheme for Trusts (CNST), which stems from the Major government and handles all clinical negligence claims against member NHS bodies, further strengthened the audit culture, as trusts which achieve the relevant NHS Litigation Authority (NHSLA) risk management standards and have the fewest claims attract a significant reduction in their (costly) membership contribution. Here Deery (2008) has shown the damaging effects on midwifery, where the prestige of having a history of few or no claims, and the possibility of a discounted premium, have meant that mandatory updating (focusing on the medical management of care and interventions in midwifery) has been prioritised above developing schemes such as midwife-led care.

Since 2002 Strategic Health Authorities monitored trusts' performance and standards, providing potential 'customers' with guidance on available clinical care and also specifying how, and by whom, this care should be delivered. By 2009, however, the Labour government's stated aim was to free providers from such control and to 'devolve decision-making from central government control to local organisations and communities so they are more responsive to the needs and wishes of their local people'. To this end, it was 'committed to delivering an all-foundation trust model for the NHS as soon as possible' (Department of Health, 2009). This trust status, which allowed for greater financial autonomy and freedom from SHA control, could be achieved by hospitals that had demonstrated their 'entrepreneurship' and 'excellence'.

Demonstrating fitness for trust status is itself time-consuming, and if NHS staff spend most of their time focusing on targets, audits and efficiency savings, they cannot at the same time focus on providing the kind of care that patients often need. The potentially negative effects of inappropriately target-driven health care were clear in a number of reports from 2005: one linked malnutrition among elderly hospital patients to the inability of over-stretched nursing staff to sit with patients and help them eat, while another found that nurses have to spend much of their time completing paperwork (Revill, 2005; Age Concern, 2006; Boseley, 2006). Most dramatically, in early 2009 the Health Commission found an alarmingly high death rate in the Mid Staffordshire NHS Foundation Trust and concluded that pursuing targets rather than patient care might have contributed to an unusually high death rate. The Mid Staffordshire Trust is, hopefully, an extreme example of the 'growing disconnect . . . between a target-driven culture and the best interests of . . . patients' (Edemariam, 2009). However, the more general problem remains of how to reconcile the 'nurturing rationality' (Davies, 1989: 170) that good-quality care requires with the demands of the contemporary public-sector workplace.

The impact on midwives: two case studies

The case studies discussed in this section demonstrate the effects of policy changes on two groups of front-line workers in midwifery services. The first study was conducted between 1997 and 2000 in the north of England, at a time when the NHS was still experiencing the impact of the New Public Management reforms introduced by the Conservatives, and maternity services were constantly reconfiguring, with time on the 'shop floor' increasingly task-filled in a performance-driven culture. The study took an action research approach (Deery, 2005; McNiff, 2005) that involved working with a typical group of eight white British NHS community midwives in a collaborative, non-hierarchical and democratic way in order to explore their support needs and achieve change (Deery and Kirkham, 2000). The approach facilitated the midwives devising, and putting into practice, their own model of clinical supervision, described in the nursing literature as a supportive mechanism meant to create time, space and safety (Wilkins, 1998) in order to reflect on practice. Each midwife was interviewed twice, before and after the experience of clinical supervision. They also participated in two focus groups before clinical supervision. Individual interviews and focus groups lasted up to two hours and were taped, transcribed and then analysed using a relational voice-centred methodology (Mauthner and Doucet, 1998).

The second case study was undertaken more recently (2006–08), again in the north of England. By that time New Labour's promise to make public services accountable to the public, and the accompanying 'management by metrics' (Dopson, 2009: 47), was fully under way, as was the commitment to consumer 'choice'. The study involved midwives from three maternity units, all of which had been subject to reconfiguration processes that had involved 'customer empowerment and localised decision-making' (Dopson, 2009: 49), and one of its aims was to identify the cultural and organisational changes that might enable NHS maternity care to be more effective and efficacious. When the study began, each unit was at a different stage of developing 'alongside' midwife-led care (that is, care for a woman in labour, by a midwife only, but in close proximity to an obstetric unit). During the course of the study, radical reconfiguration took place, with two of the sites merging in August 2008, leaving a birth centre managed and run by midwives at site C and all 'high risk' obstetric care at site A, while the well established midwife-led unit on site A was relocated away from the obstetric unit and renamed a birth centre. Data collection methods included focus groups and individual interviews with midwives. This chapter presents some of the findings from preliminary interviews and these focus groups.

Too much to do, and not enough time
In addition to the pressures common to other NHS workers, including the focus on auditing and paperwork, midwives experience particular demands on their time that have become more acute in recent years. Not only is there an ongoing shortage of midwives that increases the average work load (Ball *et al.*, 2002; Carlisle, 2008), but by the time of the second study New Labour's acceptance of the European Working Time Directive, which many welcomed as a positive step for women doctors, was having adverse knock-on effects on the midwifery profession. Blocked by the Conservatives, the directive was enacted into UK law as the 1998 Working Time Regulations, and in 2004 its provisions were extended to junior doctors, whose working hours were limited by law, first to fifty-eight hours a week and then, by 2009, to forty-eight hours. Although this helps women doctors balance their work and family commitments, it means that doctors are not available for all the work they previously did; one effect is that some midwives have had to extend their skills and role to undertake the examination and assessment of the newborn – something that was previously the responsibility of a paediatrician.

New Labour's commitment to patient 'choice' has created further pressures on already stretched maternity services. It has supported a 'with woman' approach that expects midwives to offer choice and plan care for women and their families. Here the focus is the mother as the consumer of maternity care, and the aim is to ensure that health care is personalised and equitable within a safe system, for example increasing breastfeeding rates and offering women more choice about place of birth, their access to midwives, the place and time of postnatal care and the choice and place of antenatal care. These changes all mean that midwives have been expected to extend their role even further, to take on more responsibility and to change their ways of working within existing time frames. In this context, midwives have come to be seen as interchangeable workers who must prioritise keeping the system ticking over (Deery and Kirkham, 2006), rather than individuals who can support women best if they build a relationship with them. Meanwhile, the pursuit of 'efficiency' has meant that women have been discharged earlier from hospital after giving birth. This has increased pressure on hospital-based midwives attempting to support women and establish breast feeding before they return home, and created greater demands on midwifery services in the community.

Because over 99 per cent of midwives are women (Keen, 2009) the conflict between family needs and workplace demands is particularly widespread and acute in the profession. Although there have been attempts at providing more 'family-friendly' working conditions, such as 'term-time contracts', these have been difficult to implement, as the atypical nature of midwifery work means that a twenty-four-hour service almost always has to be offered, within a resource constrained NHS.

The result of all this, unsurprisingly, has been stress (Sandall, 1998; Deery, 2008). Midwives in the case studies have clearly been overworked, with their professional responsibilities spilling over into their 'own time':

> I get myself all worked up . . . at the end of the week you've got a pile of stuff that needs sorting out . . . you're always off late at night and then when you get home you've forgotten to do something so you have to sit down and do it at home . . . in your own time . . . (Study 1)
> I feel that it's difficult being a good midwife and you know providing the care that you need to for that woman, as well as the amount of time that you need to put into guiding . . . is really hard and I think that you end up doing a lot of that time in your own time which then has the knock-on effect of not getting off on time. (Study 2)
> I've got a case load and I don't get any time allocated to do my paperwork and I've got a lot of social problems in my areas . . . and you're balancing all the time. (Study 2)
> Sometimes I get pulled in from community to do a shift on here, so you can do your full-time hours and then you're pulled in to do a night shift and you're doing nights and days in the same week. (Study 2)

Midwives experienced particular problems because of the promises that have been made to mothers about the service they can expect:

> I mean there's all this government stuff and everybody gets a copy in their notes and they're [the women] all told what they should expect and they're all told they'll get a named midwife and they'll be seen at the time of their appointment time and the midwife will come and see you when you get home and if you arrive late they say 'where have you been? . . . I've been waiting for you' . . . You can't do eleven visits between nine and twelve . . . How can you possibly do that . . . not and give quality care to somebody . . . (Study 1)
>
> we've got four hundred women between us . . . we have to give a time when we visit . . . and if not we ring the person and give a reasonable excuse as to why not . . . (Study 1)

Research participants in the second study were additionally stressed by the effects of reconfiguration of maternity services:

> I need the work, I need the money and I feel really aggrieved that I've worked in a place and where I'll now have to travel for forty minutes to get to work and my choice was I would work somewhere where I was five minutes away from where I live and where I can reach my children at school if I need to. (Study 2)

They also complained that women were being discharged too early from hospital:

> I was speaking to a community midwife the other day and in the past two weeks she's noticed a big increase in the amount of women that are coming home . . . who haven't established breast feeding, who are needing extra support and visits which, you know, they just can't provide in the time. (Study 2)
>
> They just get tossed out there and nobody gives a damn. 'Let's just get them through, get them home and discharge them as quick as possible,' and so be it. (Study 2)
>
> There's so much change going on at the moment, in terms of shipping women out quicker and management are on your back to get rid of patients quicker and you just feel constantly harassed that you can't do your job properly. It's awful, it's depressing. (Study 2)

Underlying issues: the strengthening of 'men's time'
The problem is not simply that there are too few midwives for too many women, but that midwives are increasingly subject to directly contradictory temporal pressures. On the one hand, they are expected to provide personalised support. This requires an open-ended approach to time that enables relationships to develop, and it cannot be pushed

neatly into a slotted timetable or work schedule. On the other hand, midwives are under pressure to ensure that all women receive 'appropriate' antenatal and postnatal care, and keep to a scheduled timetable of visits. This reflects a culture dominated by considerations of prudent use of resources, strengthening performance indicators and monitoring quality. The result is a rigid prioritisation of clock time over relational time that reflects the transformation of childbirth from a 'natural' process to a form of medicalised assembly-line production within a system that has rationalised service delivery. When clinical practice is carried out according to such an industrialised conveyor-belt model there is no continuity of relationship between the woman and the midwife (Deery and Kirkham, 2006) and time spent building relationships with women and colleagues is disregarded by performance indicators.

The case studies indicate that such a model is not only stressful for midwives; it is also to the detriment of mothers:

> We used to spend hours with them in their homes and, you know, you really were their friend . . . but you're so busy now . . . that personal touch is lost. (Study 1)
> I wish I could give them more of my time and I'm always saying I'm sorry . . . I'm sorry I haven't been in . . . I'm sorry I haven't been able to help you feed your baby . . . I'll be back in half an hour. (Study 2)
> I just think you're not giving your best, you can't give your best. There's always someone on your back saying, 'Can't she go home, can't she do this, can't she do that,' so you're rushing to do everything all the time, and, the poor women, it's awful. (Study 2)

Conclusion

As part of its commitment to social justice New Labour promised to help women balance their family and workplace commitments. This promise was certainly not delivered to the midwives in the case studies. New Labour also promised to increase choice for consumers of public services and ensure that providers are accountable. The case studies discussed in this chapter show that the very mechanisms of choice and accountability can prove counterproductive and produce a reduction in the quality of service provided.

Childbirth is in many ways the paradigm example of 'women's time': experienced only by women, its 'natural' and unpredictable processes are particularly difficult to timetable or streamline in accordance with man-made workplace norms, while appropriate professional support for the practical and emotional needs of new mothers is often both open-ended and time-consuming, involving the development of a relationship rather than a tick-list of tasks. The case studies show that, as with other forms of care work, recent policies have strengthened the hegemony of 'men's time'; a contradiction appears where an increased emphasis on quantifiable targets, efficiency savings and the rationalisation of service delivery that is supposed to promote a personalised, women-centred service makes this impossible in practice. The results are both a poorer service and an increasingly stressed profession.

The implications of these findings extend far beyond the midwifery services, and affect everyone who has ever given or received care – and that is all of us. (We all need care as infants, most of us need it when old or sick.) The chapter therefore indicates that, if social needs for care are to be addressed, we need to pay more attention to the use and nature of time. In particular, we need a radical redistribution of public and private time to recognise the social, economic and civic value of women's traditional responsibilities. Even more fundamentally, we need to recognise that the provision of good-quality care and the development of human relationships require a fluid and open-ended approach to time that transcends 'men's time' considerations of cost efficiency. We therefore need to challenge current policy directions in the name of both gender justice and the well-being of society as a whole.

Note

1 These terms reflect gendered social roles rather than innate attributes. They do not imply that all women or all men share the same relationship with time.

Bibliography

Adam, B. (1995) *Timewatch. The Social Analysis of Time* (Cambridge: Polity Press).

Age Concern (2006) *Hungry to be Heard. The Scandal of Malnourished Older People in Hospital* (London: Age Concern).

Ball, L., Curtis, P., and Kirkham, M. (2002) *Why Do Midwives Leave?* (London: Royal College of Midwives).

BBC News Channel (2007) 'Police condemn "target culture"', 15 May, http://news.bbc.co.uk/1/hi/uk/6656411.stm (accessed 7 July 2010).

Blair, T. (1998) *The Third Way: New Politics for the New Century* (London: Fabian Society).

Boseley, S. (2006) 'Minister admits malnutrition risk', *Guardian*, 30 August.

Bryson, V. (2007) *Gender and the Politics of Time. Feminist Theory and Contemporary Debates* (Bristol: Policy Press).

Bryson, V. (2008) 'Time-use studies: a potentially feminist tool?', *International Journal of Feminist Politics* 10:2, 135–53.

Buckler, S., and Dolowitz, D. P. (2000) 'Theorizing the third way: New Labour and social justice', *Journal of Political Ideologies* 5:3, 301–20.

Carlisle, D. (2008) 'Will Darzi bring about a renaissance in maternity services?', *Health Service Journal*, 3 July.

Childs, S. (2004) *New Labour's Women MPs* (London: Routledge).

CNST, www.nhsla.com/Claims/Schemes/CNST/ (accessed 7 July 2009).

Cook, H. (2002) 'Empowerment', in G. Blakeley and V. Bryson (eds) *Contemporary Political Concepts. A Critical Introduction* (London: Pluto Press).

Cooper, A. (2008) 'Welfare: dead, dying or just transubstantiated?' *Soundings* 38, 29–41.

Coote, A., Harman, H., and Hewitt, P. (1990) *The Family Way: a New Approach to Policy-making* (London: Institute for Public Policy Research).

Corker, M., and French, S. (1999) 'Reclaiming discourse in disability studies', in M. Corker (ed.) *Disability Discourse* (Buckingham: Open University Press).

Crinson, I. (2005) 'The direction of health policy in New Labour's third term', *Critical Social Policy* 25, 507–16.

Cushing, P., and Lewis, T. (2002) 'Negotiating mutuality and agency in care-giving relationships with women with intellectual disabilities' *Hypatia*, 17:3, 173–93.

Davies, K. (1989) *Women and Time. Weaving the Strands of Everyday Life* (Lund: University of Lund).

Davies, K. (1994) 'The tensions between process time and clock time in care work', *Time and Society* 3:3, 277–303.

Deery, R. (2005) 'An action research study exploring midwives' support needs and the effect of group clinical supervision', *Midwifery* 21:2, 161–76.

Deery, R. (2008) 'The tyranny of time: tensions between relational and clock time in community-based midwifery', *Social Theory and Health* 6:4, 342–63, doi:10.1057/sth.2008.13.

Deery, R., and Kirkham, M. (2000) 'Moving from hierarchy to collaboration: the birth of an action research project', *Practising Midwife* 3, 25–8.

Deery, R., and Kirkham, M. (2006) 'Supporting midwives to support women', in L. Page and R. McCandlish (eds) *The New Midwifery: Science and Sensitivity in Practice*, 2nd edn (London: Elsevier).

Department of Health (1993) *Changing Childbirth*, Part 1, *Report of the Expert Maternity Group* (London: Stationery Office).

Department of Health (2009) *Background to NHS Foundation Trusts*, www.dh.gov.uk/en/Healthcare/Secondarycare/NHSfoundationtrust/DH_406 2852 (accessed 7 July 2009).

Dopson, S. (2009) 'Changing forms of managerialism in the NHS: hierarchies, markets and networks', in J. Gabe and M. Calnan (eds) *The New Sociology of the Health Service* (London: Routledge).

Drewry, G. (2005) 'Citizens as Customers', EGPA Conference, Bern, 31 August–2 September, http://www.public-admin.co.uk/brochures/cutomers_charters_paper.pdf (accessed 7 July 2009).

Dworkin, R. (1993) *Life's Dominion: an Argument about Abortion, Euthanasia, and Individual Freedom* (New York: Knopf).

Edemariam, A. (2009) 'A hospital is able to tick all the boxes yet still utterly fail patients', *Guardian*, 19 March.

Fisher, P. (2008) 'Well-being and empowerment: the importance of recognition', *Sociology of Health and Illness* 30:4, 583–98, DOI: 10.1111/j.1467-9566.2007.01074.x.

Fitzpatrick, T. (2004) 'Social policy and time', *Time and Society* 13:2–3, 197–219.

Fraser, N. (2000) 'After the family wage: a postindustrial thought experiment', in B. Hobson (ed.) *Gender and Citizenship in Transition* (Basingstoke: Macmillan).

Goffman, E. (1963) *Stigma: Notes on the Management of Spoiled Identity* (New York: Prentice-Hall).

Harman, H. (1993) *The Century Gap* (London: Vermilion).

Harman, H. (1997) *Speech at the Launch of the Centre for Analysis of Social Exclusion at the London School of Economics* (London: Department of Social Security).

Hewitt, P. (1993) *About Time. The Revolution in Work and Family Life* (London: Rivers Oram Press).

Hochschild, A. R. (1983) *The Managed Heart: Commercialization of Human Feeling* (Berkeley CA: University of California Press).

Hughes, D., Deery, R. and Lovatt, A. (2002) 'A critical ethnographic approach to facilitating cultural shift in midwifery', *Midwifery* 18: 43–52.

Keen, A. House of Commons Hansard written answer of 2 February, www.publications.parliament.uk/pa/cm200809/cmhansrd/cm090202/text/90202w0019.htm (accessed 7 July 2009).

Kelly, R. (2000) *Plugging the Parenting Gap: the Case for Paid Parental Leave* (London: Fabian Society).

Kittay, E. (2002) 'Love's labour revisited', *Hypatia* 17:3, 237–50.

Labour Party (1997) *Manifesto*, http://labour-party.org.uk/manifestos/1997/1997-labour-manifesto.shtml (accessed 7 July 2009).

Labour Party (2001) *Manifesto*, http://labour-party.org.uk/manifestos/2001/2001-labour-manifesto.shtml (accessed 7 July 2009).

Labour Party (2005) *Manifesto*, www.practicallaw.com/5-200-6210 (accessed 7 July 2009).

Levitas, R. (2001) 'Against work', *Critical Social Policy* 21:4, 449–65.

Lister, R. (2003) *Citizenship. Feminist Perspectives* (Basingstoke: Macmillan).

McNiff, Jean (2005) *All you need to Know about Action Research* (London: Sage).

Mauthner, N., and Doucet, A. (1998) 'Reflections on a voice-centred relational method. analysing maternal and domestic voices', in J. Ribbens and R. Edwards (eds) *Feminist Dilemmas in Qualitative Research. Public Knowledge and Private Lives* (London: Sage).

Okin, S. (1990) *Justice, Gender and the Family* (New York: Basic Books).

Opportunity Now (2008) *Women and Work: the facts*, www.springboardconsultancy.com/pdfs/women-and-work.pdf (accessed 7 July 2009).

Powell, M. (2000) 'New Labour and the third way in the British welfare state: a new and distinctive approach?', *Critical Social Policy* 20, 39–60.

Rawls, J. (1971) *A Theory of Justice* (Oxford: Clarendon Press).

Rawls, J. (2001) *Justice as Fairness* (Cambridge MA: Harvard University Press).

Revill, J. (2005) 'Paperwork mountain keeps nurses from care', *Observer*, 27 November.

Rustin, M. (2008) 'Contradictions in the welfare state', *Soundings* 38, 42–55.

Sandall, J. (1998) 'Occupational burnout in midwives: new ways of working and the relationship between organisational factors and psychological health and well-being', *Risk Decision and Policy* 3:3, 213–32.

Sevenhuijsen, S. (1998) *Citizenship and the Ethics of Care* (London: Routledge).

Thompson, E. P. (1967/1999) 'Time, work-discipline and industrial capital', in E. P. Thompson (ed.) *Customs in Common* (London: Penguin Books).

Trades Union Congress, *Working Time*, www.tuc.org.uk/h_and_s/index.cfm?mins=344 (accessed 7 July 2009).

Tronto, J. (1993) *Moral Boundaries. A Political Argument for an Ethic of Care* (London: Routledge).

White, Sue (2008) 'Computers can hinder child protection', *Guardian*, 19 November.

Wilkins, P. (1998) 'Clinical supervision and community psychiatric nursing', in T. Butterworth, J. Faugier and P. Burnard (eds) *Clinical Supervision and Mentorship in Nursing*, 2nd edn (Cheltenham: Nelson Thornes).

Williams, F. (1999) 'Good-enough principles for welfare', *Journal of Social Policy* 28:4, 667–87.

Williams, F. (2001) 'In and beyond New Labour: towards a new political ethics of care', *Critical Social Policy* 21, 467–93.

Wissenburg, M. (2001) 'The "third way" and social justice', *Journal of Political Ideologies* 6:2, 231–5.

Woolf, M. (2009) 'Paternity leave scheme shelved by Lord Mandelson', *Sunday Times*, 31 May.

Acknowledgements

The action research study was partly funded by the West Yorkshire Workforce Confederation and the ethnographic study was funded by the Health Foundation. We are grateful to both funding bodies and all those who participated in the research studies.

7

Promoting social justice, perpetuating social injustice? New Labour and disabled people

Anne Chappell and Chris Gifford

Much has been written about the contradictory nature of New Labour's social policy (see for example, Clarke 2005), and these contradictions apply also to New Labour's approach to social justice itself (Powell 2002). One of the most notable areas of contradiction arises from New Labour's attempt to combine the logic of global free markets with a commitment to offsetting the worst effects of capitalism in the name of social justice. This chapter explores tensions in New Labour's social policy with particular reference to the government's approach to disability issues. It shows that the New Labour approach to social justice drew on contrasting models of disability: the individualised model of disability (sometimes known as the medical model) and the social model of disability. The chapter shows that these models are consistent with contractarian and solidaristic conceptions of citizenship respectively, and that the government's shifting position between the two models created tensions within policy. By making the origins of these tensions explicit the chapter provides a framework for understanding competing approaches to the inclusion, and corresponding exclusion, of disabled people in modern societies.

This chapter will examine three policy discourses which exemplify New Labour's approach to disability. These are, first, policy discourses which promote social justice and draw on the social model of disability; secondly, discourses which draw on individualised notions of disability while framing these in social justice rhetoric; and, thirdly, discourses which emphasise the disciplining of disabled people and also draw on the individualised approach. The chapter concludes that although disabled people saw some important gains under New Labour governments, these were undermined by New Labour's individualised approach and its focus on labour market participation. It also finds little prospect of significant policy change.

Discourses of disability and citizenship

New Labour's approach to social policy was complex, reflecting its ideological eclecticism. The most useful analyses are based on tax-onomies of policy discourses (see Levitas, 2005) and citizenship (see Dean, 2002) as these address competing and contradicting values, strategies and positions. In this chapter, New Labour's social justice and inclusion discourses are examined in relation to both the social and individualised model of disability, while its disciplining and exclusion-ary discourse is related to the individualised model. These it is argued underpin competing citizenship agendas.

The first model of disability referred to in this chapter is known as the social model. This tool for understanding disability takes as its staring point the notion that 'disability' is a social construct, founded on the socially and historically specific meanings given to the presence of impairment in an individual. In the social model, the difficulties encountered by disabled people flow from environmental barriers and the prejudice, disadvantage and discrimination meted out to them, as opposed to the limitations caused by impairment. In the social model, impairment and disability are *not* synonymous. 'Disability' is created by the social and economic organisation of society (for example, schooling, work, poverty, access, cultural representation, etc.) and not by the presence of impairment in individuals. The social model has developed from the disabled people's movement. Its par-ticular explanatory power is that it incorporates the experience of all disabled people, regardless of the manner of their impairment. In contrast, the individualised model divides disabled people from each other by focusing on impairment. The social model, therefore, is a springboard for disabled people to demand economic, social and political change (see Oliver, 1996, for a more detailed explanation of the social model).

Nonetheless, it is the individualised model that remains the more conventional way of explaining disability. The individual model identi-fies impairment (that is, the deficiency located within a person's body or mind) as synonymous with disability. Thus all restrictions on a per-son's activity, including social and economic exclusion, flow as inevita-ble consequences of the presence of impairment within the individual. Within this approach, disabled people have to be rehabilitated or nor-malised to aid their integration into mainstream society, through the provision of impairment specific health and wealth services and pro-fessional interventions. This means that people with impairments are expected to strive to be 'normal' by behaving like non-disabled people.

The premise of the individualised model is that if disabled people are unwilling or unable to be rehabilitated they face social sanctions.

Here we are particularly concerned with how these models inform political discourses and policies that, in turn, construct disabled people in relation to the state and the wider political community. The key concept is citizenship, understood as a 'contested site of social struggles' and the 'right to have rights' *and* obligations (Isin *et al.*, 2009: 1). As Marshall showed (1963), citizenship is progressive in that it implies a challenge to systematic disadvantage and exclusion. Nevertheless, as the dominant form of national citizenship has been challenged by globalisation and the rise of social movements, a considerable uncertainty underlies the direction of citizenship. Not least for disabled people, the legacy of the Labour government is a mixture of opportunity alongside continued social injustices.

The social model of disability aligns most clearly with a solidaristic conception of citizenship. Drawing upon the work of Dean (2007), solidaristic citizenship institutionalises rights and duties that explicitly address structural social injustice. It is underpinned by an understanding that human beings are fundamentally social and interdependent and that the goal of citizenship is to ensure social cohesion and protection. This has parallels with Marshall's seminal theorisation of citizenship as a continued accumulation of rights and entitlements by disadvantaged groups as part of a wider conflict between market inequities and the principle of equality (Marshall, 1963). The culmination of modern citizenship development for Marshall was social citizenship institutionalised in the post-war welfare state. In line with solidaristic citizenship, Marshall endorsed universalist political intervention to address systemic inequality. Drawing explicitly on Marshall, Rummery argues that for the disabled citizen this is 'about whether the state is meeting its obligations to enable you to meet yours: whether you are enabled, or prevented, from being a "fully competent member of society", "living the life of a good citizen" and "promoting the welfare of the community"' (2006: 636).

The solidaristic citizen is first and foremost a social citizen committed to the equal social worth of all, who 'assumes responsibility – mediated by the state – for others as much as for themselves' (Dean, 2007: 580). Such a conception need not lead to conformity and passivity if it is underpinned by 'meaningful participation in processes of deliberative democracy' (Stewart, 2000: 65). From this perspective, structures of political participation are essential for generating social solidarity and social justice in societies characterised by plurality and diversity. This corresponds with the growing emphasis on the importance of disabled people's *voice* and enabling political participation in decision making, not just about services but in society more generally (Oliver, 1996; Rummery, 2006). The proposition in this chapter is that the general direction of the New Labour project was not in line with solidaristic citizenship and was not realised for disabled people. Nevertheless, we propose that in areas such as disability rights, political participation in decision making and control over resources there is some room for optimism.

There remained a strong liberal and contractarian aspect to Marshall's theory of citizenship in his conception of citizens who claim their rights as individuals from the state and fulfil their citizenship duties through contractual employment. Indeed, it is the hegemony of the individualist able-bodied worker-citizen that has been identified within the social model as the root of disabled people's oppression in capitalist society. In contradistinction to solidaristic citizenship, the individualist model of disability gives rise to a disabling conception of citizenship that is focused on the individual's impairment and behaviour, as opposed to the underlying injustice experienced by disabled people as socially and politically disadvantaged social group. Integral to this conception of citizenship is the idea of self-interested and competitive individuals capable of entering into market contracts (Stewart, 2000; Dean, 2007). This is then the 'hallmark of full adult status' (Stewart, 2000: 58). From such a perspective the market provides equal opportunities for individuals to access resources and empower themselves. Correspondingly, social disadvantage is the consequence of a lack of capacity and suggests individual failure. Access to rights then is conditional on fulfilling civic duty, which means ensuring that individual interests and ambitions are 'fulfilled without burdening others or unfairly prejudicing the interests of others' (Dean, 2007: 580). Dean argues that underpinning this is a disciplinary notion of responsibility that subjects those considered irresponsible to penalties and sanctions and stigmatisation (*ibid.*). Indeed, the focus becomes eliciting obedience to rules as part of a system of 'governance of irresponsibility' (*ibid.*: 581). In this chapter it is argued that this model of disability and citizenship has been most clearly evident in Labour's policies such as Welfare-to-work and in the treatment of those with mental health problems.

Social justice, the social model and disability policy

Since the mid-1990s (indeed, before New Labour took office in 1997) there have been clear policy gains for disabled people. This section of the chapter will examine some of the advances in disability policy by showing how they have been shaped (at least in part) by the social model and locating them in New Labour's social justice agenda. The policy areas to be explored here are:

- The Disability Discrimination Act 1995 and its extended and strengthened versions enacted in 2002 and 2004.
- The White Paper *Valuing People: A New Strategy for Learning Disability for the Twenty-first Century* (DoH, 2001a).
- The report of the Prime Minister's Strategy Unit (2005) *Improving the Life Chances of Disabled People.*
- Direct Payments and personalised budgets

The Disability Discrimination Act
As disabled people and their organisations have become increasingly politicised and able to articulate policy demands by drawing on the social model they have made more demands on central government for interventions to improve the their lives. Barnes and Mercer note the way that:

> disability issues acquired a political and policy importance in the last quarter of the twetieth century that provided a stark contrast with earlier years . . . Governments began to reconsider the aims and consequences of disability policies. (2005: 528–9)

A vital campaign for disabled people has been for anti-discriminatory legislation. This campaign has had clear links with notions of social justice and the social model, as it seeks to outlaw discrimination against disabled citizens (in ways similar to legislation which outlaws discrimination on the grounds of sex, marital status and ethnic origin). Demands for such legislation have argued that the unequal treatment of disabled people originates from discrimination against a socially disadvantaged group rather than restrictions caused by impairment.

When the Disability Discrimination Act (DDA) was passed in 1995 it provided the first legal protection for disabled people against discrimination, but it was regarded as a half-measure by sections of the disabled people's movement. This was because of the individualised model of disability and citizenship that underpinned it, its numerous get-out clauses and exemptions, and because, initially, it lacked a mechanism to enforce compliance (Priestley, 1999; Barnes and Mercer, 2001). Yet Priestley also notes that 'the passage of the Act must be seen as an important advance for the disabled people's movement' (1999: 208). Since the DDA was first implemented there have been significant additions to its scope; for example, the inclusion of educational institutions and issues of public access into its remit. As Morris explains, 'in its concept of "reasonable adjustment" the legislation goes a long way to promoting the social model of disability' (2005: 6–7).

The revised versions of the DDA mean that legal protection for disabled people has shifted from being reactive (discrimination has to occur before a disabled person can seek redress) to being proactive (employers and other organisations must take the needs of disabled people into account or face legal sanction). This demonstrates the influence of a more solidaristic citizenship agenda. By 2009 this agenda was moving forward as the government introduced plans for a comprehensive piece of legislation to rationalise and clarify existing laws against sexism, racism, ageism and disablism in a new Equalities Bill (Government Equalities Office, 2009).

The 2001 White Paper

Valuing People: A Strategy for Learning Disability Services in the Twenty-first Century (DoH, 2001a) was the first White Paper for thirty years aimed at overhauling services for people with learning difficulties. Fryson and Simons refer to its 'radical tone' and 'breadth of ambition' in taking a proactive and joined-up approach to improving the lives of people with learning difficulties (2003: 153). It is evident also that *Valuing People* has been shaped by the wider agenda of New Labour's focus on citizenship, inclusion and social justice: 'The Government is committed to enforceable civil rights for disabled people in order to eradicate discrimination in society' (DoH, 2001a: 23):

> Being part of the mainstream is something that most of us take for granted . . . Inclusion means enabling people with learning disabilities to do these ordinary things, make use of mainstream services and be fully included in the local community. (DoH, 2001a: 24)

Although there have been some criticisms of *Valuing People* (see Burton and Kagan, 2006), the White Paper was generally well received by professionals, families and, most significantly, people with learning difficulties themselves (Grant and Ramcharan, 2002; Walker, 2002). Since its publication in 2001 there have been further documents which review the progress of the objectives of *Valuing People*. People with learning difficulties, their carers and advocates have been involved in the consultation processes for these documents. Greig's report on the progress of *Valuing People* (2005) demonstrated social model values with its 'nothing about us without us' philosophy and jargon-free writing style.

One of the key objectives of *Valuing People* was its emphasis on a multi-agency partnership approach to service development, which includes people with learning difficulties and their families in the growth of inclusive services. The principal mechanism to achieve this has been the Learning Disability Partnership Board. The LDPBs include a number of stakeholders, including service users, to develop long-term strategic change in the planning and implementation of services. The inclusion of service users on LDPBs is clearly influenced by the social model/ social justice agenda, as people with learning difficulties are regarded as experts whose voices must be heard. There is evidence, however, that LDPBs have not always met these objectives. In practice they can be more of a forum for service users to give feedback on plans for service development than an opportunity for service providers and people with learning difficulties to make key budgetary, planning and delivery decisions (see Riddington *et al.*, 2008). Overall, therefore, the solidaristic citizenship achievements of *Valuing People* have been partial and the policies outlined have been 'strong on vision but short on the detailed implantation plans to make the vision a reality' (DoH, 2008: 11).

The Life Chances *report*
New Labour's emphasis on social justice was taken further by the Prime Minister's Strategy Unit Report (2005) *Improving the Life Chances of Disabled People*. The influence of the social model is clearly evidenced in this document. The report went far beyond the narrow question of services into discussion of the much wider social, economic and environmental barriers of housing, transport, employment and crime. Indeed, environmental barriers were regarded as the root of the problems experienced by disabled people, and the report set a clear objective of full civil rights for disabled people within twenty years (PMSU, 2005). The report recognised, for example, that disabled people are frequently victims of crime and harassment (2005: 10). This was portrayed not as an inevitable manifestation of fear of difference of persons with an impairment, but as a sign of prejudice and discrimination against disabled people. This is a clear indicator that the thinking behind this document was shaped by New Labour's social model and social justice discourses.

Direct Payments
For many in the disabled people's movement, the major policy victory was the introduction of Direct Payments, described by Barnes as, 'potentially one of the most significant developments in British social policy since the establishment of the modern welfare state' (2002: 3).

The disabled people's movement campaigned hard for the right to be able to control the resources spent on the services for disabled people. Direct Payments were introduced in 1996 and meant that disabled people apply for public money to employ personal assistants to deliver care in the way desired by the disabled person. The rationale for Direct Payments was that disabled people are experts in the organisation of their own care and they should exercise control of the support they receive. Direct Payments are an opportunity for disabled people to exercise autonomy; that is, disabled people may require the provision of personal care, but through Direct Payments they can decide *when*, *how* and *by whom* this care is provided. They have been the result of a synthesis of contrasting discourses: on one side, the user-led empowerment values of the social model and, on the other side, the shifting position of the state as it moved from being a direct provider of services to taking a regulatory role and expecting disabled people to choose their service providers.

One limitation of Direct Payments has been the low take-up by some groups of disabled people, notably those with learning difficulties or mental health problems (Riddell *et al.*, 2005). Some groups are less likely to apply, and staff in some local authorities have been sceptical as to the capacity of people with learning difficulties or mental health problems to manage the payments (Ridley and Jones, 2003; Newbigging with Lowe, 2005). However, the Labour government sought to expand the Direct Payment idea into a system of individualised budgets that would bring all funding requirements (e.g. health, social care, transport) into one budget for each disabled person. This initiative has been described as a 'leap forward in disability rights' (Community Care, 2005).

The success of Direct Payments and the more recent proposal of individualised budgets identified disabled people as citizen consumers. The nature of this consumerism, was, however, shaped by the social model values of empowerment and autonomy and implied more solidaristic citizenship for disabled people. Direct payments have seen a number of disabled people become engaged as citizens rather than as clients within the conventional organisation of services. They provide a significant example of where disabled people are enabled 'to participate in society *and* fulfil their citizenship obligations' (Rummery, 2006: 644).

Social justice, the individualised model of disability and New Labour

The second theme of New Labour's social justice agenda that will be discussed in this chapter draws on an individualised model of disability.

This section will argue that the New Labour government misunderstood the different ways of conceptualising disability, so that its disability policy contained important contradictions while being seen to draw on the rhetoric of social justice. Two policy examples will be examined here:

- Social exclusion and mental health services
- Welfare-to-work initiatives

Social exclusion and mental health services
When New Labour came to power in 1997 the tackling of 'social exclusion' was a major policy objective. Social exclusion can be understood as a shorthand for a combination of linked problems, such as poverty, unemployment, poor housing and poor health (Cabinet Office, 2009). New Labour's concept of social exclusion also had a moral element, as the circumstances of those who are socially excluded are, from this perspective, worsened by their socially undesirable and criminal behaviour which can be passed on through the generations:

> There exists a vast majority with good habits of work, virtuous conduct between citizens, stable family structure and a minority who are disorganised, welfare dependent, criminal and crimogenic, who live in unstable and dysfunctional families. (Young, 2001: 11)

People with mental health problems have been defined as a group who are at serious risk of stigma and discrimination, extremely vulnerable to unemployment, poverty and social isolation, and who find it difficult to access the services they need (Social Exclusion Unit, 2000; Sainsbury Centre for Mental Health, 2002). People with mental health problems thus came within the remit of the Social Exclusion Unit, established in 1998. The tone of the SEU's approach to mental health issues emphasised the commonality of mental illness and the ordinariness of those who experience it. Similar approaches to mental health policy were also evident in the government's commitment to raise standards of care and tackle discrimination and social exclusion; for example, through the National Service Framework (Dobson, 1999).

These areas of policy can be seen to draw on notions of social justice. They emphasised that the main problems faced by people with mental health problems relate not simply to their diagnosis but to the isolation, poverty, discrimination and poor standards of care they encounter. As Dobson (1999) puts it, 'Mental illness is not well understood; it frightens people and all too often it carries a stigma.'

Yet, at the same time, elements of the individualised model of disability were evident. These interventions are based on a medical (i.e.

individualised) definition of mental health and illness and suggested that people with mental health problems are partly responsible for their poor quality of life:

> Most people who suffer from mental illness are vulnerable and present no threat to anyone but themselves. Many of these patients have not been getting the treatment and care they need partly because the system has found it so hard to cope with the small minority of *mentally ill people who are a nuisance or a danger to both themselves and others*. (Dobson, 1999, emphasis added)

This individualised approach placed particular emphasis on the extent to which people with mental health problems take their medication regularly, thereby complying with the notion of being a good patient and following medical advice. In this way, policy initiatives to address the social exclusion of people with mental health problems which drew on a social justice agenda slid very quickly into an individualised perspective which moved away from the question of people's economic and social environments into a medicalised approach. The tension between individualised and social model perspectives on disability is also highlighted in the controversy surrounding the 2007 Mental Health Act, which will be examined later in the chapter.

Welfare-to-work
New Labour's commitment to tackling poverty and social exclusion was founded on the principle of paid work. This, it was argued, was the key to both improving people's incomes so that they are lifted out of poverty and tackling social exclusion by ensuring that they are full participants in society, i.e. they enjoy social citizenship (Barnes and Mercer, 2005.) As Roulstone points out, there was a clear assumption by the Labour government that work is 'good for disabled people' (2002: 628). Therefore a central component of New Labour's social justice agenda was to expand participation in the labour market through Welfare-to-work programmes. The intention was to help unemployed people and support them in employment to ensure that benefit claimants fulfil their societal obligations.

The social model operates from a materialist basis and it identifies economic exclusion as 'the ultimate cause of the various other exclusion experiences by disabled people' (Oliver and Barnes, 1998: 95). Nonetheless, New Labour's Welfare-to-work programme attracted great controversy in regard to its expectations that disabled people should enter the labour market. As discussed earlier in this chapter, the conventional approach to disability policy was driven by the individualised model. In this model, disabled people remain outside the labour market because their impairment renders them unable to work and they form part of the 'deserving poor'. However, New Labour's strategies to increase their participation in the labour market challenged this assumption. As Jolly points out, in terms of unemployment, the category of disabled people was being redrawn so that 'they are no longer classified as the "deserving poor" but *en masse* with other disadvantaged and marginalised sectors of society' (2000: 803).

As the Welfare-to-work initiatives were rolled out and applied more vigorously, disabled people were recategorised as part of the undeserving poor (along with lone parents, young people and older workers). In addition, stories in the media about disabled people allegedly abusing the benefit system added to demands to introduce stricter systems of classifying impairment based on the individualised model of disability (see Grover and Piggott, 2005: 711). Although the rhetoric of Welfare-to-work drew very clearly on the language of citizenship, inclusion and social justice, benefits, particularly Invalidity Benefit, were portrayed as too easy to claim, and it was argued that once disabled people were in receipt of such benefits they were trapped as claimants and denied re-entry to the world of work. The image was that disabled people were abandoned in the benefit system. Using this imagery, government intervention was portrayed as 'rescuing' people from the twilight world of long-term claiming and facilitating their re-entry to mainstream society via Employment and Support Allowance and back-to-work providers. The language of these interventions emphasised that 'no one is written off' (Purnell, 2008) and that these reforms were about 'enhancing support and control for disabled people' (Department for Work and Pensions, 2008).

Certainly, there is some evidence that disabled people who found jobs through Welfare-to-work found the experience beneficial. Heenan's research indicates that, despite reservations, the disabled people whom she interviewed appreciated the support to help them enter the world of work: 'for many it has been a positive, life-changing experience' (2002: 379).

Yet it is clear that there has been conflict here between the different models of disability evident in the Welfare-to-work agenda. The rhetoric drew on notions of social justice, while the acceptance of supply-side economic orthodoxy pointed to deficiencies in the labour market (i.e. disabled people) as the explanation for their exclusion from the market. Welfare-to-work has been about making disabled people market-ready, and as such it has drawn on an individualised model of disability and a contractarian notion of citizenship. As is noted elsewhere,

Welfare-to-work strategies put pressure on disabled people to 'conform to a deregulated labour market' (Holden and Beresford, 2002: 198; Fisher, 2008 and this volume). At the same time, the government's expectations of employers were much less stringent:

> Employers have an important role in welfare promoting the well-being of their employees as well as in relating to wider corporate social responsibility. The Government will consult with employers, listen to their concerns and seek to reduce the regulatory burden on them. (DWP, 2008: 12)

Reducing the regulatory burden on employers may make disabled people appear a more attractive and cheaper work force, yet it is *increasing* the regulatory responsibilities of employers (e.g. through the DDA) that will afford more protection to disabled people as they enter a competitive and discriminatory labour market. New Labour administrations took the view that labour markets are largely neutral arbiters of individual capacity rather than institutionalised forms of social disadvantage and injustice. While the rhetoric of Welfare-to-work has been about social inclusion and social justice, the reality for disabled people is of incorporation into an individualist-contractarian form of citizenship that has historically been shown to reproduce their social exclusion and thereby undermine social justice.

New Labour and the disciplining of disabled people

The final section of this chapter will examine the way that disabled people were disciplined and controlled through New Labour discourses. In these discourses, the behaviour of disabled people was labelled as problematic, antisocial, out of control and potentially dangerous. A range of interventions were developed to contain such behaviours. This section of the chapter will discuss the:

- Mental Health Act 2007.
- Development of the label of 'antisocial behaviour' and its application to disabled people.

The authors will argue that disabled people, in addition to the social justice discourses addressed earlier, could experience punitive interventions from the state. The individualist notion of citizenship evident in Welfare-to-work was extended further to the point where the overriding concern was eliciting obedience.

The development of community care policy meant the closure of long-stay hospitals, and for over two decades there has been significant concern that the loss of psychiatric beds has outstripped the provision of alternative community-based facilities, leading to serious failings in mental health services (Audit Commission, 1986). During the 1990s, there was a growing sense of crisis in mental health services (Payne, 1999).The individualist ideology of the then Conservative government interpreted the failings of the mental health system as being caused primarily by patients who did not take their medication (see Jones 1993; Payne, 1999). A series of violent acts committed by individuals with mental health problems added to the pressure on the government to review the 1983 Mental Health Act, with particular focus on ensuring that people with personality disorders could be detained in hospital against their will if they were deemed a danger to themselves or others. This strand of policy emphasised the dangerousness of people with mental health problems (Butler and Drakeford, 2005: 159) despite evidence to the contrary about the reality of the dangers posed by this group of people (see Laurence, 2003). The preoccupation with dangerousness has produced a gendered and racialised account of mental illness, with people with conditions like schizophrenia and personality disorders regarded as a threat to the wider community in the public space (rather than a danger to themselves in the private space).

In 2002 the New Labour government published the first draft of the new Mental Health Bill. The Bill proved to be extremely controversial and, despite being redrafted a number of times, did not become law until July 2007. Campaigners against the law won some concessions, for example, in relation to the right to advocacy, but one of the most contentious parts of the Act remains. The Mental Health Act 2007 introduced a new power of supervised community treatment for people with mental health problems who have been detained in hospital. People with mental health problems in hospital can be discharged only if they agree to a Community Treatment Order (CTO), which ensures that they are continuing to take their medication while living in the community. If people with mental health problems do not comply with the terms of their CTO they can be detained in hospital, against their will if necessary. Although the government said that CTOs would be used only for a small number of people, by 2009 the indications were that they were being applied more extensively. According to a report in the *Guardian* (Gould, 2009: 3), in the first twelve months of the new system the government expected about 450 people with mental health problems to be released from hospital in England and Wales on CTOs, but the figure is closer to 1,600 (Gould, 2009: 3). In Scotland, which has a separate Mental Health Act (2005), the expected number of CTOs has also been exceeded (Jackson, 2007: 11).

It has been argued that one of the main reasons for the over-use of the CTO is that the implementation of the Mental Health Act has been dominated by fears as to the dangerousness of a very small number of people. This concern has been applied to large numbers of people with mental health problems who are not a danger to members of the public, while putting pressure on mental health professionals to practice in a defensive way (see Jackson, 2007).This aspect of mental health policy was governed by questions of surveillance, discipline and risk, rather than by New Labour's wider social justice agenda (see Beresford, 2003).

Earlier in this chapter we indicated how New Labour expressed concern about the vulnerability of disabled people as victims of crime and harassment, drawing on a social model/social justice agenda. Yet, through its preoccupation with antisocial behaviour, the New Labour government also actively reclassified disabled people as perpetrators of nuisance offences. This situation developed through the management of what Flint refers to as the politics of behaviour, particularly among tenants of social housing (Flint, 2004). Squires highlights the speed with which the New Labour government accepted antisocial behaviour as a widespread problem and 'embarked upon such a wholesale process of ambitious civic and moral renewal through quasi-criminal enforcement mechanisms' (2008: 4).

The focus on antisocial behaviour in New Labour discourse was linked with the desire to tackle social exclusion, including the behavioural elements of social exclusion, as noted earlier in this chapter. Antisocial behaviour was viewed as a sign of social disorganisation and poor community control (see Jacobson et al., 2008). In practice, much of the machinery aimed at tackling antisocial behaviour was focused on young people 'hanging around' in economically deprived areas (Squires, 2008).

Although antisocial behaviour may be found in different types of housing tenure, a link between social housing and antisocial behaviour has been established in policy circles and sections of the media. The sale of council housing after 1980 and restrictions on the building of new housing meant that areas of social housing became characterised by vulnerable groups of people living closely together, based on allocation decisions which tenants are unable to control (see for example, Flint, 2004; Squires, 2008). Disabled people feature as a priority group for social housing and are overrepresented in this housing sector (DoH, 2001b). Indeed, as Hunter et al. argue, the overall shortage of social housing has meant that vulnerable groups are knowingly placed in hard-to-let tenancies (2007: 67), often in poor-quality housing where there is frequent concern about undesirable behaviour.

There is also evidence that the administrative machinery of the Antisocial Behaviour Order (ASBO) has been catching groups of disabled people in its net. Young and Matthews (2003) argue that deviance has been 'defined up' so that there exist a greater number of behaviours which are viewed as unacceptable and subject to sanction. These behaviours are particularly evident in socially excluded neighbourhoods which are regarded as requiring more assertive management (by the authorities and the community itself). The Social Exclusion Unit (2000: 25) found that 17 per cent of perpetrators of more serious forms of antisocial behaviour had mental health problems and a further 4 per cent had learning difficulties.

Similar findings have been made by some voluntary organisations. A campaign launched by the British Institute for Brain Injured Children argued that some disabled people are being pursued for alleged antisocial behaviour, when their behaviours are part of their impairment and not within their ability to control (BIBIC, 2005). The National Autistic Society (2004) made similar claims regarding the way that the behaviours of people with autistic spectrum disorder can be misinterpreted as antisocial behaviour. The inclusion of hearsay evidence in the pursuit of ASBOs has serious implications for groups about whom the public may hold prejudiced or discriminatory views, such as disabled people. Ramcharan *et al.* (2006) suggest that people with learning difficulties are four and a half times more likely to have an ASBO imposed on them than the rest of the population. As Brown (2004: 206) points out, 'Antisocial behaviour involves the use of the neighbourhood in deviancy control.'

Thus 'commonsensical', even prejudiced, notions of what falls into the category of 'acceptable behaviour' can be a factor in complaints about the behaviour of others. Moreover, the fact that an alleged perpetrator of antisocial behaviour is a disabled person and that her/his behaviour may be linked with her/his impairment does not warrant a cessation of the ASBO application. It also means that possible mitigating factors behind the antisocial behaviour are not taken into account (Brown, 2004). This is particularly problematic for vulnerable groups, like disabled people, whose 'antisocial behaviour' may be a reaction to a campaign of harassment or provocation from neighbours (see, for example, Hunter *et al.*, 2007). Squires (2006) emphasises that the dominant policy thrust has been towards the enforcement of policy along criminal justice lines, rather than the provision of support.

These policy discourses and practices that subject disabled people to disciplinary discourses and emphasise containment, surveillance and sanction are in direct opposition to those which offer support, autonomy and social justice. Welfare-to-work leaves disabled people to the arbitrariness of the market, yet in the case of mental health policies they are constituted as subjects of state power and become part of the 'governance of irresponsibilities' (Dean, 2002: 201). Even the most minimal forms of citizenship and justice are potentially eroded when discipline and obedience become the overriding objectives in the relationship between the state and the individual.

Conclusion

New Labour offered a qualified citizenship to disabled people that drew on a mix of social and individualist policy approaches and discourses. There was some evidence of the realisation of social justice for disabled people in the areas of rights, voice and resources. Underlying this was an emergent form of solidaristic citizenship that reflected the gains and possibilities of social movements in late modernity. Yet a highly individualised approach to social exclusion and to labour market participation remained hegemonic and worked against progress in other areas. Furthermore, the symbolic identification of some disabled people as undesirable and a potential threat to the wider community led to their substantive exclusion from citizenship

As Bryson and Fisher argue in the concluding chapter of this volume, David Cameron's 'progressive Conservatism' (Cameron, 2009) endorsed many of the assumptions that have underpinned New Labour thinking on social justice; these assumptions include its concept of the civic state, which seeks to blend the state and the market, and stresses the importance of the communal over the individual. By the time of the 2010 general election, populist concern around welfare scroungers and antisocial behaviour had combined with economic recession, growing unemployment and the widely perceived need for public spending cuts to provide a political climate which was far from conducive to developing social justice for vulnerable people. In this context, there is little prospect of any break with the New Labour approach that promoted the governance of individuals in the pursuit of rigid conformity and behaviours that were in line with labour market requirements; as this chapter has shown, this approach has been highly damaging to disabled people's social inclusion.

Bibliography

Audit Commission (1986) *Making a Reality of Community* Care (London: MSO).

Barnes, C. (2002), 'Introduction. Disability, policy and politics', *Policy and Politics* 30:3, 311–18.

Barnes, C., and Mercer, G. (2001) 'The politics of disability and the struggle for change', in L. Barton (ed.) *Disability, Politics and the Struggle for Change* (London: David Fulton).

Barnes, C., and Mercer, G. (2005) 'Disability, work and welfare: challenging the social exclusion of disabled people', *Work, Employment and Society* 19:3, 527–45.

Beresford, P. (2003) 'Shaping our Lives: National User Network, a Key Issue for the Future: Relating Disability Studies to the Diversity of Disabled People', paper delivered to the conference 'Disability Studies: Theory, Policy and Practice', University of Lancaster, 4–6 September.

British Institute for Brain Injured Children (2005) '"Ain't misbehavin'": young people with learning and communication difficulties and antisocial behaviour', *Campaign update*, November.

Brown, A. P. (2004) 'Antisocial behaviour, crime control and social control', *Howard Journal* 43:2, 203–11.

Burton, M., and Kagan, C. (2006) 'Decoding valuing people', *Disability and Society* 21:4, 299–313.

Butler, I., and Drakeford, M. (2005) *Scandal, Social Policy and Social Welfare* (Bristol: Policy Press).

Cabinet Office (2009) www.cabinetoffice.gov.uk/social_exclusion_task_force/context.aspx (accessed 18 August 2009).

Cameron, D. (2009) *Making Progressive Conservatism a Reality*, www.demos.co.uk (accessed 13 May 2009).

Clarke, J. (2005) 'New Labour's citizens: activated, empowered, responsibilized, abandoned?', *Critical Social Policy* 25:4, 447–63.

Community Care (2005) www.communitycare.co.uk/Articles/2005/01/27/47869/personalised-budgets-greeted-as-a-leap-forward-in-disability.html (accessed 17 August 2009).

Dean, H. (2002) *Welfare Rights and Social Policy* (Harlow: Pearson).

Dean, H. (2007) 'The ethics of Welfare-to-work', *Policy and Politics* 35:4, 573–89.

Department of Health (2001a) *Valuing People: A New Strategy for Learning Disability for the Twenty-first Century*, CM 5086 (London: Stationery Office).

Department of Health (2001b) *Health Survey for England, 2001: Disability* (London: Stationery Office).

Department of Health (2008) *Summary of Responses to the Consultation on Valuing People Now: From Progress to Transformation* (London: HM Government).

Department for Work and Pensions (2008) *Raising Expectations and Increasing Support: Reforming Welfare for the Future*, www.dwp.gov.uk/policy/welfare-reform/legislation-and-key-documents/raising-expectations/ (accessed 18 August 2009).

Dobson F. (1999), Foreword by the Secretary of State, *National Service*

Framework for Mental Health, www.dh.gov.uk/prod_consum_dh/groups/dh_digitalassets/@dh/@en/documents/digitalasset/dh_4096624.pdf (accessed 21 January 2010).

Fisher, P. (2008) 'Well-being and empowerment: the importance of recognition', *Sociology of Health and Illness* 30:4, 583–98.

Fisher, P. (2010) 'An alternative model for social justice and empowerment from the perspective of families with disabled children', in V. Bryson and P. Fisher (eds) *Redefining Social Justice: New Labour Rhetoric and Reality* (Manchester: Manchester University Press).

Flint, J. (2004) 'The responsible tenant: housing governance and the politics of behaviour', *Housing Studies* 19:6, 893–909.

Fryson, R., and Simons, K. (2003) 'Strategies for change: making *Valuing People* a reality', *British Journal of Learning Disabilities* 31:4, 153–8.

Gould, M. (2009) 'Hazards of a health safeguard', *Society Guardian*, 13 May: 3.

Government Equalities Office (2009) *A Fairer Future: The Equality Bill and other Action to make Equality a Reality*, www.equalities.gov.uk/ (accessed 18 August 2009).

Grant, G., and Ramcharan, P. (2002) 'Researching *Valuing People*', *Tizard Learning Disability Review* 7:3, 27–33.

Greig, R. (2005) *The Story so far . . . Valuing People: a new Strategy for Learning Disability in the Twenty-first century* (London: HM Government).

Grover, C., and Piggott, L. (2005) 'Disabled people: the reserve army of labour and welfare reform', *Disability and Society* 20:7, 705–17.

Grover, C., and Piggott, L. (2007) 'Social security, employment and incapacity benefit: critical reflections on *A New Deal for Welfare*', *Disability and Society* 22:7, 733–46.

Heenan, D. (2002) '"It won't change the world but it turned my life around": participants' views on the personal adviser scheme in the New Deal for disabled people', *Disability and Society* 17:4, 383–401.

Holden, C., and Beresford, P. (2002) 'Globalization and disability', in C. Barnes and M. Oliver (eds) *Disability Studies Today* (Cambridge: Polity Press).

Hunter, C., Hodge, N., Nixon, J., Parr, S., and Willis, B. (2007) *Disabled People's Experiences of Antisocial Behaviour and Harassment in Social Housing: a Critical Review* (Sheffield: Disability Rights Commission/Sheffield Hallam University).

Isin, E. F., Nyers, P., and Turner, B. S. (2009) 'The Thinking Citizenship series', *Citizenship Studies* 13:1, 1–2.

Jackson, C. (2007) 'Good in parts', *Mental Health Today*, September: 10–11.

Jacobson, J., Millie, A., and Hough, M. (2008) 'Why tackle antisocial behaviour?', in P. Squires (ed.) *ASBO Nation: The Criminalisation of Nuisance* (Bristol: Policy Press).

Jolly, D. (2000) 'A critical evaluation of the contradictions for disabled workers arising from the emergence of the flexible labour market in Britain', *Disability and Society* 15:5, 795–810.

Jones, K. (1993) *Asylums and After: A Revised History of the Mental Health Services from the early Eighteenth Century to the 1990s* (London: Athlone Press).

Laurence, J. (2003) *Pure Madness: How Fear drives the Mental Health System* (London: Routledge).

Levitas, R. (2005) *The Inclusive Society? Social Exclusion and New Labour*, 2nd edn (Basingstoke: Macmillan).

Marshall, T. H. (1950/1963) 'Citizenship and social class' in his *Sociology at the Crossroads* (London: Heinemann).

Morris J. (2005) *Citizenship and Disabled People: A Scoping Paper prepared for the Disability Rights Commission*, www.leeds.ac.uk/disability-studies/archiveuk/morris/Citizenship%20and%20disabled%20people.pdf (accessed 19 July 2009).

National Autistic Society (2004) *Youth Offending Teams and Antisocial Behaviour*, www.nas.org.uk/nas/jsp/polopoly.jsp?d=2523&a=5382 (visited 21 January 2010).

Newbigging, K., with Lowe, J. (2005) 'Implementing direct payments in mental health', Joseph Rowntree Foundation (February), www.jrf.org.uk/publications/implementing-direct-payments-mental-health (visited 21 January 2010).

Oliver, M. (1996) *Understanding Disability: From Theory to Practice* (Basingstoke: Macmillan).

Oliver, M., and Barnes, C. (1998) *Disabled People and Social Policy: From Exclusion to Inclusion* (Harlow: Longman).

Payne, S. (1999) 'Outside the walls of the asylum? Psychiatric treatment in the 1980s and 1990s', in P. Bartlett and D. Wright (eds) *Outside the Walls of the Asylum: The History of Community Care, 1750–2000* (London: Athlone Press).

Powell, M. (2002) 'New Lbour and social justice', in M. Powell (ed.) *Evaluating New Labour's Welfare Reforms* (Bristol: Policy Press).

Priestley, M. (1999), *Disability Politics and Community Care* (London: Jessica Kingsley).

Prime Minister's Strategy Unit (2005) *Improving the Life Chances of Disabled People*, www.cabinetoffice.gov.uk/search.aspx?search=disabled+2005 (accessed 21 January 2010).

Purnell, J. (2008) *Oral Statement 'No one written off': Reforming Welfare to reward Responsibility*, www.dwp.gov.uk/newsroom/ministers-speeches/2008/21-07-08.shtml (accessed 18 August 2009).

Ramcharan, P., McClimens, A., and Roberts, B. (2006) 'People with learning difficulties should not get ASBOs', www.communitycare.co.uk/Articles/2006/06/22/54665/People+with+learning+difficulties+should+not+get+ASBO's.html (accessed 8 November 2006).

Riddell, S., Pearson, C., Jolly, D., Barnes, C., Priestley, M., and Mercer, G. (2005) 'The development of direct payments in the UK: implications for social justice', *Social Policy and Society* 4:1, 75–85.

Riddington, C., Mansell, J., and Beadle-Brown, J. (2008) 'Are partnership boards really valuing people?', *Disability and Society* 23:6, 649–65.

Ridley, J., and Jones, L. (2003) 'Direct what? The untapped potential of direct payments to mental health service users', *Disability and Society* 18:5, 643–58.

Roulstone, A. (2002) 'Disabling pasts, enabling futures? How does the changing nature of capitalism impact on the disabled worker and jobseeker?', *Disability and Society* 17:6, 627–42.

Rummery, K. (2006) 'Disabled citizens and social exclusion: the role of direct payments', *Policy and Politics* 34:4, 633–50.

Sainsbury Centre for Mental Health (2002) *An Executive Briefing on 'Working for Inclusion'*, briefing 15, www.scmh.org.uk/publications/working_for_ inclusion.aspx?ID=294 (accessed 21 January 2010).

Social Exclusion Unit (2000) *Report of Policy Action Team 8: Antisocial Behaviour* (London: Cabinet Office).

Squires, P. (2006) 'New Labour and antisocial behaviour', *Critical Social Policy* 26:1, 144–68.

Squires, P. (2008) 'Introduction. Why antisocial behaviour? Debating ASBOs', in P. Squires (ed.) *ASBO Nation: The Criminalisation of Nuisance* (Bristol: Policy Press).

Stewart A. (2000), 'Never-ending story: inclusion and exclusion in late modernity', in P. Askonas and A. Stewart (eds) *Social Inclusion: Possibilities and Tensions* (Basingstoke: Macmillan).

Walker, C. (2002) '"Revolutionising" care for people with learning difficulties: the Labour government's learning disabilities strategy', in R. Sykes, C. Bochel and N. Ellison (eds) *Social Policy Review 14* (Bristol: Policy Press/ Social Policy Association).

Young, J. (2001) *Crime and Social Exclusion*, www.malcolmread.co.uk/ JockYoung/crime&socialexclusion.htm (accessed 22 May 2009)

Young, J., and Matthews, R. (2003) 'New Labour, crime control and social exclusion', in J. Young and R. Matthews (eds) *The New Politics of Crime and Punishment* (Cullompton: Willan).

Acknowledgements

The authors would like to thank Paul Watt and Pauline Noden for their comments on an earlier version of this chapter.

8

An alternative model for social justice and empowerment from the perspective of families with disabled children

Pamela Fisher

Based on research conducted in relation to the experiences and perspectives of families with disabled children, this chapter critiques the dominant understanding of social justice as applied in health and social policy and in some areas of related practice under New Labour. From the New Labour perspective, social justice was largely equated with a form of 'empowerment' based on a relatively narrow notion of the reflexive agent of late modernity (Giddens, 1991).[1] Seen from this perspective, traditional economic, social and cultural roles are diminishing and divisions between the left and right are becoming obsolete; therefore citizens, untrammelled by their former structured identities, now have greater freedom to creatively forge their personal destiny. Under New Labour, Giddens's vision of increasing individualisation and choice was translated into a policy direction that equates self-empowerment with paid employment. As a result, social justice was largely interpreted as the imperative to 'empower' citizens to assume the 'worker-citizen' role.

The 1997 New Labour manifesto aspired towards a society 'in which more people get on, do well, and make a success of their lives' and where there are more 'successful entrepreneurs' (New Labour, 1997). An interventionist role was nevertheless envisioned for the state in order to ensure greater 'equality of opportunity'. The 'Third Way' would contribute to greater social justice by rectifying the New Right error of conceptualising the individual as separate whilst avoiding the pitfalls of the Old Left that had not afforded individuals with sufficient opportunities to advance themselves (Blair, 1998: 3). Implicit in this is the right – but also the duty – to comply with the New Labour vision of social justice. Social justice has therefore been primarily about enabling ontologically separate[2] individuals to achieve independence through paid employment in the public sphere. At the Labour Party spring conference on 1 March 2008 Gordon Brown (2008) announced that 'opportunity and security' were attainable 'not just for some, but for all who *play by the rules*' (my italics). He added, 'This is what I mean by fairness to hardworking families.' This discourse automatically excluded those who are not able or who choose not to comply with Brown's contractual understanding of social justice. At the same time, it also closed down the potential for alternative understandings of social justice.

In this chapter I argue for an enlarged understanding of social justice – one that does not impose a 'one size fits all' model of 'empowered' citizenship that is exclusively based on relationships of equivalent rights and responsibilities. Social justice should involve endowing citizens with rights to develop and pursue alternative forms of empowerment, including those associated with the private sphere. At the same time, I suggest that individual empowerment is often achieved intersubjectively rather than through rugged individualism. My standpoint owes much to previous work in which the concept of a feminist 'ethics of care' is posited as an alternative model of citizenship (Corker and French, 1999; Cushing and Lewis, 2002; Fisher, 2007; Kittay, 2002; Sevenhuijsen, 1998; Williams, 1999, 2001, 2002).

Drawing on interview and observational data collected for an ESRC study, *Parents, Professionals and Babies with Special Care Needs: Identifying Enabling Care*,[3] I show here how parents of disabled children have been attempting to conceptualise a form of empowerment that they see as embedded in relationships of interdependence. I suggest that these nascent discourses of empowerment are often undermined when parents access health and social services on behalf of their children, where they encounter discourses and practices that are embedded in the neo-liberal model of economic self-sufficiency, shored up further by biomedical understandings of disability based on individual deficiency. At a broader level, the chapter highlights the importance of according recognition[4] to the diverse ways people seek to construct authentic routes towards well-being and empowerment.

The discussion below starts with a consideration of how social justice was interpreted within New Labour policy, which, I suggest, was discursively restricted to neo-liberal aspirations of narrow self-sufficiency. After a brief description of the study, based on the experiences of families with disabled children, I outline my analytical framework of recognition and misrecognition, as conceptualised by Honneth (1996, 2001, 2003), Sointu (2005, 2006) and Yar (2001), explaining why families with disabled children are vulnerable to patterns of disrespect whenever they access health and social services. Subsequently I draw on ethnographic and interview data to show how families with disabled children are constructing alternative forms of empowerment in the private sphere and within informal neighbourhood networks. Finally, I suggest that these alternative forms of empowerment may offer a blueprint for a form of social justice in which the right of social inclusion is not conditional on compliance with the 'worker-citizen' model of citizenship.

Social justice according to New Labour

Central to this chapter is the idea that social justice under New Labour was characterised by the contradictory aims of encouraging citizens to take responsibility for their own well-being whilst also requiring that they should find it within the boundaries laid down by 'expert' opinion. The White Paper *Choosing Health: Making Healthy Choices Easier* (DoH, 2004) unequivocally identified the ideal service user as an informed consumer (Hughes, 2004; Powell and Hewitt, 2002) and the role of the National Health Service (NHS) and other organisations as that of enabling individuals to promote their own health and well-being. The virtuous citizen is expected to reflexively achieve her sense of well-being and empowerment through incorporating expert advice into her deliberations. As it was put in *Choosing Health*, 'People want to be able to make their own decisions about choices that impact on their health and to have credible and trustworthy information to help them do so. They expect the Government to provide support by helping to create the right environment' (DoH, 2004: 3). In seeking their 'authentic' route towards empowerment citizens were expected to avail themselves of 'expert' assistance that is ideologically embedded within the prevailing neo-liberal order. Such an interpretation, however, is not consistent with the understanding that everyone's authenticity and quest for well-being are unique and should not be curtailed by the dominant order (see Taylor, 1991).

As argued above, New Labour policy located 'normal' citizenship within an individualised and contractual framework (Fisher, 2007, 2008) which was reflected in family policies that promote a highly instrumental approach to parenting. Whilst the importance of family life was stressed as a forum in which the values of good citizenship are learned (see, for example, *Supporting Families:* Home Office, 1998), good parenting was seen as quasi-contractual in nature, based as it was on the idea that the identities of family members must be regarded as essentially independent and atomistic. As Gillies (2005: 77) puts it, *Supporting Families* 'depicts parenting not as an intimate relationship, but as an occupation requiring particular knowledge and skills'. The result was that parenting practices were increasingly isolated from the quality of interpersonal relationships and the 'skills' of good parenting were constructed as detachable entities in ways that define family relationships in contractual terms between independent human actors. Parents were expected to improve and regulate their parenting skills with reference to 'expert' training.

Similarly the types of values that parents were expected to instil were based on an understanding that empowerment is achieved individually, mainly through engaging in paid work. In 1997 the then Social Security Secretary, Harriet Harman, stated: 'Work is the only route to sustained financial independence. But it is also much more . . . It is a way of life . . . Parents don't just work to support their families financially, they also work to set an example to their children' (Harman 1997, cited in Lister, 2000: 39–40). Since 1997 the policy connection between well-being, empowerment and economic self-sufficiency through remunerated work within the public sphere has been clearly entrenched (see DWP, 2005, 2008a, b). In the Green Paper *No one Written off: Reforming Welfare to Reward Responsibility* (DWPa, 2008) and the subsequent White Paper, *Raising Expectations and Increasing Support: Reforming Welfare for the Future* (DWP, 2008b), the discourse pathologised dependence that constructs people with disabilities (and by extension those who care for them) as 'failing' to live up to 'commonsense' expectations of economic self-sufficiency:

> many disabled people do not have the sort of choice and control over their lives that non-disabled people take for granted. This is partly explained by the fact that, because of their support needs, many disabled people rely on resources made available by the State . . . Too often, services are structured in a way that can reinforce dependency instead of providing support in a way that enables disabled people to achieve their aspirations and access the same opportunities as non-disabled people. (DWP, 2008a: 58)

Social justice is therefore construed as enabling as many people as possible to avoid the 'ignominy' of dependence by pursing self-empowerment through their participation in the work force. Any validation of life and work in the private sphere remains conspicuously absent.

Towards an alternative vision of social justice

This last point is an important one to consider in relation to many of the research participants referred to in this chapter, who were parents – mainly mothers – of disabled babies and children. Employment was not an option for most of these parents, who were full-time carers. It was not uncommon for parents to attend up to ten appointments in a single week. While keeping up with appointments alone is more than enough to preclude a parent from engaging in paid work, many of the mothers could be regarded as socially excluded on a number of other dimensions – many were lone parents, some had disabilities and one belonged to a stigmatised minority. In stating this I wish to underline the fact that most research participants were highly circumscribed in their ability to seek empowerment and well-being through participating in paid employment. Equally, many of their children were unlikely to be in a position to take up full-time paid employment in future adult life. Therefore parents and children alike were vulnerable to the oppressive discourses of welfare that construct well-being and empowerment around economic self-sufficiency. Their quest to construct positive understandings of the value of their lives with their disabled babies was being impeded by forms of 'misrecognition' which made them vulnerable to patterns of disrespect. As Robertson (2001: 122) points out, 'education or welfare systems that operate on the premise of normality and the reduction of difference will always leave some people out. It is part of their logic.'

As someone who is interested in differing understandings of social justice, and who bases much of her work on constructionist and feminist positions, I take the view that people are inevitably shaped by dominant narratives but that they do not internalise these uncritically. Reflexivity and the potential for self-empowerment are shaped by environmental and structural factors and by experiences of recognition or misrecognition. From this perspective, identity is not based on ontological separateness but is constructed intersubjectively. As Butler (2003, cited in Magnus, 2006: 50–3) argues, the subject is not free to tell their own story, since 'every "I" begins in and through others'.

For the parents and disabled babies project in depth I conducted interviews in Sheffield with twenty-five families with babies and young children with special health and social care needs. The families were divided into two groups. The first group of participants provided retrospective accounts of their experience, including experience of medical and social care services, since the birth of their child. The second group involved families who had children up to two and a half years of age at the start of the project. These participants offered a longitudinal perspective through participating in a number of interviews conducted over a period of up to eighteen months. The approach in the interviews with the parents was conversational, and prompts arose from what the interviewees told me. There was also a strong ethnographic component to the methodology that involved me observing mothers (and occasionally fathers), children and professionals in a variety of clinical social services and social service and home settings. I also became involved within the wider support networks of parents. It should be noted that the families who participated in this study were from differing socio-economic groups. Those recruited from marginalised populations such as unemployed lone parents, particularly if they were disabled or from minority ethnic groups, appeared to suffer from more intensive forms of misrecognition, often in the form of heightened surveillance. Finally, focus groups were conducted to include the perspectives of a range of medical and social care professionals working with the families.

Analytical framework

I have stated above that families are challenging dominant narratives in relation to disability and that I am arguing here that their agency to do so is curtailed by a symbolic order constituted through biomedical understandings of individual pathology and neo-liberal scripts of self-sufficiency. To clarify this position further, I draw on the politics of recognition as represented by Honneth (2001, 2003), Sointu (2006) and Yar (2001). Intersubjective recognition, these writers assert, provides the bedrock for the development of the inwardly reflective competent actor required in modern Western individualism (Sointu 2006). It is within relationships of recognition that people attain what Yar (2001: 299) refers to as a 'practical relation to self', that is, the necessary self-esteem to empower them to take advantage of opportunities and successfully deal with life's setbacks. Similarly, Honneth (2001, 2003) has influentially argued that our human dependence on intersubjective recognition is enacted in three distinct spheres of life: (1) the private sphere through relationships of intimacy and love, (2) the 'legal order' which is required to provide equality in law and (3) the public sphere, which provides the forum for self-esteem derived from abilities that are respected and valued by others. In all three domains 'the establishment of one's understanding is inextricably dependent on recognition or affirmation on the part of others', and all three types of recognition lead to human beings enjoying dignity and integrity (Yar 2001: 59). Honneth's clear distinctions between private and public forms of recognition have been problematised elsewhere (Fisher and Owen, 2008). In this chapter I draw on his central argument that subjects achieve a positive sense of self though relationships of intimacy and love and also through societal recognition of achievement. From this perspective intersubjective recognition is central to the processes of individual empowerment.

Societal recognition tends to be based on notions of individualised success (in particular financial self-sufficiency), or, as Honneth (2003: 141) puts it, achievement is evaluated according to a 'value standard whose normative reference point is the economic activity of the independent, middle-class, male bourgeois' (Honneth, 2003: 141). Achievement, understood this way, is therefore attached to dominant understandings of masculinity whilst also being contingent on access to power and on the mechanisms of complex structures embedded in socio-economic relations. Seen from this perspective, the parents (mainly mothers) of disabled children *and* the children themselves constitute subordinate groups on the basis that they are rarely engaged in paid employment and their activities are necessarily based primarily in the private sphere. When the parents of children venture into the public sphere with their children they are often positioned by others as supplicants who are seeking to access resources and services. This means that their quest to construct positive understandings of the value of their lives with their disabled babies is being impeded by forms of 'misrecognition' within the public sphere which position them as inferior and vulnerable to patterns of disrespect. Processes of recognition and misrecognition also determine how material resources are distributed in society.

From chaos to resistance

The birth of a disabled child, the onset of a serious illness and acquired disabilities are events that throw life narratives into disarray (Ezzy, 2000; Frank, 1995; Fisher and Goodley, 2007; Fisher, 2007). People affected by unanticipated crises often describe their feelings by using metaphors that evoke a sense of disorientation. Commonly, they may speak of losing their path in life or their map (see Frank, 1995: 5), or they may describe themselves as wrecks (Dworkin, 1993: 311) that have run aground, washed up 'on the rocks' of their ruined lives. The worst aspect of this is apparently the sense of losing an anticipated life course in which past, present and future run together in a coherent whole that makes sense (Carr, 1986). According to Carr (1986: 96), a 'responsibility' is placed on those who undergo an interrupted life narrative to create a new story which gives the narrator 'something to live up to' by reinterpreting the past in a way that enables the construction of a new future.

The birth of a disabled child was identified by some parents – although by no means all – as devastating. Words such as loss, grief, anger and numbness were used to describe feelings experienced around the time of diagnosis. One woman of Pakistani origin, whom I shall call

Sofia (all the names of the research participants and their children have been anonymised), put it in the following way when she described her emotions on learning that her son had cerebral palsy:

> It's very difficult, you can't take it in. You feel as if somebody has come over, hit you with something and is constantly just battering your head, it's just this feeling of empty numbness. ... What happens then is, it turns into anger and frustration, and then grief, it is grief. ... I remember taking him upstairs and sitting by the window and just holding him and he was laughing and gurgling and just doing what he was doing, this chubby gorgeous, beautiful little baby, big brown eyes. I just held him and I just cried for him, I cried for the loss of his life in terms of what he could have been, I cried for the loss of my normal baby.

Despite an initial feeling of crisis, prompted by both emotional and practical turmoil, many parents developed new understandings around disability and identity that countered dominant discourses based on individualised deficiency (see Fisher, 2007; Fisher and Goodley, 2007). The extract below is taken from an interview with a woman, let's call her Linda, with children diagnosed with autism and learning difficulties:

> I wouldn't change 'em. I've been told and I've read in books that if I were to continue with my family there would be the possible chance of another child being autistic, but that wouldn't bother me. I wouldn't be bothered at all about having another child with autism, because they are lovely kids.

Motherhood: from discourses of 'normality' to an appreciation of diversity

There are some who may argue that Linda was simply constructing a narrative that was consistent with dominant ideas of motherhood. Presenting as a responsible mother involves self-governance around what can and cannot be voiced (Miller, 2005). Experiences that are not consistent with the construct of ideal motherhood may be suppressed and can lead women to question their own abilities as women. Below, Linda's statement tends to suggest that the positive relationship she enjoys with her children is not based on an over-idealised interpretation of motherhood:

> You do have days like that, where you can't quite get your head around why your children are the way they are, but in a positive way there are children who are very much like the next children down the road, whereas mine aren't, mine are unique, and in a way I'm sort of glad they

are the way they are, because they've taught me something as well and everybody around me. I think you've got to have a child in your family with some form of disability to really be able to understand it.

Linda continued to explain how the experience of having a disabled child had transformed her perspective:

I think they've taught me to look at people in different ways now, like if I'm in town, and I see a man and he walks past and he's talking to himself, if you don't really know what's going on, you are going to think, Oh, he's drunk, or, Oh, he shouldn't be out on his own, him, he's a loony. And that's small-minded people who don't understand, but now I look at people differently and I think he may have got a learning difficulty. It doesn't necessarily mean that he needs to have someone with him all the time. Why shouldn't he be independent?

When I asked another parent, Karen, whose son had been diagnosed as having severe learning difficulties and autism whether she would wish him to be any different, she replied:

I don't know. . ... erm. . . it's hard to say really. I mean, it would be nice for Antonio to be able to do what every other child can do but yet I wouldn't want to take his identity away from him because that's his identity, that's who he is. I mean, I think that if I took it away from him I don't think he'd actually be Antonio. He wouldn't be the child I've brought up, he'd probably be a different child.

Notwithstanding the pressures to internalise pre-given understandings, the parents' narratives are characterised by openness to complexity and interdependence that potentially opens up wider interpretations of empowerment. While the experience of having a disabled child was sometimes described as a shock, it had often led to what Gur-Ze'ev *et al.* (2001: 96) have described as a '. . . moment of rupture [when] new possibilities arise from the very fact that the self-evident, the facts, do not have the last word and the violence of the normalisation process is broken, postponed or questioned'. Under certain circumstances, there is the possibility that such 'a moment of rupture' may lead to a process whereby new understandings are constructed that counter normalising practices and their ideological foundations. The parents participating in this study appeared to be discovering a 'degree of authorship' (MacIntyre, 1985) within the private sphere where they were able to find some space away from the 'symbolic violence' of the public sphere (Bourdieu, 1991).

The relationships that the parents enjoyed with their children tended to evoke Diprose's (2002) notion of 'corporeal generosity', which she

Pamela Fisher

defines as embodied, intersubjective and formed with reference to social and familial situations. Unlike dominant notions of generosity that tend to be based on an economy of exchange between individuals, corporeal generosity involves openness to others and to difference – welcoming the new potentials that these may open up. As the moral philosopher Levinas (see Bauman, 1991: 214) has argued, the Other necessarily eludes our full understanding, but the ethical relationship begins with the willingness to be open to everybody's unique subjectivity. Similarly Diprose (2002: 01) argues, 'There is a reciprocity of giving, but not reciprocity in the content of what is given, and generosity is only possible if neither sameness nor unity is assumed as either the basis of the goal of an encounter with others.' This is an understanding of identity – and of empowerment – that defies the forms of codification or standardisation associated with the rational ends of contractual relationships. The relationships between the parents and children were not based on predetermined rights and obligations but pointed instead to a type of solidarity which does not presume relationships of equivalence.

Recognition and an ethic of care

Morality based on corporeal generosity is associated with the values of mutualism and interdependence and is, therefore, less concerned with the idealised forms of self-sufficiency that so often underpin the delivery of health and social care interventions. According to Williams (2001), these emerging values could form the basis of what she terms 'an ethic of care', an ethic which would usefully provide an alternative model to the discourses embedded in current social policy that situate paid work as the first responsibility of citizenship. Such an ethic of care would validate all caring activities undertaken in both the public and private sphere and would enable both men and women to participate in caring activities and combine these with paid employment. Williams (2001: 474) argues that the current emphasis on paid employment is based upon a traditional notion of a male worker, 'a relatively mythical self-sufficient being whose care needs and responsibilities are rendered invisible because they are carried out somewhere else, by someone else'. Personal autonomy, according to Williams (2001, 2002), is always embedded in relationships of interdependence in which diversity is valued and the voices of marginalised groups heard. An ethic of caring is necessarily implicated in struggles for 'recognition' (Fraser and Honneth, 2003) and, as Williams (2002: 505) points out, this necessarily raises issues around *how* social and health care services are delivered. A shift from individualised citizenship informed by neo-liberalism to one constructed around an ethic of caring would necessitate a democratisation of the relationships between service users and providers. It would require an acknowledgement of the value of experiential knowledge and the nascent forms of alternative empowerment that may be acquired in the private sphere. This, I suggest, opens up the possibility for a more inclusive understanding of social justice.

An ethic of care could, Williams (2001, 2002) suggests, form the basis for a new type of citizenship that recognises everybody as interdependent and having the potential and responsibility to be caring and cared for. Crucially, an ethic of caring would provide the basis for an alternative to counter the notion that empowerment and authenticity are necessarily associated with ontological separateness, and that equates dependence with failure. This reflects the position of mutual aid within certain 'self-care' movements that have made attempts to provide an alternative to the management, commodification and curricularisation of professional care. In *The Careless Society* McKnight (1995) has argued that formerly 'competent' communities have been colonised and disempowered by a burgeoning welfare 'industry' that seeks its own expansion by constructing needs as unfortunate individual absences or deficiencies. Complex social problems are therefore redefined as individual pathologies that require individualised remedial tools and techniques to correct. The agents with labelling powers are the caring professionals who disempower their 'clients' by constructing them as a class of deficient individuals in need. Through these processes, families and communities falter and collapse. McKnight's main argument is that 'care' should be reclaimed as a quality and power that is inherent within people, families and communities rather than a service provided by professionals. This is consistent with Williams' (2001, 2002) notion of an 'ethic of care' which values interdependence and diversity whilst empowering people to develop their own authentic ways towards well-being.

Misrecognition and the limits of empowerment

Many of the parents involved in this study were in the process of constructing life scripts embedded in an ethic of care by rejecting interpretations that pathologise dependence. Families were building networks of interdependence that often extended into their local communities, and these were not based on the assumption that each individual should contribute according to a contractually based 'rights and responsibilities' agenda. Quite often relationships based on an appreciation of difference – on corporeal generosity – were deemed to be more mutually rewarding. However, these bids towards counter-hegemonic forms of empowerment were often undermined by parents' and children's encounters with health and social care providers, where the dominant ideology still equated empowerment with self-sufficiency. One mother, Sadie, described the consultant's first assessment of Tom in the following terms:

> It was all, 'he's got this facial palsy and we don't know what that's about' and 'he's got floppy legs and his muscle tone's poor' and 'he's not responding as he should'. He was sort of like a 'write-off' by the end of the appointment. . . . We both came out of there really deflated and feeling like we'd got this real loser baby that had everything wrong with him, and it was terrible.

Experiences of denigration were by no means limited to negative interpretations around children's lack of viability for 'normal' independent citizenship. Parents were also subjected to additional forms of misrecognition if their way of life did not correspond to dominant narratives around neo-liberal 'achievement' as identified by Honneth (2003). Often multiple forms of misrecognition converged to position them as 'deviant' and 'dependent'. As mentioned above, some of the parents who participated in this study led marginalised lives as a result of poverty, disability, their religious beliefs and/or because they were lone parents.

Emma, quoted below, was a lone mother living on benefits in a disadvantaged area of Sheffield. The extract quoted shows how the tragedy model of disability can combine with social disadvantage in ways that denigrate both children and parents:

> I can just remember not liking him [the consultant]. Um . . . I think it were . . . at one point when he was talking to us about Clare [daughter] and it seemed he were talking down to us.

Emma and her baby had been subjected to misrecognition related to the biomedical model of disability and to Emma's socio-economic marginalisation. Both types of misrecognition are embedded within neo-liberal and medical narratives based on a view of identity as essentially individualised. Reliant on narrow understandings of self-sufficiency, these narratives tend to shore up binaries such as 'normal' and 'deviant' and 'independent' and 'dependent'.

There is a further important issue to consider in relation to misrecognition and professional practice that is encouraged to focus on the identification of 'deviance'. In recent years, particularly in the wake of the death of Victoria Climbié in 2000, the health and social services have themselves been subject to an unprecedented level of surveillance in how professionals manage 'risk'. The devolved mechanisms of governance that were supposedly intended to empower public-sector agencies have arguably resulted in increased government control – although with less central accountability (Clarke and Newman, 1997). As a result, practitioners are obliged above all to make 'defensible' decisions. The 'risk agenda' therefore reinforces processes of misrecognition by promoting an over-zealous policing of people's lives (Furedi, 1997), which is in turn linked with an increasing tendency to perceive individuals' 'needs' for resources and services in terms of personal failings (Kemshall, 2002). As Kemshall (2002) has stated, the current preoccupation with risk often means that needs are pushed aside and professional activity becomes almost uniquely focused on the identification of individual failings.

Some of the parents' experiences in this study suggest that the assessment of risk is measured according to the extent of a person's deviation from the ideal form of citizenship as defined by hegemonic understandings that codify people as individually competent or incompetent. In other words, standards of defensibility are decided according to service users' apparent level of conformity to neo-liberal standards of citizenship, as defined by centrally prescribed performance criteria. This results in multiple forms of misrecognition. Below I provide some examples of this.

Sylvia is an outstandingly capable and intelligent woman who enjoys a rich and mutually rewarding relationship with her children, family and others in her neighbourhood. However, as a lone parent and wheelchair user unable to pursue economic self-sufficiency, Sylvia does not conform to the standards of self-sufficient citizenship deemed appropriate for parenthood. As a result, she has been subjected to an intensified form of surveillance. After the birth of her daughter, Sarah, who was diagnosed with cerebral palsy, Sylvia felt that she was singled out in ways that invalidated her sense of self. In the extract below she is relating an incident that occurred in hospital after Sarah's birth. Sylvia was discussing her imminent discharge from hospital with a health visitor who wanted to 'inspect' Sylvia's home to assess it for its suitability for a child,

> and so I said, 'Well, you know, I don't feel at all happy about this inspection.' I said, 'You don't do it for anybody else and it seems to me that you're only doing it because I'm disabled – we need to talk about this.' I said to her, 'Could you give me the list of standards,' and she said, 'What do you mean?' I said, 'Well, obviously this isn't something that is subjective, it needs to be objective, so there must be a list of standards that are

all right. If you give me a list of standards then I'll know whether it's Royal Doulton plates or Marks & Spencer's plates – whatever it is, I'll get them. Whatever your best is for Ruth, my best will be much better, I can assure you'. She just looked at me like I was this awful woman.

The impact of misrecognition is not restricted to negative evaluations that disempower those labelled deficient or even to risk assessment exercises that equate 'dependence' with risk. Recognition and misrecognition are also closely bound up with the distribution of resources in society. Consistent with materialist arguments and the experiences of other movements for economic and social rights, the struggle for resources was a potent source of counter-hegemonic discourse for the parents of disabled children. Parents involved had often encountered enormous difficulty in accessing the resources they were entitled to. The allocation of resources, underpinned by 'achievement' values (see Honneth, 2001, 2003) often failed to give recognition to the value of their lives with their children.

When Sadie's son, Thomas, was diagnosed as 'deaf', Sadie was anxious to learn sign language so that she could communicate with him. She discovered, however, that there was no support for families of 'deaf' children to get free sign language learning. Sadie had been forced to give up her lucrative work, and the family were in the process of selling their house. If Sadie had been an unemployed lone parent seeking to join the work force by undertaking vocational training, the necessary support would have been immediately forthcoming. Her wish to learn sign language, as it was not vocationally relevant, was regarded as ineligible. As far as Sadie was concerned, the fact that monetary resources were not available to her in order for her to learn sign language was evidence that her relationship with Thomas was not valued. Experiences similar to Sadie's were a recurrent theme in many of the interviews with parents, who often associated the struggle for resources with issues of misrecognition. One parent, who had recently had a request for a special-care seat for her child with postural difficulties rejected, explained, 'Sometimes I feel as though I'm scrounging.' When I asked her if she would appeal, she replied, 'No, because I feel as though they'd make me feel like a scrounger. And I'm not scrounging, I'm fighting for my baby.'

I wish to emphasise here I do not intend to detract from the excellent practice within health and social care that is often evident. The research revealed many examples of practice in which professionals showed an understanding that enabling care is dependent on relationships of recognition in which difference is not constructed as a problem. I have the impression, however, that empowering care such as this is achieved *despite* the dominance of narratives that act to define acceptable 'normality' within ever more circumscribed boundaries. Gleeson and Knights (2006) have written about 'ecologies of practice', that is, micro-cultures in which professionals are neither 'victims', whose practice is determined entirely by the dictates of the audit culture, nor purely strategic operators who seek to challenge managerialist structures. It has previously been argued (Fisher and Owen, 2008) that 'ecologies of practice' involve a high component of emotional labour (Hochschild, 1983) in order to 'repair' stigmatised or, to use Goffman's term (1963), 'spoiled' identities. I would suggest that genuinely empowering interventions are often achieved in situations where practitioners do not attribute 'deficient' identities to service users but provide the space for alternative scripts of empowerment to be written.

Conclusion

Ostensibly, empowerment is a benign concept that appears entirely congruent with commonsense notions of social justice. In this chapter it is suggested that empowerment is interpreted in policy and practices for families with disabled children as assistance to achieve normative citizenship. Social justice has become narrowly focused on the concern to provide opportunities to enable compliance with a dominant form of citizenship. This is one that equates empowerment with the model of the citizen worker (see Chappell and Gifford in this volume). Implicit within this is the assumption that families who 'fail' to achieve the standardised norm are 'deficient'.

The parents interviewed for this study were asserting their right to construct their lived relationships with their families and children, friends and service providers in a way that is linked with the rights of recognition. This is being achieved through intersubjectively acquired understandings of recognition that value alterity – that is, each person's particularity and authenticity. In doing this, they are also challenging discourses around health and well-being that locate these as individual responsibilities (Crawford, 2006). However, reflexivity that questions pre-given understandings and may lead to the construction of authentic forms of well-being and empowerment does not occur within a vacuum. Whilst families are renegotiating the tragedy model of disability through an appreciation and enjoyment of their relationships with their children, they are, at the same time, encountering the 'symbolic violence' of seeing their children's unique authenticity and selfhood being effectively erased by forms of care that are underpinned by neo-liberal interpretations. The resulting forms of misrecognition are further intensified by surveillance procedures that pathologise parents living in disadvantaged circumstances or leading less conventional lives. Difference or social marginalisation comes to be seen as a dangerous form of deviance and only forms of empowerment and well-being that adhere to 'expert' agendas and interventions are viewed as legitimate.

Openness to difference and singularity is integral to the rights of recognition, but it will remain absent in situations in which empowerment continues to be equated with individualised agency within the public sphere. This may have also been the case before 1997, but it was undoubtedly reinforced by the remoralisation of citizenship based on labour market participation that has taken place under New Labour (Rake, 2001; Lister, 2000). While significant and welcome strides forward in relation to the integration of marginalised groups into employment have been achieved under New Labour, there has also been an equally strong tendency to equate empowerment exclusively with these terms. Honneth (2001, 2003) has argued that our human dependence on intersubjective recognition must be realised in both the private *and* public domains of life. In the private sphere, the parents of disabled children appear to be constructing understandings of well-being and empowerment around relational models that extend beyond a narrow 'rights and responsibilities' agenda. However, the common experience of the refusal of recognition in the public sphere needs to be addressed.

The refusal of recognition faced by the families in this study is a form of coercive identification that is embedded in unequal relations of power (Honneth, 1996).It is ironic that the ideal notion of the empowered citizen, promoted so energetically by New Labour policy, increased the pressure to be recognised in the public sphere while, at the same time, creating a culture which may undermine this. In the Equality Bill (Government Equalities Office, 2009), it was stated that the gap between employment rates of disabled and non-disabled people had been reduced from 34.5 per cent to 26.3 per cent since 1998. While this is a development that can be regarded as positive in many ways, there is no acknowledgement within the Bill that the social justice should go further than enabling everyone to assume one model of citizenship. I suggest here that a discursive space needs to become available in which a range of understandings of empowered citizenship may be debated and considered as potentially viable alternatives. This would include a validation of activities within the private sphere and would also require greater acknowledgement within policy and practice that individual empowerment is often achieved within relationships of interdependence. Parity of access to opportunities within formal employment is important, but understandings of social justice should mean much more than this. Perhaps the insights of the families discussed in this study point to aspirations towards a new model of social justice beyond New Labour?

Notes

1 According to Giddens, self-identity in late modernity is not fixed or stable; instead it is a project for individuals to constantly reflect and work on.
2 From this perspective identity is seen as individualised. In other words, individual identity is not constructed within social relationship but exists as pre-given prior to these.
3 This study ('Parents, Professionals and Babies with Special Care Needs: Identifying Enabling Care') was funded by the Economic and Social Research Council. It was conducted jointly by the University of Sheffield and the University of Newcastle.
4 The terms 'recognition' and 'misrecognition' are central to the analysis in this chapter. The terms are discussed in greater detail below in the section 'Analytical framework'.

Bibliography

Bauman, Z. (1991) *Modernity and the Holocaust* (Cambridge: Polity Press).

Beck, U. (1992) *Risk Society: Towards a New Modernity* (London: Sage).

Bourdieu, P. (1991) *Language and Symbolic Power* (Cambridge: Polity Press).

Brown, G. (2008) *A Common Purpose for the Age of Ambition*, New Labour conference, 2008, www.labour.org.uk/spring08/gordon_brown_speaks_to_ conference (accessed 20 January 2010).

Butler, J. (2003) *Kritik der ethischen Gewal*, Adorno Lectures, 2002, Frankfurt am Main: Institut für Sozialforschung an der Johann Wolfgang Goethe-Universität.

Carr, D. (1986) *Time, Narrative and History* (Bloomington IN: Indiana University Press).

Charmaz, K. (1995) 'Grounded theory', in J. A. Smith, R. Harré and L. V. Langenhove (eds) *Rethinking Methods in Psychology* (London: Sage).

Charmaz, K. (2004) 'Premises, principles, and practices in qualitative research: revising the foundations', *Qualitative Health Research* 14:7, 976–93.

Clarke, J., and Newman, J. (1997) *The Managerial State* (London: Sage).

Crawford, R. (2006) 'Health as a meaningful social practice', *Health: An Interdisciplinary Journal for the Social Study of Health, Illness and Medicine* 10:4, 401–20.

Diprose, R. (2002) *Corporeal Generosity* (New York: State University of New York Press).

DoH (2004) *Choosing Health: Making Healthier Choices Easier*, Executive summary, www.dh.gov.uk/en/Publicationsandstatistics (accessed 10 August 2006).

DWP (2005) *Health, Work and Well-being: Caring for our future: A Strategy for the Health and Well-being of Working-age People*, www.dwp.gov.uk (accessed 10 August 2006).

DWP (2008a) *No one Written off: Reforming Welfare to reward Responsibility*, www.dwp.gov.uk (accessed 12 June 2009).

DWP (2008b) *Raising Expectations and increasing Support: Reforming Welfare for the Future*, www.dwp.gov.uk (accessed 12 June 2009).

Ezzy, D. (2000) 'Illness narrative: time, hope and HIV', *Social Science and Medicine* 50, 605–17.

Fisher, P. (2007) 'Experiential knowledge challenges "normality" and individualised citizenship: towards "another way of being"', *Disability and Society* 22:3, 283–98.

Fisher, P., and Goodley, D. (2007) 'The linear medical model of disability: mothers of disabled babies resist with counter-narratives', *Sociology of Health and Illness* 29:1, 66–81.

Fisher, P., and Owen, J. (2008) 'Empowering interventions in health and social care: recognition through "ecologies of practice"', *Social Science and Medicine* 67:12, 2063–71, http://dx.doi.org/10.1016/j.socscimed.2008.09.035.

Frank, A. W. (1995) *The Wounded Storyteller: Body, Illness and Ethics* (Chicago and London: University of Chicago Press).

Fraser, N., and Honneth, A. (2003) *Redistribution or Recognition? A Political-Philosophical Exchange* (London and New York: Verso).

Furedi, F. (1997) *Culture of Fear: Risk-taking and the Morality of Low Expectation* (London: Cassell).

Furedi, F. (2004) *Therapy Culture* (London: Routledge).

Giddens, A. (1991) *Modernity and Self-identity: Self and Society in the late Modern Age* (Cambridge: Polity Press).

Gillies, V. (2005) 'Meeting parents' needs? Discourses of "support" and "inclusion" in family policy', *Critical Social Policy* 25:1, 70–90.

Gleeson, D., and Knights, D. (2006) 'Challenging dualism: public professionalism in "troubled times"', *Sociology* 40:2, 277–96.

Government Equalities Office (2009) *A Fairer Future: The Equality Bill and other Action to make Equality a Reality*, www.equalities.gov.uk/ (accessed 5 July 2009).

Gummer, B. (1998) 'Decision-making under conditions of risk, ambiguity and uncertainty: recent perspectives', *Administration in Social Work* 22:2, 75–93.

Gur-Ze'ev, I., Masschelein, J., and Blake, N. (2001) 'Reflectivity, reflection and counter-education', *Studies in Philosophy and Education* 20, 93–106.

Home Office (1998) *Supporting Families* (London: HMSO).

Honneth, A. (1996) *The Struggle for Recognition: The Moral Grammar of Social Conflicts* (Cambridge: Polity Press).

Honneth, A. (2001) 'Recognition or redistribution? Changing perspectives on the moral order of society', *Theory, Culture and Society* 18:2–3, 43–55.

Honneth, A. (2003) 'Redistribution as recognition: a response to Nancy', in N. Fraser and A. Honneth, *Redistribution or Recognition? A Political-Philosophical Exchange* (London and New York: Verso).

Hughes, K. (2004) 'Health as individual responsibility. possibilities and personal struggle', in P. Tovey, G. Easthorpe and J. Adams (eds) *The Mainstreaming of Complementary and Alternative Medicine: Studies in Social Context* (London: Routledge).

Kemshall, H. (2002) *Risk, Social Policy and Welfare* (Buckingham: Open University Press).

Lister, R. (2000) 'Dilemmas in engendering citizenship', in B. Hobson (ed.) *Gender and Citizenship in Transition* (Basingstoke: Macmillan).

MacIntyre, A. (1985) *After Virtue* (Notre Dame IN: University of Notre Dame Press).

Magnus, K. D. (2006) 'The unaccountable subject: Judith Butler and the social conditions of intersubjective agency', *Hypatia* 21:2, 81–103.

McKnight, J. (1995) *The Careless Society: Community and its Counterfeits* (New York: Basic Books).

Miller, T. (2005) *Making Sense of Motherhood. A Narrative Approach* (Cambridge: Cambridge University Press).

New Labour (1997) *New Labour because Britain deserves better*, Archives of Labour Party Manifesto, www.labour-party.org.uk/manifestos/1997 (accessed 07 June 2009).

Powell, M., and Hewitt, M. (2002) *Welfare State and Welfare Change* (Buckingham: Open University Press).

Rake, K. (2001) 'Gender and New Labour's social policies', *Journal of Social Policy* 30:2, 209–32.

Robertson, C. (2001) 'Autonomy and identity: the need for new dialogues in education and welfare', *Support for Learning* 16:3, 122–7.

Rose, N. (1999) *Powers of Freedom* (Cambridge: Cambridge University Press).

Sointu, E. (2005) 'The rise of an ideal: tracing changing discourse of well-being', *Sociological Review*, 255–74.

Sointu, E. (2006) 'Recognition and the creation of well-being', *Sociology* 40:3, 493–510.

Stronach, I., Corbin, B., McNamara, O., Stark, S., and Warne, T. (2002) 'Towards an uncertain politics of professionalism: teacher and nurse identities in flux', *Journal of Educational Policy* 7:1, 110–38.

Taylor, C. (1991) *The Ethics of Authenticity* (Cambridge MA: Harvard University Press).

Williams, F. (2001) 'In and beyond New Labour: towards a new political ethics of care', *Critical Social Policy* 21:4, 467–90.

Williams, F. (2002) 'The presence of feminism in the future of welfare', *Economy and Society*, 31:4, 501–19.

Yar, M. (2001) 'Recognition and the politics of human(e) desire', *Theory, Culture and Society* 18:1–3, 57–76.

Acknowledgements

This chapter is an adapted version of a paper that was first published in 2008: P. Fisher, 'Well-being and empowerment: the importance of recognition', *Sociology of Health and Illness* 30:4 (2008), 583–98.

9

New Labour and Northern Ireland: delivering peace,
prosperity and social justice?

Catherine McGlynn and James W. McAuley

Tony Blair's skilful diplomacy and unflagging commitment to restarting
negotiations in Northern Ireland were key factors in securing a peace
accord, which officially brought to an end one of the bloodiest conflicts
in post-war Europe. Despite this, the major early reviews of the rise of
New Labour make little or no reference to Northern Ireland as a central
issue (see for example material in Coddington and Perryman, 1998;
Driver and Martell 1998; Heath *et al.*, 2001). Northern Ireland for
many remained a place apart.

Even within the context of the UK state's strong sub-national differences in policy-making (see Schumuecker, 2008; Wincott, 2006)
Northern Ireland has stood out, and the settlement that brought devolution to the province is based on a complex understanding of citizenship and allegiance that has not been applied elsewhere in the UK.
In light of this, it would be easy to assume that policies in Northern
Ireland depart from the conceptions of citizenship and social justice
that informed New Labour's approach to social policy. However, we
will argue that Blair's administration used peace itself as a model
of social justice because it was assumed that this would produce a
peace dividend of private investment, new employment and growing
prosperity – factors that were essential to the New Labour emphasis
on employment and inclusion as the mechanisms that would deliver
their vision of social justice. It is apparent, though, that the situation in
Northern Ireland has not developed as intended. This is partly because
the so-called peace dividend was paid out in a society that is strongly
horizontally stratified but also because central interference has been
inimical to progression from the definite vertical segmentation that has
fractured Northern Irish civil society.

We propose an alternative to New Labour's reliance on the worker
citizen, making use of Lister's ideas of citizenship as participation to
consider ways in which the legitimacy of citizenship could be extended

outside the workplace. In order to outline our argument we will provide contextual information on the background to the peace process in Northern Ireland, the debate about the consociational settlement laid down in the resulting Belfast Good Friday Agreement of 1998 (hereafter the GFA) and the manner in which New Labour sought to make employment the key indicator of normality and security in Northern Ireland.

Northern Ireland: conflict and peace process

Following a war of independence in Ireland after the First World War, negotiations were conducted that resulted in partition of the island through the 1920 Government of Ireland Act. Twenty-six counties formed an Irish Free State (later the Republic of Ireland), reflecting the aspirations for independence of an Irish nationalist movement that had become increasingly focused on an ethnic (Gaelic and Catholic) conception of Irishness. Six counties of the province of Ulster remained within the UK, albeit with a new devolved parliament, reflecting the unionist preferences of the Protestant majority in the industrialised heartland of the north. The resulting socially conservative unionist administration 'focused obsessively on intra-Protestant relations to the virtual exclusion of changes within Northern Ireland' (Paterson, 1996: 10). A clientist approach to the distribution of jobs and services created an employment differential that meant Catholic men were twice as likely to be unemployed as their Protestant counterparts (Cebulla and Smyth, 1996). The Catholic nationalist minority's major response was abstentionism, with only a handful committed to a violent republican campaign to overthrow the state, illustrated by the ill fated IRA campaign of 1958 to 1962 that petered out because of lack of support.

In the 1960s a new unionist Prime Minister, Terence O'Neill, sought to promote reconciliation between unionists and nationalists through public investment to attract new business and gestures such as visiting Catholic schools (Harris, 1991; Mulholland, 2000). It was assumed that modernising Northern Ireland's economic base would reverse the steep post-war economic decline, generating enough prosperity to integrate the minority without structural change that would challenge the unionist hierarchy (Buckland, 1981). Modernisation, however, also encouraged the formation of a civil rights movement dedicated to genuinely equal citizenship in areas such as housing provision, public-sector employment and treatment by the security forces. Police overreaction to civil rights marches sparked Catholic nationalist frustration and Protestant unionist insecurity into violence on the streets and led to the re-emergence of organised extra-constitutional forces tagged republican and loyalist, devoted respectively to destroying or maintaining the union with the UK. The resulting conflict, known as the 'Troubles', resulted in the loss of more than 3,500 deaths, with civilians making up the largest group of victims (Hayes and McAllister, 2001).

Northern Ireland's parliament was suspended in 1972 and the British government attempted to foster a peace settlement based on two key elements. The first was a power-sharing government that instituted in some manner the differing constitutional preferences of the majority of each community, beginning with a short-lived devolved administration in 1974, created by the Sunningdale Agreement. The second element was high public spending to bolster the weak and rapidly deindustrialising Northern Ireland economy and encourage acquiescence at the least to the presence of the British state (Bean, 2008). This emphasis on the importance of the state as an investor and employer continued even through the years of the neo-liberal Thatcher administration (see Cunningham, 2001; McKay and Williams, 2005; O'Dowd, 1987).

Attempts to draw all the relevant actors into a peace process were stepped up under the Major administration in the 1990s. However, the early promise of these negotiations faltered. The Irish Republican Army (IRA) through their political representatives, Sinn Féin, were excluded from talks after bombs in Manchester and London in 1996 and the teetering Major administration was too dependent on Ulster Unionist votes at Westminster to push the talks forward. The election of a Labour government kick-started the stalled process, not least because Blair himself dealt with negotiations with astonishing reserves of energy and diplomacy. Sinn Féin was readmitted to talks and an agreement was forged that paved the way for the return of devolution to Northern Ireland. Maintaining the institutions endowed by the GFA has proved a difficult task but after a number of suspensions of the Northern Ireland Assembly the St Andrews Agreement of 2006 resuscitated devolution. Unfortunately the Assembly did not flourish after the two largest parties the Democratic Unionist Party (DUP) and Sinn Féin agreed to form an executive, and by early 2010 personal scandals and disagreements over the thorny issues of devolved policing and justice powers had created new obstacles for the fragile institutional settlement.

New Labour's prescription for Northern Ireland – a settlement that recognises different constitutional preferences and a belief that addressing Northern Ireland's economic weakness will temper the alienation that encourages violent action against the state and/or fellow citizens – did not differ in key respects from the approaches of previous Labour and Conservative administrations. However, having secured the GFA and seemingly put a stop to large-scale organised political violence, it is apparent that New Labour sought to extend their version of social justice to a newly peaceful and potentially prosperous part of the UK. Before outlining and assessing how this was done some further context needs to be provided on the consociational framework of citizenship laid down by the GFA.

Consociational citizenship versus civil society

Consociational theory contends that there are a number of highly segmented societies which lack cross-cutting political cleavages and affiliations (Lorwin, 1971; Steiner, 1981). The model of peaceful and enduring consociational democracy used in segmented post-war societies such as Belgium and the Netherlands has long been proposed as a means of fostering stable and relatively peaceful democratic settlements in societies such as Cyprus and Lebanon that have been beset by much more violent division. The model rests on the assumption that 'overarching co-operation at the elite level can be a substitute for cross-cutting affiliations at the mass level' (Lijphart, 1968: 200).

The parliamentary systems of consociational democracies are by necessity top-heavy and top-down political arrangements. Grand coalitions of interests are drawn into the executive and decisions are ratified and rejected through mechanisms such as proportionality in voting and the power of mutual veto. Such principles are reflected in the outcome of the Northern Irish peace process, a system that is 'the clearest example of fully blown consociationalism that exists today' (Reynolds, 1999: 614). At its core rests an Assembly elected by the single transferable vote (STV) system of proportional representation and an executive coalition that shares out Ministerial responsibility using the D'Hondt mechanism of allocating portfolios, with parties taking it in turn to select their chosen posts with the order decided by the strength of their vote. Cross-community consent is required to approve both the budget and the nominees for the dual premiership. These communities are designated unionist and nationalist, and the consociational settlements are seen as an appropriate method of government for a society divided along the fault line of ethno-nationalism. As the former Secretary of State for Northern Ireland, Peter Mandelson, put it, the system means that 'Orange and Green [unionist and nationalist] can live side by side in mutual respect, as keen to protect each other's rights as their own' (cited in MacIntyre, 2000: 536).

Citizens of a consociational polity are presented as divided from each other by a primary allegiance, usually based on ethnicity, religion or language. They are vertically aligned and the leadership of their group bears their claims in a political arena that is insulated from sudden demands for change from below. Such settlements have been criticised for being insufficiently democratic (Horowitz, 2001). It has also been argued that institutionalising different cultural and political identities stifles the possibility of common citizenship and arrests the forces of social change, most notably by ignoring the possibilities for reconciliation at the informal level of civil society (Dixon, 1997; Taylor, 2009).

Defenders of such settlements argue that they are based on a realistic acceptance of pre-existing divisions and that they present an opportunity for democracy in societies that may otherwise collapse (Lijphart, 1985; McGarry and O'Leary, 2006). In the specific context of Northern Ireland it is argued that civil society is also vertically segmented and cannot offer an alternative forum for change (McGarry and O'Leary, 1995) and also that whilst ethnic outbidding (Gormley-Heenan and MacGinty, 2008) has led to the rise of the DUP and Sinn Féin, both these parties have been forced to moderate their stance in order to gain this success and to work together (Mitchell *et al.*, 2002). Finally, defenders of such settlements propose a paradoxical effect of consociational settlements whereby recognising difference is the first step to transcending it (O'Leary, 1989), although this does require political parties to move beyond the early stages of cementing their support through strident calls for intra-bloc unity (Luther, 1999).

The institution of consociational modes of democracy was not an approach unique to New Labour. The much-quoted description of the GFA by Northern Irish nationalist politician Seamus Mallon as the Sunningdale Agreement for slow learners reflects the resistance by successive administrations to any system based solely on integrating Northern Ireland either into a completely unitary state or subscription to a shared national identity. Throughout the conflict there was growing acceptance of the explanation that the roots of sectarian division related to ethno-nationalism, and a settlement that recognised the identities and claims of both sides was presented as the logical solution to such a problem (McAuley *et al.*, 2008).

The GFA did recognise a positive role for civil society actors in transcending difference through the creation of a Civic Forum of civic leaders and voluntary-sector interests. It was envisaged that the Forum would bring 'the resources and goodwill of civil society to bear in support of the work of the assembly' (Woods, 2001: 79). Unfortunately, it has struggled to find a role for itself and has for the most part been sidelined by the day-to-day activities of the Assembly and the civil service (Taylor, 2006). However, whilst it must be accepted that it would be naive to ignore the fact that ethno-nationalism divides civil society in the same manner it does institutional politics (Wolff, 2002), New Labour's approach to the distribution of social goods and services meant that formalising the vertical stratification of politically salient cultural identities has not been the only block to transcending difference and fostering a sense of common cause between citizens in Northern Ireland.

New Labour, social justice and peace: the worker citizen

As Shirlow and Shuttleworth (1999) pointed out soon after the GFA was signed, one of the assumptions behind the peace process was that there would be a resulting economic dividend, and that post-conflict economic reconstruction would ease social exclusion, something that would in turn curb the possibility of further violence. The normalisation of Northern Irish society was seen to be evident in the opening of branches of Tesco and Marks & Spencer as much as it was in the absence of soldiers in the street. It was taken as read that prosperity and peace were interdependent by New Labour, meaning that 'perhaps more than in any other administration political, security, economic and social policy were seen as mutually supporting and reinforcing' (Cunningham, 2001: 147).

Just as the acceptance of the need to recognise different constitutional preferences was not unique to New Labour's approach to Northern Ireland, neither was such faith that prosperity would guarantee peace and vice versa entirely new. In the first instance this was because of the apparent causal connection between poverty and a propensity to paramilitary violence based on the concentration of both violent incidents and protagonists in areas of high socio-economic need. The unemployment differential between Catholic and Protestant men persisted throughout the conflict, as fair employment legislation failed to address long-standing structural reasons for the gap (Cebulla and Smyth, 1996).

This situation endured along with the lower average wage of Catholic women, even though they were more likely than Protestant women to be in full-time employment (Coulter, 1999). Significant job creation was required if these inequalities were to be addressed without any loss of work in Protestant communities (Teague, 1997). Projects such as the Castle Court shopping centre in Belfast were deliberately designed to generate wealth and reduce the scope of republicans to exploit poverty and joblessness as evidence of the British state's indifference to the needs of those who were not committed to the union (Bean, 2008; McDonald, 2009).

What made New Labour's approach different from previous administrations' was that employment was more than a method of ensuring at least a minimal begrudging acceptance of the authority of the British state; it was the key feature of New Labour's vision of social justice. Employment was central to the New Labour agenda and its commitment to 'an open world order and co-operation in Europe' (Gamble and Kelly, 2001: 173), and the need to prepare citizens for work in a globally competitive market was seen as one of the main challenges facing the new government (Driver and Martell, 2006). The tone was set by the Commission for Social Justice, which was inaugurated by the Labour leader John Smith and which reported in the year of his death: 'The extension of economic opportunity is not the only source of economic prosperity but also the basis for social justice' (Commission for Social Justice, 1994: 95). It was assumed that training citizens for employment would ensure that the UK could maintain a buoyant job market in a globalised economy. It was also believed that this would ensure 'inclusion and thus the achievement of social justice' (Kenny, 2007: 35). This shifted the focus of New Labour from the eliding of social justice with equality through redistribution to a more restricted equating of social justice with overcoming social exclusion (Plant, 1999).

This change of focus was accompanied by a shift from emphasis on rights to inclusion in the mainstream of work as the basis of a citizenship that is heavily rooted in obligation (Lister, 1998a; Lund, 1999). It is important to note that governmental responsibility for maintaining high levels of employment in order to ensure inclusion lay in the supply side of skilled employees, meaning that 'the stress is on the employability of workers, not job creation' (Tonge, 1999: 230). This focus on employment as the central obligation of a citizen but also the wellspring from which they gain their rights through individual empowerment meant that the good citizen of New Labour's imagination was a worker. Having discharged its responsibility of equipping individuals with skills, the government then obliged these worker citizens to make the most of the economic opportunities offered.

In the context of Northern Ireland, attracting new investment to employ the potential work force was particularly important because of the hope that economic regeneration would supplant the need for intensive public subsidy (Shirlow and Shuttleworth, 1999). Economic growth would then help close the employment differential by creating more jobs instead of attempting to redistribute existing opportunities.

This approach was articulated in a speech by Blair reiterating his commitment to the peace process, which was facing difficulties after the suspension of the devolved institutions. Blair reminded his audience that progress included 'new jobs, new investment and a new way of life, as anyone who walks through Belfast city centre, or that of Derry or any other town, can see' (Blair, 2002). In his view, peace had brought the prosperity that had transformed Northern Ireland. Interestingly, his choice of words is similar to the rhetoric of the unionist Prime Minister, Terence O'Neill, who proclaimed, for example, that 'new industries for Newry mean new hope for all its people' (O'Neill, 1969: 130).

Problems with New Labour's model

New Labour's approach to Northern Ireland, then, was a combination of the long-standing two-track approach of power sharing between unionist and nationalists and remedies for Northern Ireland's consistent economic under-performance. Having secured power sharing, albeit with a number of suspensions, the government then sought to augment the simple connection between job creation and citizenship (that those who saw the economic benefit of the union would be at least grudgingly acquiescent to the existence of the existence of Northern Ireland) towards integration into a wider UK vision of workers as active and empowered citizens, safe from slipping into the position of 'demoralised rights claimers' (Dwyer, 1998: 497). This would allow Northern Ireland to be normalised, i.e. to follow a centralised prescription for creating the good life and good citizens.

Producing concrete benefits from peace did not mean the drop in state subsidy that Labour would have wished. As with regeneration programmes elsewhere in the UK, 'the recent growth in private-sector investment fuelling Belfast's regeneration has been largely underpinned by pump priming and strategic support from the state' (Bean, 2008: 23). However, the peace dividend was also cast as increased prosperity for individual citizens, meaning that those who had signed up to a risky peace agreement with long-standing enemies could demonstrate that the gamble had brought about a genuine improvement in the quality of life for all.

There are a number of ways in which New Labour's conception of the worker citizen can be critiqued. In the specific context of Northern Ireland the focus on employment has created three interrelated problems that have limited the prospects for the creation of the hoped-for consociational paradox, whereby differences can be transcended and cross-cutting cleavages created by the very settlement that formalises vertical segmentation. The first is that the new job market of Northern Ireland has not in itself been a guarantor of prosperity. The second is that the emphasis on inclusion rather than inequality has meant that Northern Ireland remains an intensely unequal society and that this played a part in the persistence of low-level spontaneous violence that has been one of the biggest threats to peace in Northern Ireland. The third is that while it would be convenient to blame the long-standing ethno-national divide for the limited transition to a bottom-up mode of civil society politics in Northern Ireland, New Labour have played a part in limiting the opportunities for citizens to work together by interfering in the embryonic new politics created by the Assembly in its first sittings.

Tomlinson (1997) points out that concentration on maintaining the supply side of skilled workers led to a lot of rhetoric about the responsibility of government and of individuals but little about the responsibility of industry to ensure that all this education and training resulted in work that did not waste such honed talents. Initially the period following the signing of the GFA coincided with a rapid decrease in the unemployment figures and Blair was keen to highlight this by pointing out that 'the transformation in the economy has been enormous: unemployment at its lowest since 1975, down 65 per cent since the Agreement' (Blair, 2002).There was also a narrowing of the unemployment differential between Catholics and Protestants to 1.7 in 2007, accounted for in part by the improving performance in education by those from a Catholic background and their strong representation in the growing service sector (Northern Ireland Statistics and Research Agency 2009).

The fact that it was industries such as tourism and sales that accompanied Northern Ireland's decrease in joblessness signifies that increasing employment did not automatically mean increased prosperity for all citizens. Whilst arguing that private services were associated with prosperity, and that the lack of a thriving private sector had been integral to Northern Ireland's economic problems, a report by the Department for Enterprise Trade and Industry in Northern Ireland (2004) admitted that the only real evidence of increased competitiveness in Northern Ireland was the creation of 6,000 call centre jobs. Horgan (2005) points out that Northern Ireland was deliberately marketed to overseas investors as a low-wage economy and links this state of affairs to the fact that half of all children living below the poverty line were in families where at least one adult was working.

Equating social justice with inclusion rather than equality meant that New Labour ignored the nature of regeneration in Northern Ireland, which has perpetuated the huge disparity in incomes between different working groups (Shirlow and Shuttleworth, 1999; Horgan, 2005). This polarisation of employment between highly paid professionals and low-pay service workers is reflected in increasing residential segregation of socio-economic groups, which was until recently augmented by educational segregation through the eleven-plus examination for secondary education (Cebulla and Smyth, 1996; Coulter, 1999). The influx of new jobs was in large part poorly paid, insecure and uninspiring, and this contradicted the Commission for Social Justice's optimism that attracting investment would foster benefits of equal worth for both companies and workers. The jobs boom increased the ranks of the working poor, rather than generating genuine opportunity which would ensure that life chances were not just based on the socio-economic position of one's parents.

This reinforcement of Northern Ireland's horizontal stratification impacted upon the new consociational settlement in a potentially dangerous manner. The murder of two soldiers by the Real IRA at the Massareene barracks in County Antrim in 2009 was a reminder that there are those who oppose the GFA and wish to destroy the settlement by force. However, for the most part, large-scale organised political violence has declined and peace as defined by the absence of sustained paramilitary campaigns has come to Northern Ireland. At the same time there has been an increase in local and unplanned violence in areas with high levels of deprivation.

Urban working-class districts experienced a disproportionate amount of violence during the years of the conflict, and for areas such as inner-city Belfast the signing of the GFA did not remove this violence entirely. The persistence of such unrest has intensified physical segregation between poorer members of both communities in post-GFA Northern Ireland. Boundaries are clearly demarcated by flags and murals, and sometimes physically, by the many 'peace walls', gates and other features of security architecture (Jarman, 2008). Territoriality has intensified since 1998 and violence is particularly reflected at the interface areas, where the social and physical lines are most readily identifiable between the two communities (Jarman, 2003; Shirlow, 2006).

Following Labour's idealisation of the worker citizen one could argue that the stubborn persistence of unemployment in these areas means that the residents have been excluded from a 'moral community in which citizens can earn access to their social rights through a combination of hard work, responsible behaviour and personal contribution' (Dwyer, 2002: 274). In October 2005, whilst unemployment had dropped to 3.2 per cent in Northern Ireland, the rate tripled in inner-city wards such as Falls and Shankill (West Belfast Taskforce and Greater Shankill Taskforce, 2007). This could, therefore, offer an explanation for why these areas have seen so much unrest.

The focus on employment, however, meant Labour avoided the importance of other areas of social policy that interact with citizens' sense of security and well-being, principally housing. For working-class Protestants, living in communities that are declining in size leaves them vulnerable to being 'overrun' by what they perceive to be the old enemy. For the young and growing Catholic community, unable to secure accommodation because segregation keeps them 'penned' into existing areas, housing has become a source of anger and frustration.

These concerns connect through the emotive issue of Protestant Orange Order parades through Catholic nationalist areas to overall political narratives of betrayal and discrimination. In Shirlow's words, 'segregation influences the localised nature of the politics of territorial control and resistance, where the imperatives of communal difference, segregation and exclusion still predominate over the politics of shared interests, integration, assimilation and consensus' (Shirlow, 2006: 227). This territoriality and sense of threat also led to the intensification of attacks on newly arrived immigrant communities, as the hounding out of Romanian families from loyalist south Belfast in 2009 demonstrated. In addition, the Orange Order marching season saw another round of protests about marches through areas such as Ardoyne escalate into rioting.

In post-Agreement Northern Ireland the strident ethnic outbidding undertaken by Sinn Féin and the DUP to ensure their primacy within their respective communities means that they have sought to present social and economic issues through a filter of threat from the other side. In 2001 there was a stand-off at the Holy Cross primary school in North Belfast. Residents of Glenbryn prevented Catholic pupils and their parents using a route through the area to the school gates. They claimed that the school run was a cover for republican infiltration of a loyalist area and desisted from this tactic only when plans for CC-TV and gating were confirmed. Political representatives of both communities sought to state the case for their side. The local DUP MP, Nigel Dodds, argued that the protests were 'the result of the government continually ignoring the plight of isolated communities who have been the subject of an organised campaign of intimidation for over thirty years' (*Shankill Mirror*, 2001). On the other side Sinn Féin MLA Gerry Kelly claimed that a regeneration scheme in North Belfast was a direct reward for loyalists for their actions at Holy Cross (*An Phoblacht*, 2001).

Such rhetoric does in part explain why a series of local and haphazard outbreaks of violence have developed such political significance, but this conflict is also rooted in the extreme inequalities of Northern Irish life. By arguing this we do not mean to say that such actions are cries for social justice marked as demands for group protection. And it is simplistic to assume that issues of socio-economic need could be used as a rallying point to undermine sectarian affiliation. As Coulter (1994) and McAuley (1994) point out, sectarian and class identity need not be mutually exclusive, and for many in Northern Ireland the perceived relationship with social deprivation and threats to one's group from outside makes immediate sense. However, whilst deprivation is not solely the cause of the attitudes and anxieties that fuel local conflicts it is the element that sharpens insecurity and makes expression of these anxieties so damaging both to the individuals concerned and to a society that is trying to move away from political violence. The relentless focus on inclusion and employment meant that New Labour's approach to Northern Ireland ignored the deleterious impact of inequality on the well-being of a community.

Whilst examples such as Holy Cross demonstrate how local politicians have used social issues to strengthen difference there is also evidence that the consociational framework of the Assembly allowed some modes of politics that have moved beyond the ethno-national divide. McLaughlin (2005) points out that by the time of its suspension in 2002 the Northern Ireland Assembly had abolished school league tables, set up the office of Children's Commissioner, established means-tested bursaries for those in higher education and offered free public transport to pensioners. The controversial passage of legislation to enact the recommendations of the Burns Report (Department of Education for Northern Ireland, 2001) by removing the eleven-plus exam from the education system was aided in part by co-operation between Sinn Féin and the Progressive Unionist Party, who served as the political representatives respectively of the IRA and the loyalist paramilitary group the Ulster Volunteer Force (Shirlow et al., 2010).

In fact, one of the biggest deterrents to the creation of cross-cutting cleavages on social and political issues has been interference from the centre. A good example of this was the Assembly's approach to private finance initiatives (PFIs). Horgan (2006) documents how an interdepartmental working group established an alternative model to centralised versions of public–private partnerships, which were deemed to be unpopular and unsuitable. The proposed model would involve social partnership with groups such as trade unions and voluntary organisations, which would have significant input on where and how the private sector would be involved. When direct rule was reimposed after sus-pension this model was abandoned and a Strategic Investment Board was set up in 2003 to actively promote New Labour's model of PFI in services such as water, roads and health.

New Labour's approach to social policy in Northern Ireland was often at variance with local perceptions of priorities. For example, Paris *et al.* (2003) point out that throughout the conflict spending on social housing in Northern Ireland remained comparatively high, with a much smaller role for housing associations than in England, Scotland and Wales. However, whilst the Assembly was suspended Labour embarked upon contracting the provision and maintenance of housing to such groups despite vocal protests from local politicians. Arguably, the nor-malisation that New Labour sought to bring to Northern Ireland was that of their overall commitment to minimising direct state provision and inviting co-operation from private and voluntary interests in the running of services. Resistance to this programme in Northern Ireland suggests the possibility of a consensus between politicians from dif-ferent communities in terms of political accountability for services and redistribution of wealth, something that puts greater focus on citizens' rights and entitlements than Labour's focus on employment, self-reliance and obligation.

An alternative model: citizenship as participation

In proposing an alternative model of citizenship and social justice for Northern Ireland it must be acknowledged that the consociational structures laid down by the Good Friday Agreement are unlikely to be dismantled any time soon (although the GFA continues to be chal-lenged by sections of loyalism and republicanism). The settlement has been a key part of a process that has supported a move away from political violence and created a devolved Assembly with opportunities for a Northern Irish model of social policy. However, proponents of the system have been vague about how to bring about the consociational paradox, by which we mean using a system that institutionalises dif-ference to address other structural inequalities that stretch across com-munity divides. It is not enough to say that 'the hope is that these issues might provide a focus that will enable politicians and citizens to move in time, beyond the constitutional issue, but that is something that will happen of its own accord, if it happens at all' (O'Neill, 2009: 97).

Reviewing New Labour and approaches to citizenship in Northern Ireland, it is apparent that such a term was limited to a constricted version of its potential meaning. This is inevitable in part, given the acceptance of a consociational settlement that prioritised elite negotiation. However, it also stems from the focus on obligations in general and employment in particular. It follows that an alternative model would broaden out the manner and arenas in which individuals could be legitimately viewed as active citizens.

Lister has suggested that citizenship should be conceived as participation, by which she means the expression of human agency in a much more broadly defined political arena (Lister, 1998b, 1998c). Broadening out how, where and by which means citizens are deemed to participate would have the advantage of dispelling notions that groups who were less visible in the formal sphere were passive. She claims that, in Northern Ireland, broadening citizenship activity from the formal political sphere to grass-roots community activism has been key in strengthening confidence within communities and can therefore 'act as a prerequisite for cross-community work' (Lister, 1998c: 231).

In this context, it is worthy of note that although conflict has deterred the establishment of a thriving network of groups operating between communities (what others have called bridging capital), when Northern Ireland's poorer districts are compared with others in the UK with a similar socio-economic profile they have high levels of civic engagement within their communities (McEvoy and Mika, 2002). A good example of the way participation in informal networks can improve conditions for local communities and support the development of peaceful conditions to underpin formal political action is the reintegration of those imprisoned for paramilitary offences during the conflict.

Prisoner release was a central component of the Agreement, but Rolston (2007) points out that there was no formal programme of reintegration for former combatants. This was left to voluntary community groups and to self-help groups founded and organised by the former combatants themselves. This successful reintegration led to a successful leadership role for many former prisoners in defusing incidents at interface areas and to successful negotiation across community lines to prevent further violence (Shirlow et al., 2010).

Lister's application of citizenship as participation to Northern Ireland ignores the imbalance in confidence between the two communities and the insecurity and sense of loss and disintegration inherent in loyalist thinking and the belief that the Accord has offered a continual process of concessions to Irish republicanism (McAuley and Tonge, 2007). In addition, although broadening the political arena to give due recognition to participation through care and support, as well as more traditionally accepted means of discharging one's citizenship, obligation is a vital step for ensuring participation and confidence at the grass roots. Negotiation and consensus are still required at the formal level of politics to ensure that these modes of participation influence policy.

In its earliest incarnation the Assembly did enact legislation that dismantled barriers to services such as transport and education and looked at social partnerships that would ensure that private finance was accountable to community needs in the provision of public services. Such programmes would suggest a possible affinity with redistribution of wealth and power. In its newer incarnation the picture is more uncertain. Whilst Sinn Féin see community activism as a legitimate and vital activity, the socially more conservative DUP are mistrustful of a grass-roots sphere that they see as an area where paramilitaries have sought to legitimise themselves through activism.

Conclusion

Tony Blair played a key role in bringing a stalled peace process towards the consensus required to return devolved power to Northern Ireland. Jonathan Powell once went so far as to compare him directly to Gladstone, both in terms of his fascination with Ireland and the depth of his personal commitment to finding a solution (Seldon, 2007: 116).

The fruits of Blair's labours, the consociational settlement that underpinned the GFA, offered a complicated version of self-determination based upon recognition to different political and cultural identities. The concrete benefit of this has been a drop in political violence. However, the institutional and rhetorical sharpening of ethno-national differences has exacerbated tensions and anxieties for deprived communities.

Considering Lister's ideas of citizenship as participation, it becomes clear that, within the confines of a society that is highly segmented vertically and horizontally, both communities have been able to exhibit sufficient agency to mitigate some of these problems. Therefore they should not be presented as passive victims of post-Agreement life. However, in the justifiable drive to celebrate the achievements of the peace process the debilitating effects of increased tension and estrangement cannot be brushed aside.

New Labour's handling of the peace process was based on the assumption that the Agreement would provide political justice through recognition and the resulting stability would produce a peace dividend that would promote social justice through including the marginalised as worker citizens. This formula was implemented in partnership with the marketing of Northern Ireland as a low-wage economy and a boom that produced more jobs without reducing the stark inequality of income and life experience in Northern Ireland. As that boom fades it is apparent that Northern Ireland's political elite will have to address these structural inequalities in partnership with the communities they serve if differences are to be genuinely transcended.

Bibliography

An Phoblacht (*The Republican*) (2001) 'Glenbryn rewarded for bigotry', 27 September.

Bean, K. (2008) *The New Politics of Sinn Féin* (Liverpool: Liverpool University Press).

Blair, T. (2002) Speech at Belfast on 17 October, www.nio.gov.uk (accessed 20 April 2009).

Buckland, P. (1981) *A History of Northern Ireland* (Dublin: Gill & Macmillan).

Cebulla, A., and Smyth, J. (1996) 'Disadvantage and new prosperity in restructured Belfast', *Capital and Class* 60, 39–60.

Coddington, A., and Perryman, M., eds (1998) *The Moderniser's Dilemma: Radical Politics in the Age of Blair* (London: Lawrence & Wishart).

Coulter, C. (1994) 'Class, ethnicity and political identity in Northern Ireland', *Irish Journal of Sociology* 4, 1–26.

Coulter, C. (1999) *Contemporary Northern Irish Society* (London: Pluto).

Commission for Social Justice (1994) *Social Justice: Strategies for National Renewal* (London: Vintage).

Cunningham, M. (2001) *British Government Policy in Northern Ireland, 1969–2000* (Manchester: Manchester University Press).

Department of Education for Northern Ireland (2001) *Education for the Twenty-first Century: Post-primary Review Body* (the Burns Report), www. deni.gov.uk (accessed 26 June 2003).

Department of Enterprise Trade and Industry for Northern Ireland (2004) *The Future of Private Services in Northern Ireland: Final Report*, www.detini.gov. uk (accessed 4 April 2009).

Dixon, P. (1997) 'Paths to peace in Northern Ireland' I, 'Civil society and consociational approaches', *Democratisation* 4:2, 1–27.

Driver, S., and Martell, L. (1998) *New Labour: Politics after Thatcherism* (Cambridge: Polity Press).

Driver, S., and Martell, L. (2006) *New Labour* (Cambridge: Polity Press)

Dwyer, P. (1998) 'Conditional citizens? Welfare rights and responsibilities in the late 1990s', *Critical Social Policy* 57, 493–519.

Dwyer, P. (2002) 'Making sense of social citizenship: some user views on welfare rights and responsibilities', *Critical Social Policy*, 22:2, 273–99.

Gamble, A., and Kelly, G. (2001) 'Labour's new economics', in S. Ludlam and M. J. Smith (eds) *New Labour in Government* (Basingstoke: Macmillan).

Gormley-Heenan, C., and MacGinty, R. (2008) 'Ethnic outbidding and party modernisation: understanding the Democratic Unionist Party's electoral success in the post-Agreement environment', *Ethnopolitics* 7:1, 43–61.

Harris, R. (1991) *Regional Economic Policy in Northern Ireland, 1945–1988* (Aldershot: Gower).

Hayes, B., and McAllister, I. (2001) 'Sowing dragon's teeth: public support for political violence and terrorism in Northern Ireland', *Political Studies* 49:5, 901–22.

Heath, A. F., Jowell, R. M., and Curtice, J. K. (2001) *The Rise of New Labour: Party Policies and Voter Choices* (Oxford: Oxford University Press).

Horgan, G. (2005) 'Child poverty in Northern Ireland: the limits of Welfare-to-work policies', *Social Policy and Administration* 39:1, 49–64.

Horgan, G. (2006) 'Devolution, direct rule and neo-liberal reconstruction in Northern Ireland', *Critical Social Policy* 26:3, 656–68.

Horowitz, D. (2001) 'The Agreement: clear, consociational, risky', in J. McGarry (ed.) *Northern Ireland and the Divided World* (Oxford: Oxford University Press).

Jarman, N. (2003) 'Managing disorder: responses to interface violence in north Belfast', in O. Hargie and D. Dickson (eds) *Researching the Troubles: Social Science Perspectives on the Northern Ireland Conflict* (Edinburgh: Mainstream).

Jarman, N. (2008) 'Security and segregation: interface barriers in Belfast', *Shared Space* 6, 21–33.

Kenny, C. (2007) 'Does New Labour have a consistent conception of social justice?', *Politics* 27:1, 32–9.

Lijphart, A. (1968) *The Politics of Accommodation* (Berkeley CA and Los Angeles: University of California Press).

Lijphart, A. (1985) *Power-sharing in South Africa* (Berkeley CA: University of California Press).

Lister, R. (1998a) 'From equality to social inclusion: New Labour and the welfare state', *Critical Social Policy*, 18:2, 215–25.

Lister, R. (1998b) 'Citizenship on the margins: citizenship, social work and social action', *European Journal of Social Work* 1:1, 5–18.

Lister, R. (1998c) 'Citizen in action: citizenship and community development in a Northern Ireland context', *Community Development Journal* 33:3, 226–35.

Lorwin, V. R. (1971) 'Segmented pluralism', *Comparative Politics* 3:2, 141–75.

Lund, B. (1999) '"Ask not what your country can do for you": obligations, New Labour and reform', *Critical Social Policy* 61, 220–43.

Luther, K. R. (1999) 'A framework for the comparative analysis of political parties and party systems in consociational democracy', in K. R Luther and K. Deschouwer (eds) *Party Elites in Divided Societies: Political Parties in Consociational Democracy* (London: Routledge).

McAuley, J. W. (1994) *The Politics of Identity* (Aldershot: Aldgate)

McAuley, J. W., and Tonge, J. (2007) '"For God and for the Crown": contemporary political and social attitudes among Orange Order members in Northern Ireland', *Political Psychology* 28:1, 33–54.

McAuley, J. W., McGlynn, C., and Tonge, J. (2008) 'Conflict resolution in asymmetric and symmetric situations: the case of Northern Ireland', *Journal of Asymmetric Conflict* 1:1, 88–102.

McDonald, H. (2009) 'Hey, Gordon, whatever happened to the peace dividend?' www.guardian.co.uk, 24 April 2009 (accessed 1 May 2009).

McEvoy, K., and Mika, H. (2002) 'Restorative justice and the critique of informalism in Northern Ireland', *British Journal of Criminology* 42, 534–62.

McGarry, J., and O'Leary, B. (1995) *Explaining Northern Ireland* (Oxford: Blackwell).

McGarry, J., and O'Leary, B. (2006) 'Consociational theory, Northern Ireland's conflict and its Agreement 2. What critics of consociation can learn from Northern Ireland', *Government and Opposition* 41:2, 249–77.

MacIntyre, D. (2000) *Mandelson and the Making of New Labour* (London: HarperCollins).

McKay, R., and Williams, J. (2005) 'Thinking about need: public spending on the regions', *Regional Studies* 39, 6.

McLaughlin, E. (2005) 'Governance and social policy in Northern Ireland, 1999–2004: the devolution years and postscript', in M. Powell, L. Bauld and K. Clarke (eds) *Social Policy Review Seventeen: Targeting Social Need* (Bristol: Policy Press).

Mitchell, P., O'Leary, B., and Evans, G. (2002) 'The 2001 elections in Northern Ireland: moderating "extremists" and the squeezing of the moderates', *Representation* 39:12, 23–36.

Mulholland, M. (2000) 'Assimilation versus segregation: Unionist strategies in the 1960s', *Twentieth Century British History* 11:3, 284–301.

Northern Ireland Statistics and Research Agency (2009) *2007 Labour Force Survey: Religion Report* (Belfast: OFMDFM).

O'Dowd, L. (1987) 'Trends and potential of the service sector in Northern Ireland', in P. Teague (ed.) *Beyond the Rhetoric: Politics, the Economy and Social Policy in Northern Ireland* (London: Lawrence & Wishart).

O'Leary, B. (1989) 'The limits to coercive consociationalism in Northern Ireland', *Political Studies* 37, 562–88.

O'Neill, S. (2009) 'Recognition, equality, difference: achieving democracy in Northern Ireland', in R. Taylor (ed.) *Consocational Theory: McGarry, O'Leary and the Northern Ireland Conflict* (Abingdon: Routledge).

O'Neill, T. (1969) *Ulster at the Crossroads* (London: Faber).

Paris, C., Gray, P., and Muir, J. (2003) 'Devolving housing policy and practice in Northern Ireland, 1998–2002', *Housing Studies* 18: 2, 159–75.

Paterson, H. (1996) 'Northern Ireland, 1921–1968', in A. Aughey and D. Morrow (eds) *Northern Ireland Politics* (London: Longman).

Plant, R. (1999) 'Crosland, equality and New Labour', in D. Leonard (ed.) *Crosland and New Labour* (Basingstoke: Macmillan).

Reynolds, A. (1999) 'A constitutional Pied Piper: the Northern Irish Good Friday Agreement', *Political Science Quarterly* 114:4, 613–37.

Rolston, B. (2007) 'Demobilisation, reintegration and ex-combatants: the Irish in international perspective' *Social and Legal Studies* 16:2, 259–80.

Schumuecker, K. (2008) 'Social justice in the UK: one route or four?', in

G. Craig, T. Burchardt and D. Gordon (eds) *Seeking Fairness in Diverse Societies* (Bristol: Policy Press).

Seldon, A., with Snowdon, P., and Collings, D. (2007) *Blair Unbound* (London: Simon & Schuster).

Shankill Mirror (2001–02) 'Dodds welcomes protest move', Christmas/January.

Shirlow, P. (2006) 'Segregation, ethno-sectarianism and the "new" Belfast', in M. Cox, A. Guelke and F. Stephen (eds) *A Farewell to Arms? Beyond the Good Friday Agreement* (Manchester: Manchester University Press).

Shirlow, P., and Shuttleworth, I. (1999) 'Who is going to toss the burgers? Social class and the reconstruction of the Northern Irish economy', *Capital and Class* 69, 27–46.

Shirlow, P., Tonge, J., McAuley, J. W., and McGlynn, C. (2010) *Abandoning Historical Conflict?* (Manchester: Manchester University Press).

Steiner, J. (1981) 'Research strategies beyond consociationalism', *Journal of Politics* 43, 1241–50.

Taylor, R. (2006) 'The Belfast Agreement and the politics of consociationalism: a critique', *Political Quarterly* 77:2, 217–26.

Taylor, R. (2009) 'The injustice of a consociational solution to the Northern Ireland problem', in R. Taylor (ed.) *Consocational Theory: McGarry, O'Leary and the Northern Ireland Conflict* (Abingdon: Routledge).

Teague, P. (1997) 'Catholics and Protestants in the Northern Ireland labour market. Why does one group perform better than the other?', *Economy and Society* 26:4, 560–78.

Tomlinson, J. (1997) 'Economic policy: lessons from past Labour governments', in B. Brivati and T. Bale (eds) *New Labour in Power: Precedents and Prospects* (London: Routledge).

Tonge, J. (1999) 'New packaging, Old Deal? New Labour and employment policy innovation', *Critical Social Policy* 19:2, 217–31.

West Belfast Taskforce and Greater Shankill Taskforce (2007) *Strategic Review and Stocktaking*, www.detini.gov.uk (accessed 10 March 2009).

Wincott, D. (2006) 'Social policy and social citizenship: Britain's welfare states', *Journal of Federalism* 36:1, 169–88.

Wolff, S. (2002) 'The peace process in Northern Ireland since 1998: success or failure of post-Agreement reconstruction?', *Civil Wars* 5:1, 87–116.

Woods, J. (2001) 'The civic forum', in R. Wilson (ed.) *Agreeing to Disagree? A Guide to the Northern Ireland Assembly* (Norwich: Stationery Office).

10

Colonising law for the poor: access to justice in the new regulatory state

Peter Sanderson and Hilary Sommerlad

Legal aid represents an interesting, if neglected, area of New Labour's policy agenda. Its significance derives not only from the fact that a disproportionate number of key figures in New Labour shadow and governmental posts earned their living from legal aid work in the 1980s and 1990s, but also from the fact that the development of policy in this area from 1995 onwards exemplifies the attempt to reconcile a discourse of social justice with the techniques of New Public Management (NPM) and the parallel discourse of commitment to the citizen as public service consumer.

This chapter will explore some of the resulting tensions in New Labour rhetoric and policy in this area. We will initially identify the ways in which legal aid could be seen to underpin the practical realisation of social justice and citizenship as envisaged by T. H. Marshall, before outlining the history of legal aid reform from 1995 onwards, culminating in the reforms which followed on from the Carter reviews of Legal Aid in 2006. In the course of this review we will explore the discursive properties of Ministerial statements and policy documents on legal aid, and the way in which the social construction of some legal aid clients and their lawyers as parasitical has been used to justify the transformation of the scheme. We will then identify ways in which the reforms have become increasingly influenced by conceptions of value for money and the demands of new regulatory state (Braithwaite, 2000). The consequent transformation which has been wrought in legal aid is, we would argue, inimical to the very ideals of social justice that New Labour politicians claimed to be promoting.

The chapter is a critical analysis of legal aid policy and discourse based on documentary and secondary sources. In addition, the authors have used data gathered in the course of a series of research projects on legal aid lawyers over the past decade (Sommerlad, 1999, 2001; Sommerlad and Sanderson, 2009, for accounts of methodology), including twelve interviews conducted by the authors specifically for this chapter with policy makers, national representatives of major advice agencies, representatives of legal aid practitioners, and partners in prominent legal aid specialist firms.

Publicly funded legal advice and representation have depended heavily on a supply base of committed solicitors and barristers working for substantially less than the large sums featuring in Ministerial statements and the front pages of popular newspapers, as well as the work of law centres and other not-for-profit (NFP) advice agencies. The development of the new form of regulation of the sector by means of cost control, contract and audit has 'colonised' the practice of legal aid lawyers in the manner identified by Michael Power (1997) in his analysis of the audit society: affected organisations begin to strive for the measurable goals imposed from outside, rather than the less tangible value-based goals (of which 'justice' is a good example) which were previously the focus of their activity. The consequent transformation of the values and practices of both individual practitioners and the organisations they work for has, we argue, had a deleterious effect on law work with the poor and socially excluded.

Legal aid as a cornerstone of citizenship

The lack of access to legal services in the 1920s to settle housing disputes and workers' accident claims prompted one of the founders of the 'Poor Man's Lawyer' movement to describe the rule of law as 'an anaemic attenuated make-believe which we flourish in the eyes of the poor as "justice"'.[1] Twenty-five years later T. H. Marshall made essentially the same point: 'the civil element [of citizenship] is composed of the rights necessary for individual freedom – liberty of the person, freedom of speech, thought and faith, the right to own property and to conclude valid contracts' and 'the right to justice. The last is of a different order from the others, because it is the right to defend and assert all one's rights on terms of equality with others and by due process of law' (1950, 10–11).

Not only are all other rights ultimately dependent on the right and ability to litigate (Cappelletti and Garth, 1981) on terms of equality with others, but the need of the disempowered for this right exceeds that of other citizens. In any society, poor people are more likely to get into trouble with the law, come into contact with state agencies, suffer violence and abuse, experience precarious and sometimes dangerous employment, live in poor-quality housing and be exploited by, for instance, private landlords. Further, as the Legal Services Research

Centre (LSRC) research into legal need and problem clusters has shown, civil justice problems are often both aspects of broader social, economic and health problems, and tend to compound such problems and cause new ones (Pleasence *et al.*, 2004; 2006) – for instance, poor people are more likely to suffer health problems, and an extensive body of research links this with civil law problems (e.g. BMA, 1998; Amato, 2000). These problems are also intimately connected with power imbalances. Two of the key dimensions of social inequality are lower levels of education and limited access to the skills and technologies which could assist in independent problem resolution, and research also suggests that the poor are more likely to feel powerless and not entitled to take action (Sandefur, 2007).

Further, access to justice has become more vital for poor people in the UK in recent decades as a result of the expansion of civil law rights and obligations related to, for example, children (Goriely, 1998), and because they have experienced the brunt of the restructuring of the economy and the related neo-liberal reconfiguration of the welfare state. As is well known, the Conservative administrations presided over a dramatic increase in poverty, and, whilst New Labour policies initially achieved a reduction in poverty, a report published by the Joseph Rowntree Foundation in 2009 (see Hills *et al.*, 2009) showed an increase in numbers of people in 'deep poverty', that is, below 40 per cent of the median. At the same time, the privatisation of large parts of state provision frequently included lighter regulation and entailed a corresponding privatisation of enforcement (Braithwaite, 2000) whilst the increased targeting of welfare increased the need for the vulnerable citizen to be able to dispute the ways in which discretion is exercised. Legal aid offers a means of combating what Colin Crouch has termed the 'degradation and residualisation of public services' (2001), of holding government to account, and challenging the stigmatisation of poverty. In addition, it is the last resort of those at the sharp end of the politicisation of the criminal justice system, and the elision between civil and criminal law, for example in antisocial behaviour legislation.

The case for providing universal access to legal advice and representation as a necessary corollary to the provision of public welfare goods and the objective of social justice is therefore a strong one, as was recognised by Tony Blair in 1996: 'legally enforceable rights and duties underpin a democratic society, and access to justice is essential to make these rights and duties real' (Bean, 1996, xiii). However, from the inception of the Legal Aid Scheme, the form of access that should be provided has been a matter of debate. On the one hand, providing state funding towards access to private solicitors' firms and barristers carries risks in terms of the development of what economists call 'moral hazard' (the danger that 'expert professionals' will use the inability of clients to assess the value of their services to extract an excessive rent from their professional licence) and politicians call a 'gravy train'. On the other, the provision of cheaper salaried services based on the American 'public defender' model appears to breach the principle that parties entering an adversarial legal system should do so on the basis of 'equality of arms'. This dilemma appears as a recurring theme throughout the history of legal aid.

The origins and expansion of legal aid, 1945–1986

As with other services which developed as bespoke products delivered by expensive professionals to a small number of private, monied clients, opening up legal services to the wider community generated difficult questions about the role of the professional, and in particular about who should administer these services and define their substance, quality, access to them and their cost. Marshall had envisaged a simplification of the processes of dispute resolution in the form of cheap, non-expert salaried advisers and the education of the ordinary citizen in the law, an option which was prefigured in the establishment of Citizens' Advice Bureau (CAB) legal advice sessions during the Second World War. But despite strong representations to the 1944 Rushcliffe Committee that the legal aid scheme should be based on such a salaried service and focused on housing, debt and benefit problems (Hynes and Robins, 2009), the committee decided in favour of the Law Society proposal for a 'judicare' scheme (Goriely, 1996, *passim*). Judicare was administered by the legal profession, and offered equal access to adversarial litigation processes, provided by solicitors in private practice, and barristers, who were paid on the basis of hourly rates with little control over quality or cost. This decision laid the ground for future public expenditure problems. It also skewed the scheme towards the interests of private solicitors, few of whom had either an interest or expertise in welfare problems: services available were therefore limited primarily to family law (and criminal defence). Where new services were established specifically to meet new legal needs, such as tribunals, no right to legal representation was granted.

By the late 1960s various factors coalesced to renew concern with access to justice. The community, anti-statist (and anti-professional) civil rights politics and new equality discourses of the time clearly identified the deficiencies in the paternalistic Beveridge welfare model and, in the case of legal aid, highlighted the failure of the scheme to serve impoverished and vulnerable communities. At the same time, the percentage of the population eligible for legal aid had fallen from nearly 80 per cent in 1949 to 40 per cent. One result was an increase in voluntary-sector involvement in tribunal representation and the provision of social welfare legal advice. The sector's strong emphasis on strategic solutions to poverty also fuelled recourse to public-law solutions. This policy work was reinforced by the political use the civil rights movement of the 1960s and 1870s made of the courts, and the related development of the law centre movement (Robins, 2008).

Together these developments contributed to an expansion of legal aid. In 1973 the 'Green Form Scheme' was introduced, enabling advisers to give advice or assistance on any matter of English law after the application of a simple means test (Hynes and Robins, 2009). In 1979 the Labour government raised eligibility levels so that 79 per cent of the population were entitled to legal aid. This period also saw the spread of law centres and the establishment of 'radical' solicitors' practices committed to a political use of law such as the judicial review of government and government agency decisions and the extension of legal regulation into such 'private' spheres as the family.

The reform programme: 1986 to the 2006 Carter Report and beyond

It is a commonplace that the expansion of social citizenship was largely halted with the election of a Conservative administration in 1979, the radical restructuring of the UK economy and the related crisis of welfare. The resulting reforms to legal aid, which began in 1986 with a cut in eligibility, largely parallel the NPM techniques applied to other areas of the public sector: a dual strategy of financial retrenchment and managerial control designed to produce cultural change which would, in turn, achieve both VFM for the taxpayer and improved quality for the consumer (Hood, 1991). These included the transfer of the legal aid scheme from the solicitors' profession to a government quango, Legal Aid Board (LAB), enacted by the Legal Aid Act 1988. Cost control was achieved through abolition of the link between legal aid fees and private fees, and reductions in scope (for instance, property and probate ceased to be matters for which a client could obtain legal aid) and eligibility. Levels of eligibility were further reduced in 1992/93 so that only 53 per cent of households could qualify for legal aid.

Control over professional work, cultural change and the quality of service delivery were addressed through the introduction of legal aid franchising. This (initially non-compulsory) system of quality assurance initiated the micro-regulation of professional work through management audits (by non-lawyers) of criminal and civil legal aid files against the transaction criteria which had been devised as proxy measures of the quality of substantive work (Sherr et al., 1994). The objective of making law firms more commercial was addressed by the requirement that firms must make annual business plans. The installation of an economic calculus to evaluate the justice system, in which law was therefore depicted as a product or service like any other, entailed only slight reference to access to justice (Smith, 1996) – instead the problem was represented as one of 'over-consumption of legality' (Abel, 2003: 287). In this consumerist discourse legal aid clients therefore figured as 'flawed consumers' (Bauman, 1997), 'abusers of the service' (Clarke, 2004), 'state-funded rotweillers' whose access to public funds placed opponents at an unfair disadvantage,[2] suggesting that the taxpayer was the real client. The narrative of the undeserving, frivolous legal aid litigant was complemented by a discourse of contempt for and mistrust of the legal aid practitioner, justifying the LAB's control over her. We discuss this discourse of contempt in greater detail below.

New Labour and the Access to Justice Act 1999
As in other areas of the public sector, New Labour's legal aid policy was more nuanced (Clarke, 2004), to the point of self-contradiction. On the one hand access to justice, a drive to raise quality, a focus on social welfare law, partnership with the voluntary sector[3] and a pervasive emphasis on the need to target social exclusion have been consistent themes. In 1999 this shift in emphasis resulted in the Access to Justice Act (AJA), which replaced the Legal Aid Board with the Legal Services Commission (LSC) as the quango overseeing the administration of legal aid funding. It also established the Criminal Defence Service (CDS) and the Community Legal Service (CLS). The CLS represented an attempt to integrate legal aid firms with generalist and specialist legal advice services, and general advice services into regional 'seamless webs', leading in 1999 to the establishment of Community Legal Service Partnerships (CLSPs). The policy change is also evident in the formidable body of research conducted by the LSRC into the extent of 'justiciable problems' (Pleasence et al., 2004, 2006) and concern with the role of 'unmet legal need' in the persistence of social exclusion (DCA/LCF, 2001, 2004).[4] This research provided an underpinning methodology for the LSC's allocation of resources designed to meet key welfare law needs in areas such as housing and community care, and to develop innovative projects such as the Money Advice Pilot.

However, these developments did not solve the issue of access. The dilemma over whether legal aid provides access just to a 'service', or to a just outcome to a cause, remains significant, in part because in other ways New Labour policy can be viewed as a continuation and development of Conservative initiatives. For instance, the AJA removed some civil legal aid cases, notably personal injury claims, from the scheme and effectively replaced their funding by Conditional Fee Arrangements (CFAs),[5] and whilst this measure was presented as increasing access to justice, insurance premiums excluded the poorest in society.[6] In addition, the legislation strengthened NPM controls over the suppliers of legal aid services and laid the basis for a system of contracts which would replace franchising, and would control the unit cost of cases and the number of cases suppliers could take on. The continuing drive to contain costs also resulted in a tightening up of the merits test which all applications for legal aid must pass, and the introduction of a hard cap on civil legal aid expenditure. Together these measures replaced an entitlement to civil legal aid services by a 'scheme of prioritising cases and resources (rationing) as a way of meeting the needs of the general public within a limited budget' (Moorhead, 2001: 550; Sommerlad, 1999). As a result, New Labour policy increased the emphasis on the 'responsibilitisation' of the individual: through the provision of advice and information about legal problems (LCD/LCF, 2001) by, for instance, the Commmunity Legal Advice Web site (Legal Services Commission, 2009) it was hoped that individuals would be able to understand and solve their legal problems by themselves.

The verdict on the AJA by one expert commentator on legal aid was damning:

> The 1949 Act was an opening of the door to justice for citizens. The 1999 Act has in effect erected a large notice over that door entitled 'Restricted Entry ... The truth is that the Government's reforms spring not from a desire to improve access to justice but from the Treasury's need to control the budget. The entire new system flows from the decision to cap the budget. (Zander, 2000)

The conclusion that the imposition of a hard cap would 'infect the whole enterprise' appears to have been borne out by subsequent developments. The continuing rise in the cost of criminal legal aid,[7] and of some civil cases, most notably immigration, produced a crisis in the CLS, the abolition of CLSPs and the commissioning of a series of reviews of the legal aid scheme.[8]

The Carter Report
These developments culminated in the decision to commission Lord Carter of Coles to review legal aid, and in particular criminal legal aid

(Carter, 2006), with the aim, as Lord Falconer argued, of forcing criminal practitioners 'to restructure . . . [to] get more control over the costs of provision' (Hynes and Robins, 2009). However, the disproportionate impact which Carter's proposals would have had on firms run by black and minority ethnic (BME) practitioners (MDA, 2006) led to its rejection by the then Minister.

Instead it was decided to impose aspects of Carter's recommendations on law firms and the NFP sector with a contract for civil legal aid, despite the fact that no research had been conducted into how this would impact on them. The resulting 'route map' for civil legal aid work produced by the LSC in 2008 (in *Focus*, LSC, 2008) introduced the following measures: fixed or graduated fees for a substantial part of civil work, a unified contract for all work, and Best Value Tendering for bulk contracts (limited to £25 or £50,000).[9] The impact of the Carter reforms on the character of legal aid provision is discussed in detail later in this chapter: the burden of our argument is that they represented the culmination of a process whereby cost containment strategies, combined with micro-management of legal aid transactions, impacted negatively on access to quality legal advice.

A further development in legal advice services was the establishment of Community Legal Advice Centres (CLACs) and Networks (CLANs), which, it was argued, would improve access to justice by providing a 'one-stop shop' responsive to local needs (LSC, 2005).[10] The proposals have been criticised on the grounds of insufficient funding, the level of quality of service they will be held to, the difficulties monopoly suppliers face in dealing with conflicts of interest between clients and their lack of independence from local authorities (Griffith, 2008).

Before discussing the impact of the post-1997 legal aid policy agenda we will explore the way in which New Labour politicians have provided a discursive justification of their strategy through a specific framing of the 'problem' of legal aid, and the character of legal aid practitioners.

Fat cats on a gravy train: the discourse of contempt

The ambivalence of New Labour policy on the form and delivery of legal aid has been matched by the character of the public announcements by Ministers responsible for legal aid. New Labour's public stances on legal aid have been characterised by twin binary oppositions. The first counterposes 'fat cat' lawyers to the taxpayer who funds their alleged excesses, while the second counterposes the 'vulnerable' who are 'most in need' of legal aid on the one hand to the undeserving and dangerous legal aid applicants, and the vexatious and litigious champions of the 'compensation culture', on the other. In 2003 the then Home Secretary, David Blunkett, was reported on the BBC giving his full backing to Tony Blair's promise to cut public spending on what he called the legal aid 'gravy train':

> On Thursday, the day of his speech to the Labour Party conference, Mr Blunkett told BBC Radio 4's Today programme the public would be 'horrified' if it knew the way asylum appeals were over-used and 'the way in which lawyers make a lot of money out of it'. (BBC, 2003)

In a competition for resources, asylum seekers struggle to achieve public support and credibility, and as a result the wave of reform of the asylum system ushered in by the Asylum and Immigration Act 2004 not only included faster removal powers and a reduction in the appeal rights of asylum seekers, but also a reduction in the length of time that legally aided immigration advisers were permitted to spend on a case, from forty hours to five (Burnett, 2008). The Lord Chancellor's response to anxiety about the consequences of this reduction was to claim that he was 'absolutely determined to ensure that the money that is spent, is spent on those who actually need the help' (Burnett, 2008), without explaining how the distinction could be made between the needy and the rest.

The implicit distinction between the deserving and undeserving recipient of legal aid was evident in the justifications offered by the Labour government for the fixed-price tendering introduced following the Carter review of procurement. Announcing the implementation of the fixed-cost case approach, the Legal Aid Minister, Vera Baird, stressed that 'in order to sustain the best-resourced legal aid system in the world we must make sure we get the best value from it. That is the only way to ensure that *those who need it most*, vulnerable people suffering from family and social welfare problems, can be sure it is there for them' (Ministry of Justice, 2007, our emphasis)

The overarching frame for legal aid discourse has been to identify expenditure on it as 'a problem'. Thus, in announcing the Carter review, Lord Falconer announced that he was 'determined to tackle the problem of legal aid' (BBC, 2007). The problem was identified as both the overall expenditure figure and also the fact of it being a larger figure per head of population than in other countries. However, whereas increasing expenditure on health, education and even prisons (see Gibb, 2008) was regarded as praiseworthy, expenditure on legal aid was presented as excessive and unacceptable. As Lord Chancellor in the Brown administration Jack Straw also identified the growth of the profession as a problem. In the course of one sentence he managed simultaneously to identify the binary opposition between lawyer and taxpayer and to use health and education as a contrasting, meritorious object of public spending: 'There are now three times as many lawyers in private practice but paid for by the taxpayer as there were three decades ago: the budget has grown faster than the health and education services' (cited in Gibb, 2008). Another aspect of Straw's verbal assault on lawyers concerned the success fees involved in civil litigation under the CFA arrangements, the very fees which he was responsible for introducing, as a substitute for legally aided civil litigation, during his time as Home Secretary. He told the *Daily Mail* that he had instructed 'the services I control to be much tougher on compensation claims, such as for injuries at work' (cited in Brogan, 2009).

As well as drawing a line between the deserving and undeserving applicant for legal aid, New Labour's rhetorical stance sought to move away from outcome-based conceptions of legal advice to a model where the key measurement was of procedural quality, and where advice was conceived of in units, so that success was measured in terms of volumes of advice units offered. In response to a critical article in the *Guardian* in 2008 the Legal Aid Minister, Lord Hunt, cited the fact that 'the LSC funded 800,000 acts of civil and family assistance, up by a third within two years' (Hunt, 2008): this figure, however, failed to distinguish a hit on an advice Web site from a matter followed through to a successful conclusion through representation in a court or tribunal. The sentiment of many practitioners is that this transmogrification of legal aid undermined its core purpose of providing access to justice, and we explore the impact of the reforms further in the following section.

Colonisation and attrition: the effects of change

In his discussion of the impact of auditing practice Power refers to the colonisation process, whereby 'the values and practices which make auditing possible penetrate deep into the core of organisational operations . . . in the creation over time of new mentalities, new incentives and perceptions of significance' (1997: 97). We would argue that colonisation has taken two forms. Firstly, the form of contractual regulation applied to legal advice provision in the last decade has radically circumscribed the capacity of legal advisers to make autonomous decisions about the amount of time and degree of expertise which they apply to particular cases: a process we have reported elsewhere (Sommerlad and Sanderson, 2009).The result has been precisely to create new mentalities, incentives and perceptions of significance.

Secondly, the use of procurement policies to transform the supplier base has had complex effects. Committed legal aid specialists concentrated in the 'high street' medium-size practice have found it difficult to remain viable, and independent advice agencies, such as Citizens' Advice, have become increasingly dependent on LSC funding for their specialist advice provision, in such a way as to significantly transform their approach to their avowed mission. This section explores the impact of the Carter reforms in the light of these two forms of colonisation.

The immediate reaction to the LSC's proposals for change post-Carter was that they would exacerbate supplier attrition, encourage 'cherrypicking' and result in poorer-quality service, especially for the most vulnerable (Law Society, 2006). For instance, Burke Niazi Solicitors' response to the LSC consultation on Carter (LSC, 2006a) detailed the losses (around 50 per cent in most categories) which fixed fees would entail and argued:

> the scheme you propose will prejudice vulnerable and disabled clients, especially those with mental difficulties, most of whom we represent, as their cases take longer to prepare . . . [it] will [also] discriminate against clients from minority ethnic groups where language barriers often mean it takes twice as long to prepare and advise on their cases. (Mental Health Lawyers' Association, 2006)

The link between attrition, cherrypicking and poor quality is implicit in these comments; however, for the sake of clarity we will discuss them separately.

Attrition

Access to justice depends on a healthy supplier base, but even prior to Carter there had been increasing concern about 'advice deserts' (Sandbach, 2004). Over the years the sector has suffered from low morale for a variety of reasons, including the administrative burden entailed in legal aid work and the discourse of contempt discussed above. Both law firms and agencies have therefore found it increasingly difficult to recruit (Sommerlad, 2001; Sommerlad and Sanderson, 2009), and there has been a steady decline in legal aid providers; for instance, the numbersof solicitors' offices holding a CLS contract went from 4,932 in 2001–02 to 3,632 in 2005–06 (Law Society, 2007). The HoCCA expressed grave concern that fixed fees would exacerbate this situation, given the very precarious financial position of many civil legal aid suppliers, and the fact that the fees are frequently considerably lower than many firms' tailored fixed fees, which were based on their average cost in handling particular categories of cases. For instance in one firm the fixed fee for housing was £174, whereas the tailored fixed fee had been £540.

It appears clear that the predicted contraction in the supplier base is taking place: 2006–07 the numbers of solicitors' offices holding a CLS contract declined to 3,437[11] and the Law Society Legal Aid spokesman stated that significant withdrawal from the CLS was taking place in rural areas such as the North West, Kent and East Anglia, where:

> there is probably only a relatively small amount of legal aid work and therefore the costs of maintaining a contract to do it – all the administration the LSC demands – becomes disproportionate and so other departments put pressure on those doing legal aid work to give it up.

Attrition of the supply base is not, however, limited to rural areas. For instance, Lambeth has seen a 50 per cent reduction in the number of law firms undertaking social welfare law through legal aid from twenty five in 2005 to thirteen in 2008, and there is no longer any firm offering legally aided employment law. Nor is attrition limited to solicitor providers; law centres and other NFP agencies have closed, or ceased to hold CLS contracts.[12] As Richard Jenner, Director of the Advice Services Alliance (ASA), observed, 'agencies that are geared towards doing straightforward cases will be fine. Our concern is that those agencies that undertake complex cases and /or cases for clients with language difficulties, disabilities or other special needs are going to struggle' (Hynes and Robins, 2009). It is predicted that the combined effect of the unified contract and the introduction of CLACs and CLANs will lead to more closures.

A managing partner of a firm in a large town in the north of England gave the following account of the impact of fixed fees on family law work:

> take stand-alone divorces, we used to get £220 and VAT, whereas now it's £197 and VAT; we only do around fifty a year of these, as it's unusual for people to just want a divorce with no other issues, but for a firm like this that loss shaves away at profit margins which are already so slim

and as a result:

> for the first time we've decided not to bid for the LSC grant-aided training contracts because I felt that I couldn't commit myself to that time because the financial situation is so precarious.

Her subsequent explanation for why the firm did do stand-alone divorces – 'because, as with all these matters, people's problems are intertwined' points to the multiplier effect of attrition in single special-isms. Similarly, another practitioner spoke of the difficulties the decline in housing lawyers posed for her clients who had suffered domestic vio-lence, but explained that her firm had been obliged to withdraw from housing because:

> our housing worker left and we couldn't replace her because you must have an experienced person because otherwise you need someone to supervise her but then you can't afford to pay an experienced person because of the low level of the fixed fee. There are now only three firms in —— [large northern city] doing legally aided housing work.

The managing partner of a legal aid firm in London described provision there as

> very fragile, like a patchwork quilt – lawyers refer clients to other provid-ers in the borough and beyond – you tinker with this at your peril . . . but they [the LSC] want to spend less on cases in London – yet it's in London that there is massive unmet need – as their own studies have shown.

He continued:

> for every civil/ family case we take on we turn away at least seven, because despite the fact that we are a large firm we do not have the capacity to take on all these cases.

All respondents spoke of the effect of attrition on the clients, who (in the words of one practitioner) 'circulate round and round as many sup-pliers as they can to see if someone can take them on – we know that because we get people who've been round to many firms before coming to us – and in the end they give up'. An informant from an NFP agency spoke of the very great difficulties she now encountered in finding a solicitor to do injunctions for battered women clients, and correspond-ingly a family lawyer said that she was sometimes overwhelmed by requests for this service. As another spokesperson pointed out, this 'shrinking and increasingly concentrated sector assumes that people will travel for help yet of course we're talking of clients who are least likely to be able to travel – i.e. have no money, no transport, problems of getting child care, etc.'

Cherrypicking
As the above comments indicate, the imposition of 'average costs per case for everybody, taking no account of whether you serve par-ticularly vulnerable communities', generates an economic logic which effectively dictates 'cherrypicking'. As a result, the following comment

was typical: 'many firms get clients whose first language is not English and for whom the particular firm is not their first port of call – they're being shunted round London – 70 per cent of social welfare clients are BME'. As the witnesses to HoCCA and responses to the LSC consultation explained, such clients generally demand more time, and the difficulties of successfully justifying the extra work incentivises cherrypicking:

> It's impossible to complete a case under the fixed fee and difficult cases therefore entail a great deal of worry as to whether you will get paid for the work you do at all, and mean you under time-record for the work you do out of fear that if the case becomes an exceptional claim (i.e. 3 times the fixed fee, entitling you to a detailed assessment of the file to see if you should be paid the full amount for the hours you have done, as under the old system) your costs will be down assessed by the LSC on the basis that it has taken you too long to do the work. This happened to quite a few of my exceptional claims in the Housing department and I had to spend hours and hours of non-chargeable time making appeal submissions to the LSC'

A managing partner spelled out the links between the financial impact on his firm of the fee structure and cherrypicking:

> we are only expected to submit exceptional claims in about 20 per cent of cases [therefore] we are effectively regularly doing large amounts of *pro bono* work on our cases, producing a loss in income to the firm of £150,000 for doing the same work, seeing the same clients, at the same quality level before fixed fees were introduced.

He went on to say that this sum represented about 3 per cent of the firm's total income, the equivalent of half the annual profit of the firm, and that this loss was therefore obliging the firm to 'filter out more cases that are likely to exceed the fixed fee level but not get into the exceptional category.' As a result, this firm used a paralegal who was doing her LPC part-time to operate its own triage service, to 'filter the work effectively'.

Another solicitor explained that the fee structure meant that her firm no longer took any homelessness cases, as these always required more than the three hours' work allowed for by the fixed fee. A trainee solicitor described how the immigration department of her (highly respected) legal aid firm cherrypicked cases:

> we have far more referrals than we can take on, so we constantly – daily – turn down a lot of cases, but when there is capacity the solicitor will look for a 'legacy case' – where we are able to avoid the fixed fee because the client initially made a claim before that date. These cases are particularly

challenging and the clients in more need of expert specialist legal advice because the history of their asylum cases here needs untangling and explaining . . . we get a lot of these referrals. That makes it difficult to judge how many of the post-1/10/07 cases we turn down directly as a result of the fixed fee. But I know that it's an incentive for avoiding such cases, and as there's so much unmet legal need, and so many legacy cases, it is not too difficult to avoid them for now. However, a lot of solicitors do fear for the future of the immigration department in this firm and immigration solicitors in general, and how we will be able to give diagnostic legal help level advice once the legacy cases have run out.

A spokesperson for the ASA expressed concern about the low take-up by advice agencies of the provision for the payment of exceptional cases, 'given that the fixed fee scheme has been running for over a year now – that suggests cherrypicking – i.e. that a lot of providers are not doing any difficult cases'. As he went on to reflect, however, it could also mean that 'maybe [some] people are getting a poorer service because they are having less time spent on their cases . . .' Other respondents also expressed concern that the logic of the reforms dictated that the quality of advice would suffer, and some alleged that the focus on cost meant that the LSC was no longer concerned about quality, and that this was evidenced by the lowering of contracting standards:

> there are five levels . . . you had to score 2 (competence plus) to get into the Preferred Supplier Pilot Scheme but now . . . all you need for any of the LSC contracts. is a 3 (competent) . . . because the LSC doesn't want to pay for 1 and 2. The thing is if you score 1 or 2 then it's likely that your average costs will be higher because there's a clear link . . . between the quality of work and the amount of time spent. (Moorhead, 2001)

The LSC specification of particular combinations of categories of work which must be bid for, the minimum limits on the size of contracts and the low fees pose an immediate threat to both the supply base and the quality of service, since this favours large firms and agencies able to do high-volume routine work. It correspondingly poses difficulties for many smaller agencies and firms, especially those committed to specialist and /or high-quality work, including a disproportionate number of BME firms whose main clientele tends to be BME. At the same time it was also predicted that the failure, when fixing the fees, to take account of the client base of particular firms or agencies would cause practitioners who specialised in complex cases to 'leave, retire and not be replaced, and, increasingly, we will have all the parties represented by non-specialist solicitors' (Professor Masson to HoCCA: 4). As a result the managing partner of a well respected legal aid practice said, 'effec-

tively what we are seeing is the rise of legal aid factories like —— and
—— [two large firms known to employ large numbers of paralegals]
in the form of both qualified legal executives and unqualified clerks, at
low rates of pay)'.

Deteriorating service

Thus, just as cherrypicking is ineluctably linked to fixed fees, so too
is the quality of service. A firm which consistently scored high in peer
review and is named as one of the pre-eminent law firms in the country
for education had had a tailored fixed fee for educational cases, including special needs tribunal cases, of £1,092, which, the managing
partner of the firm argued, reflected both their clients' needs and the
level of expertise and work they put into such cases; the fixed fee for
the work is £302. In his words, when the LSC introduced fixed fees 'all
the quality stuff went out of the window, because they're now explicitly going for the lowest common denominator'. As a result, as mental
health specialists Burke Niazi Solicitors make clear, it seems likely that
many of the providers who leave the scheme will be those who deliver
a high-quality service:

> you will be driving out the quality solicitors who put so much time and
> effort into their cases, particularly those who have strived to enhance
> their qualifications by getting on to the various panels of the Law Society
> and other professional bodies.

Conclusion

As we noted at the beginning of this chapter, equality of access to effective legal advice and representation is a cornerstone of a Marshallian
model of social and political citizenship. This is because the law is an
essential resource for the powerful – for the state in refusing entry to
asylum seekers,[13] in attempting to reduce antisocial behaviour and in
its expenditure on welfare benefits; to landlords and lenders in recover-
ing assets; and to employers in disposing of unwanted employees – and
there may be few limits to the amount that these powerful actors are
prepared to spend on maximising the possibility of achieving a result in
their favour.[14] In an adversarial system it is frequently the case that the
defendants or respondents are both ignorant of the law and lack any
corresponding resources to defend themselves – in fact they may often
be ignorant even of their right to do so. Flawed though it has been, and
tainted by its association with the socio-economic inequality which the
law implicitly endorses, legal aid nevertheless was a signifier that poor

people's problems were as important as those of the powerful. A rhetorical commitment to the cause of the socially excluded was a persistent theme in New Labour's policy portfolio from the mid-1990s onwards, and this commitment provided the background rationale for many of the post-1998 reforms to Legal Aid.

The significance of the legal aid reform programme over the past two decades is not simply in the way it has narrowed eligibility,[15] stigmatised legal aid lawyers and increased the difficulty of accessing local assistance, but also in its introduction of a calculus which has served to diminish that importance. By 2010 the Labour government legal aid policy was in effect saying that poor people's problems could be worth only two or three hours of a paralegal's time, and no more.[16]

The *reductio ad absurdum* of this paradigm is the public trumpeting of hits on legal advice Web sites or initial diagnostic phone advice as constituting an increase in access to justice, when it is impossible to gauge not merely whether any individual hit or piece of phone advice has resulted in a just outcome but also whether the 'client' has even understood the 'advice'.[17] This approach elides the distinction between the provision of a service and the achievement of a just outcome.

This reduction of civil legal aid to 'largely a *sink service* for people on means-tested benefits' (Hynes and Robins, 2009, our emphasis) corresponds to Crouch's characterisation of the neo-liberal reforms as involving the residualisation, distortion and degradation of public-sector services. It is ironic that as the dominance of the neo-liberal paradigm is challenged by its manifest failure in the economic sphere its legacy should be in part the erosion of the last legal resort of the predictable victims of that failure.

Notes

1 Gurney-Champion (1926: 21), cited in Hynes and Robins (2009).
2 Under-Secretary at the Lord Chancellor's Department Gary Streeter, who consistently deployed stigma as a strategic weapon in the attack on legal aid: 'Streeter confirms legally aided litigants are rottweilers', (1996) *New Law Journal*, 1378.
3 A pilot project with forty-two voluntary advice agencies, begun by Lord Irvine, grew to over 400 by 2002–03 (see Sommerlad and Sanderson, 2009).
4 Further work by the LSRC, referred to in the Introduction, delineated the interrelated and consequently complex character of the 'clusters' of legal problems faced by poor people.
5 CFAs had been brought in through the Courts and Legal Services Act 1990; see Yarrow and Abrams (1999).

6 At the time, the Legal Action Group (LAG) estimated that 'as much as £100 million in compensation would be lost by 75,000 people whose cases were currently funded by legal aid' (in Hynes and Robins, 2009).

7 The period between when Labour came to power and 2005 had seen a 37 per cent increase in criminal legal aid. Although this was in large part due to government policy (Orchard, Legal Action June 2003: 7, cited in Hynes and Robins, 2009), the Treasury had set a ceiling of £2 billion on legal aid expenditure.

8 This brief account telescopes a number of important developments which contributed to the eventual commissioning of the Carter Review, including personnel changes within both the Lord Chancellor's Department and the LSC, independent research which revealed CLSPs to be ineffective, largely due to under-resourcing, leading to gaps in provision; vulnerable to government policy changes and cash demands of CDS (Matrix Report, 2004).

9 This is a very broad-brush outline of what has been an extremely complex development involving judicial reviews of LSC proposals, negotiations with the various stakeholders in the CLS and the phased introduction of different parts of the proposals.

10 CLACs and CLANs connect with the recognition as a result of the LSRC work of the interconnected nature of poor people's problems; the LSC has described its objectives in establishing them as 'tackling disadvantage and promoting social inclusion; delivering legal advice services to local communities according to local needs and priorities; providing quality integrated legal advice services ranging from basic information to representation in court, which offer value for money and are supported by co-ordinated funding'.

11 The LSC has not released the figures for 2007–08.

12 The NFP providers holding a CLS contract had risen from 389 in 2001–02 to 469. However, by 2007 the number had declined to 458.

13 The extension and democratisation of the law – due in large part to legal aid – has led to its increasing use to challenge state power (Bondy and Sunkin, 2008), often on behalf of unpopular causes. When the cutbacks in welfare lead to legally aided challenges against government agencies, and when legal aid is used to fund judicial reviews of Ministers' decisions about, for instance, asylum seekers, it seems plausible to argue that the legal aid scheme may be a relatively popular target amongst Ministers: see, for example, the assertion by Phil Woolas, the Home Office Minister responsible for immigration, that a successful appellant to the Immigration Appeals Tribunal had 'no right to be in this country' and that immigration lawyers and charities were 'playing the system' (Barkham, 2008).

14 When challenged about whether the expenditure of £8,000 on prosecuting a man for gesturing at police officers through a car window was an appropriate use of public funds, the Crown Prosecution Service responded that 'at no point is cost a factor because we don't put a price on justice' (Savill, 2008).

15 Eligibility has declined from 52 per cent in 1998 to, in 2007, in the words of one respondent, 'the 29 per cent who are the poorest in society, who operate in a marginalised twilight zone'.

16 This implicit devaluation of the legal aid client and her problems necessarily entails a devaluation of her lawyer. So we have a nexus – cheap lawyers for cheap people producing substandard product. This has resulted in the delegation of legal aid work to least-cost labour, that is, to the least experienced practitioners, and this is now explicitly endorsed by LSC; yet the combination of social and legal need and the disadvantage of clients can often accentuate the complexity of poor people's problems.

17 One practitioner described this 'service' in the following way: 'It's an upfront diagnostic service rolled out by a few large organisations, some of which are not law firms . . . so what you get effectively is poor-quality initial advice which is not solicitor-led. For instance, —— have been advertising for case workers at £16,000 per annum, "no legal experience required" . . .'

Bibliography

Abel, R. (1985) 'Law without politics: legal aid under advanced capitalism', *UCLA Law Review* 32, 474–642.

Abel, R. (2003) *English Lawyers between Market and State* (Oxford: Oxford University Press).

Amato, P. R. (2000) 'The consequences of divorce for adults and children', *Journal of Marriage and the Family* 62:4, 1269–87.

Barkham, P. (2008) 'Asylum-seeker charities are just playing the system, says Woolas', *Guardian*, 18 November.

Bauman, Z. (1997) *Postmodernity and its Discontents* (New York: New York University Press).

BBC (2003) *Asylum legal aid under threat*, www. news.bbc.co.uk/2/hi/uk_news/3158266.stm (accessed 26 May 2006).

BBC (2007) *Falconer details legal aid plan*, 5 July, available on //news.bbc.co.uk/1/hi/uk/4652019.stm (accessed 20 January10).

Bean, D., ed. (1996) *Law Reform for All* (London: Blackstone Press).

Blair, T. (1996) 'Foreword', in D. Bean (ed.) *Law Reform for All* (London: Blackstone Press).

Bondy, V., and Sunkin, M. (2008) 'Accessing judicial review', *Public Law*, winter: 647–67.

Braithwaite, J. (2008) 'The new regulatory state and the transformation of criminology', *British Journal of Criminology* 40:2, 222–38.

British Medical Association (1998) *Domestic Violence: a Healthcare Issue?* (London: British Medical Association).

British Medical Association (2003) *Housing and Health: Building for the Future* (London: British Medical Association).

Brogan, B. (2009) 'Jack Straw reveals: why I want to change the law', *Mailonline*, www.dailymail.co.uk/news/article-1092695 (accessed 24 February 2009).

Buck, A., Balmer, N., and Pleasence, P. (2005) 'Social exclusion and civil law experience of civil law justice problems among vulnerable groups', *Social Policy and Administration* 39:3, 302–22.

Burnett, J. (2008) 'No access to justice: legal aid and destitute asylum seekers', PARFRAS Briefing Paper 3 (Leeds: Positive Action for Refugees and Asylum Seekers).

Cappelletti, M., and Garth, B. (1981) 'Access to justice as a focus of research', *Windsor Year Book Access Justice* 1:1, x–xxv.

Clarke, J. (2004) 'Dissolving the public realm? The logics and limits of neo-liberalism', *Journal of Social Policy* 33:1, 27–48.

Crouch, C. (2001) 'Citizenship and markets in recent British educational policy', in C. Crouch, K. Eder and D. Tambini (eds) *Citizenship, Markets and the State* (Oxford: Oxford University Press).

Department for Constitutional Affairs/Law Centres Federation (2001) *Legal and Advice Services: A Pathway out of Social Exclusion* (London: DCA Corporate Communications).

Department for Constitutional Affairs/Law Centres Federation (2004) *Legal and Advice Services: A Pathway to Regeneration* (London: DCA Corporate Communications).

Gibb, F. (2008) 'Jack Straw takes lawyers to task for their fees', *Times online*, www businesstimesonline.co.uk/tol/business/law (accessed 20 January 2010).

Goriely, T. (1996) 'Law for the poor: the relationship between advice agencies and solicitors in the development of poverty law', *International Journal of the Legal Profession* 3:1–2, 214–48.

Goriely, T. (1998) 'Making the welfare state work', in F. Regan, A. Paterson, T. Goriely and D. Fleming (eds) *The Transformation of Legal Aid* (Oxford: Oxford University Press).

Goswami, N. (2008) 'Twenty years of the lawyer: legal aid', *Lawyer*, 17 November.

Griffith, A. (2008) *CLACs: are they worth it?* (London: Advice Services Alliance).

Habermas, J. (1987) *The Theory of Communicative Action*, Vol. II, *Lifeworld and System: a Critique of Functionalist Reason* (Boston MA: Beacon Press).

Held, D. (1995) *Democracy and the Global Order* (Cambridge: Polity Press).

Hills, J., Sefton, T., and Stewart, C. (2009) *Poverty, Inequality and Policy*, report by the Joseph Rowntree Foundation, York, www.jrf.org.uk/sites/files/jrf/poverty-policy-inequality.pdf (accessed 23 April 2009).

Hood, C. (1991) 'A public management for all seasons', *Public Administration* 69:1, 3–19.

House of Commons Constitutional Affairs Committee (2007) *Civil Legal Aid* (London: Stationery Office).

Hunt, P. (2008) 'There's no crisis. Our legal aid system is the best funded in the world', *Guardian*, 10 January, www.guardian.co.uk (accessed 24 February 2009).

Hynes, S., and Robins, J. (2009) *The Justice Gap: Whatever happened to Legal Aid?* (London: Legal Action Group).

Law Society (2006) *What Price Justice?* (London: Law Society).

Law Society (2007) *Fact Sheet: Statistics for England and Wales*, 24 August, www.research.lawsociety.org.uk (accessed 9 November 2008)

Legal Services Commission (2005) *Making Legal Rights a Reality: Our strategy for the LSC* (London: Legal Services Commission).

Legal Services Commission (2006a) *Legal Aid: a Sustainable Future* (London: Legal Services Commission).

Legal Services Commission (2006b) *Legal Aid Reform: the Way Ahead* (London: Legal Services Commission).

Legal Services Commission (2008) 'Civil route map', *Focus* 58 (London: Legal Services Commission), www.legalservices.gov.uk (accessed 24 January 2009).

Legal Services Commission (2009) *Community Legal Advice*, www.community legaladvice.org.uk (accessed 24 January 2009).

Lord Carter of Coles (2006) *Legal Aid: A Market-based Approach to Reform* (London: Ministry of Justice).

Marshall, T. H. (1950) *Citizenship and Social Class* (Cambridge: Cambridge University Press).

Matrix Consultancy (2004) *The Independent Review of the Community Legal Service* (London: Department of Constitutional Affairs).

MDA (2006) *Research on Ethnic Diversity amongst Suppliers of Legal Aid Services.*

Mental Health Lawyers' Association (2006) Response of Burke Niazi Solicitors to the Carter proposals, www.mhla.co.uk/modules/smartsection/item.php?itemid=152 (accessed 10 July 2010).

Ministry of Justice (2007) 'Legal aid reform is about helping as many people as possible', press release, www.justice.gov.uk/news/newsrelease220607c.htm (accessed 10 July 2010).

Moorhead, R. (2001) 'Third Way regulation? Community legal service partnerships', *Modern Law Review* 64:4, 543–62.

Moorhead, R., Sherr, A., Webley, L., Rogers, S., Sherr, L., Paterson, A., and Domberger, S. (2001) *Quality and Cost: Final Report on the contracting of Civil, Non-family Advice and Assistance Pilot* (London: Community Legal Service).

Pleasence, P., Balmer, N. J., Buck, A., Smith, M., and Patel, A. (2006) 'Mounting problems: further evidence of the social, economic and health consequences of civil justice problems', in P. Pleasence, A. Buck and N. Balmer (eds) *Transforming Lives and Social Process* (London: Legal Services Commission).

Pleasence, P., Buck, A., Balmer, N. J., O'Grady, A., Genn, H., and Smith, M. (2004) *Causes of Action: Civil Law and Social Justice* (London: Stationery Office).

Power, M. (1997) *The Audit Society* (Oxford: Oxford University Press).

Robins, J. (2008) 'Shifting sands', *Law Society Gazette*, www.lawgazette.co.uk/features/shifting-sands-1 (accessed 25 March 2009).

Sandbach, J. (2004) 'Geography of Advice', paper presented to fifth international LSRC conference, 'Social Exclusion: a Role for Law'.

Sandefur, R. L. (2006) 'The importance of doing nothing: everyday problems and responses of inaction', in P. Pleasence, A. Buck and N. Balmer (eds) *Transforming Lives and Social Process* (London, Legal Services Commission).

Sandefur, R. L. (2007) 'Lawyers' *pro bono* service and American-style civil legal assistance', *Law and Society Review*, 41:1, 79–112.

Savill, R. (2008) '£7,000 spent prosecuting man who raised finger at police', *Daily Telegraph*, 8 September.

Sherr, A., Moorhead, R., and Paterson, A. (1994) *Lawyers: The Quality Agenda*, Vol. I, *Assessing and Developing Competence and Quality in Legal Aid: the Report of the Birmingham Franchising Pilot* (London: HMSO).

Smith, R. (1996) *Achieving Civil Justice: Appropriate Dispute Resolution for the 1990s* (London: Legal Action Group).

Sommerlad, H. (1999) 'The implementation of quality initiatives and New Public Management in the legal aid sector in England and Wales: bureaucratisation, stratification and surveillance', *International Journal of the Legal Profession* 6, 311–43.

Sommerlad, H. (2001) '"I've lost the plot": an everyday story of the "political" legal aid lawyer', *Journal of Law and Society* 28, 335–60.

Sommerlad, H., and Sanderson, P. (2009) *Training and Regulating those Providers of publicly funded Legal Advice Services: a Case Study of Civil Provision* (London: Ministry of Justice).

Yarrow, S., and Abrams, P. (1999) *Nothing to lose? Clients' Experiences of Conditional Fees* (London: University of Westminster).

Zander, M. (2000) 'Justice and access to justice', in M. Zander, *The State of Justice: the Fifty-first*, the Hamlyn Lectures (London: Sweet & Maxwell).

Statutes

Access to Justice Act 1999
Courts and Legal Services Act 1990
Legal Aid and Advice Act 1949
Legal Aid Act 1988

Glossary of terms

AJA Access to Justice Act 1999, the first major reforming Act of the 1997 administration in the field of legal aid. It established the Legal Services Commission as the body which administers legal aid, and the Community Legal Service and Criminal Defence Service.

ASA Advice Services Alliance, a national umbrella body for independent advice providers.

BME black and minority ethnic.

CAB Citizens' Advice Bureau.

CLAC Community Legal Advice Centre.

CLAN Community Legal Advice Network.

CLS Community Legal Service.

CLSP Community Legal Service Partnership.

CFA contingency fee arrangement, or 'no win, no fee' agreement, introduced to relieve the pressure on public funding of civil legal aid.

CDS Criminal Defence Service.

DCA Department for Constitutional Affairs, the government department which succeeded the Lord Chancellor's Department, and was in turn succeeded by the Ministry of Justice.

HoCCA

LCF Law Centres Federation.

LAB Legal Aid Board.

LSC Legal Services Commission.

LSRC Legal Services Research Centre.

NFP not-for-profit sector, legal advice providers from outside the private solicitor firm sector, including advice charities, Citizens' Advice and law centres.

NPM New Public Management.

VFM value for money.

11

Findings and conclusions

Valerie Bryson and Pamela Fisher

The chapters in this book explored the impact of New Labour's rhetorical commitment to social justice in a number of policy areas. They report some positive changes: for instance, the introduction of the minimum wage raised the pay of the most economically marginalised (Heppell, Chapter 2), and social inclusion for some disabled people was furthered by policies that enabled them to avail themselves of opportunities for employment previously denied to them (Chappell and Gifford, Chapter 7). Chapter 4 (Thomas) also suggests that the emphasis on employment was paralleled by policies that encouraged community-level practices that contributed towards more inclusive citizenship and improved race relations. Despite these important successes, which deserve recognition, most contributors to this book have identified some fundamental flaws in New Labour's conceptualisation of social justice, which was based on a restricted contractarian moral order of 'rights and responsibilities' that prioritised citizens' obligation to participate in paid employment above other values. Their analysis of discursive change is supported by a linguistic examination of two key political terms (Jeffries, Chapter 3).

In the sections below, the contributors' main findings are summarised and considered in relation to five separate but interconnected areas: citizen workers; stigmatisation and the construction of 'deficiency'; the delegitimisation of the private sphere; consumer choice and personalisation; surveillance and empowerment. Each of these issues is discussed in relation to how it articulates with and was shaped by a particular understanding of social justice that was constructed through New Labour rhetoric and policy. This discussion is followed by an assessment of the prospects for a more radical vision of social justice that goes beyond the New Labour model.

Citizen workers

For ideological and pragmatic economic reasons New Labour employ-ment policy was rooted in the supply side; citizens were expected to be morally autonomous individuals who were prepared to 'self-invest' by availing themselves of the opportunities provided by 'Third Way' policies that promoted the development of 'human capital'. This vision, constructed through New Labour political discourse, acted to bring about a particular understanding of social justice based on the notion of individuals 'empowered' through participation in paid employment. Within this discourse, paid work was interpreted not only as a right but also as the first duty of a good citizen, except for people with disabilities, for whom it became become both a 'duty and a right' (Williams, 1999: 672). The chapters found a number of problems with this approach.

First, by over-emphasising the contractual partnership between the state and the individual the value of community-level initiatives received insufficient acknowledgement by central government. As dis-cussed by McGlynn and McAuley in Chapter 9, this meant that 'grass-roots' initiatives, such as those in Northern Ireland, were sidelined while social justice became increasingly equated with citizen-consumer and citizen-worker models. Second, the fact that the growth in employ-ment opportunities in the UK, particularly in Northern Ireland, often tended to be concentrated in poorly paid and casualised sectors of employment remained largely unacknowledged. Because many of the jobs provided by New Labour's New Deal were of this type, they did not lead to either status or prosperity: in other words, they provided little symbolic or economic capital. After 2008 rising unemployment undermined any credibility that supply-side arguments might have had, and New Labour's focus on paid work as the prime indication of a citizen's worth left those who lost their job with no alternative source of legitimacy or respect.

New Labour's vision of social justice also relied on the understanding that citizens were morally obligated to avail themselves of the oppor-tunities for social mobility that the 'investment state' facilitated. This theme is addressed implicitly in several chapters, and it is of central concern in Chapter 5, in which Avis argues, with reference to changes within the post-compulsory education sector, that deep-seated struc-tural inequalities were discursively reduced to the level of cultural deficits. Similarly, Sanderson and Sommerlad argue in Chapter 10 that legal aid was reformed in ways that restricted its accessibility for some of the most disadvantaged members of society, who were implicitly seen as less entitled to legal representation. They suggest that reforms of legal aid pointed to a form of social justice which required citizens to take 'responsibility' by conforming to the citizen-worker model in order to be worthy of the 'right' to equality before the law.

Stigmatisation and the construction of deficiency

While Chappell and Gifford argue in Chapter 7 that the drive towards inclusion through employment offered distinct advantages, providing new opportunities for many disabled people to join the formal economy, they also find that it created a conundrum whereby progress achieved in relation to the inclusion of one group led to the greater stigmatisation of others who were unable to conform to this normative model of citizenship. Those with mental health problems or, as discussed by Fisher in Chapter 8, disabled children and their parent carers could therefore be constructed in health and social care policy and practice as 'deficient' citizens who were unable or unwilling to appropriately manage their lives. As Robertson (2001: 122) pointed out, 'In practical terms, education or welfare systems that operate on the premise of normality and the reduction of difference, will always leave some people out. It is part of their logic.' Fisher's chapter also suggests that the moral agenda of paid work provided no space for the recognition and development of alternative understandings of empowerment based on the notion that individual empowerment can be found within relationships of interdependence.

The delegitimisation of the private sphere

The construction of deficiency, discussed above, relates to an arguably gendered delegitimisation of the private sphere (and the values associated with it) that characterised New Labour social policy. The assumption that paid employment was always preferable to unpaid labour had the effect of reinforcing the 'invisibility' of domestic work whilst also devaluing work performed outside the formal economy. In Chapter 9 McGlynn and McAuley show how in Northern Ireland opportunities for building greater social cohesion were lost because 'grass-roots' community engagement remained unacknowledged within policy that over-emphasised the role of employment and consumerism within its particular vision of social justice. Fisher, in Chapter 8, suggests that nascent alternative visions of social justice associated with the private sphere received little recognition in policy. On the other hand, Thomas contends in Chapter 4 that although its political rhetoric seemed very directive, New Labour's policies in relation to race relations in Oldham left in practice plenty of scope for community engagement and for the development of 'on the ground' initiatives that were supportive of social cohesion. Here policy initiatives around social cohesion appear to have supported a more open and more flexible approach by service providers than has been possible in other areas of social welfare and health provision.

The tacit dismissal of the values of the private sphere which, according to Chapter 8, appears to have influenced how health and social care was experienced by some service users, also had implications for the well-being of those delivering the services. Here Bryson and Deery draw on the experiences of midwives to show in Chapter 6 how the expansion of regulatory mechanisms designed to promote the 'three Es' of economy, efficiency and effectiveness has undermined the traditional values of public service and resulted in a highly stressed work force. They link this with a partial and limited conception of time that reflects the values of the capitalist workplace and fails to take into account either the time needed to provide good-quality care or the domestic responsibilities of employees. Public-sector reforms also had a negative impact on the provision of legal aid, as shown in Chapter 10 by Sanderson and Sommerlad. Reform in the delivery of legal aid meant that justice itself, arguably the most central cornerstone of equal citizenship and social justice, was subordinated to the priorities of economic efficiency.

Consumer choice and personalisation

Despite some of the negative effects of New Public Management, 'Third Way' rhetoric continued with the legacy of the liberal (some would say, neo-liberal) thinking of the 1980s by endorsing and promoting the values of consumer choice. Expanding the development of quasi-markets in the public sector was expected to lead to greater choice within education, the legal services, and the health and social care sectors. Within this context, professionals employed throughout the public sector were expected to transform themselves through self-government into entrepreneurial agents that sought to improve the quality of the services they provided to 'consumers' without questioning this underlying value system.

Several chapters identify problems with the notion of 'choice'. In Chapter 5 Avis is highly critical of the introduction of the 'choice' agenda and personalisation in education, suggesting that these reinforced the notion that educational under-achievement was attributable to cultural deficiency rather than being rooted in structural inequalities.

Chapter 6 (Bryson and Deery) reveals that the promise of a person-alised service for pregnant women was undermined when a stressed midwifery service prevented midwives from developing the type of personalised service that they were expected to provide. On the other hand, Chappell and Gifford in Chapter 7, suggest that the development of a more personal service for disabled people repositioned the latter in policy and practice as autonomous citizens able to make choices in their own rights.

Surveillance or empowerment

Echoing the concerns with regulatory mechanisms within health and social care, discussed in Chapters 6 and 8, Sanderson and Sommerlad address New Labour reforms to the system of legal aid in Chapter 10. Here it is argued that, while some reforms offered advantages over previous ways of working, a significant impact was to shift professional commitment from concern that all citizens should have access to legal representation towards concern with professional competence that may be audited and mapped according to the imperatives of economic efficiency. Professional knowledge in this context was often reduced to the status of a commodity that was passed from service provider to service user, and little space was provided for knowledge that was not consistent with the pre-given framework shaped by the discourse of market and consumer choice. This meant that, although New Labour rhetoric promised greater choice for the consumer, it often resulted in an extended role of the state in surveillance and in social engineer-ing. As Finlayson (2009: 404) has argued, New Labour 'reinvented the legitimacy of state intervention . . . in part, through a revision of the concept of "social justice"'. This involved attempts to change individual orientations and dispositions towards diet, to parenting and to health, enabling the state to extend its control at the 'atomic level' while at the same time professing to believe in the extension of choice and individual empowerment.

The micro-management of individual dispositions was promoted by a range of initiatives, the most famous of which are the programme of Surestart children's centres and the 'New Deal' that were established to bring about cultural changes. From a Foucauldian perspective, Rose (1999) sees these as new moral authorities that shaped indi-vidual behaviour and dispositions through the imposition, evaluation and regulation of techniques of self-government. Notwithstanding this, Heppell reminds us in Chapter 2 that New Labour's electoral success depended on an accommodation to the highly individualised sensitivities of middle England. New Labour's vision of social justice was necessarily curtailed by this and was obliged to somehow reconcile social justice with economic efficiency by placing the policy emphasis on responsibilisation and individual responsibility. As a result, attempts to empower individuals were unavoidably bound up with issues of state surveillance.

Social justice after New Labour

By the time that Gordon Brown replaced Tony Blair as party leader in 2007 New Labour seemed to have created a new centre ground in British politics (see Beech, 2008). Partly because New Labour appeared to hold the key to electoral success, the Conservative Party had effectively accepted its terms of debate, and the rhetoric of David Cameron, who became Conservative Party leader in 2005, was often almost indistinguishable from that of his New Labour opponents. Unsurprisingly, this rhetoric included a commitment to social justice, and Cameron expressed enthusiastic support for the Centre for Social Justice, a think-tank founded in 2004 by leading party members, including the former Conservative leaders Ian Duncan Smith and William Hague, to address concerns such as

> poverty in the UK, social exclusion, broken homes and the impact of divorce upon children, teenage pregnancies, homelessness and poor housing, drug and alcohol addiction, juvenile delinquency and youth crime, anti-social behaviour, community development and the welfare of old people. (Centre for Social Justice, undated)

These concerns could have been lifted from a New Labour strategy document, and they reflect the extent to which its rhetoric had become established as the new 'common sense' of British society.

This rhetorical convergence on social issues meant that during New Labour's time in office its progress towards greater justice was widely evaluated according to a model that, as discussed above and in the previous chapters, remained in many ways profoundly limited. For ten years or so, however, even many of those who would have liked a greater commitment to equality of outcome and who were suspicious of New Labour's enthusiasm for the free market and its close links with wealthy financiers found themselves admiring Brown's apparent economic competence as Chancellor and his ability to deliver economic growth, full employment and prosperity without inflation, so that, although the gap between the richest and the rest of society was growing, all social groups, including the poorest, experienced a rise in living standards. In this context, any talk of redistribution, exploitation or structural inequalities could easily be dismissed as an 'old Labour' voice from the past, and there seemed little way of questioning the values that underpinned New Labour's model of social justice.

In an 'Appendix' to his dystopian novel *Nineteen Eighty-four* George Orwell described the principles of 'Newspeak', a language devised by the all-powerful Party to 'meet the ideological needs of Insoc, or English Socialism'. The purpose of this language was 'not only to provide a medium of expression for the world-view and mental habits proper to the devotees of Insoc, but to make all other modes of thought impossible' (1977: 241). No one would claim that the architects of New Labour had the power or inclination to develop such a project. Nevertheless, their focus on style, presentation and political 'spin' involved an unprecedented, deliberate and detailed attention to the language of political discourse and the importance of staying 'on message' that made it increasingly difficult to think outside the framework of its assumptions and 'silence[d] social, political and moral critique before it c[ould] even be expressed' (Wissenberg, 2001: 234).

Given the dominant mind set, when the economic crisis broke, the response of New Labour's leaders was to seek a return to 'normality' rather than to re-examine its assumptions about the free market, the meaning of work and the desirability of economic growth. By 2009, however, the deepening effects of economic recession had combined with an increase in poverty, including child poverty, and it seemed that the party that had promised both economic efficiency and social justice was incapable of providing either. Even so, its leaders showed little sign of questioning the compatibility and nature of these goals, while their Conservative opponents combined their rhetorical commitment to social justice with a renewed assault on 'big government' and state spending that appeared driven more by focus group than any coherent vision.

The strength of the two-party system in British politics makes it particularly difficult for alternative views to be heard. However, as Foucault (1980) argued, the ability of dominant groups to organise our understanding of society is never absolute, and their discourse can be challenged or subverted by marginalised groups at macro and micro levels. Certainly, other visions of 'the good society' had continued to be articulated throughout the New Labour years from a wide range of sources, ranging from the mass protests of the anti-globalisation and environmental movements to some academics and journalists, left-leaning pressure groups and think-tanks such as Compass or the New Economics Foundation, some minor political parties, community activists and some members of the Labour Party itself. As some of the contributions to this book show, other visions of social justice were also developed outside the public sphere in response to the everyday struggles that characterise people's daily lives. The dominant New Labour rhetoric, however, allowed little space for these.

By 2009 the economic crisis was giving some of these marginalised views more salience. In particular, public frustration and anger about the large bonuses paid to bankers and financiers and about MPs' abuse of the expenses system opened up debate around very high earnings, and there was evidence of some shift in public opinion away from the New Labour orthodoxy that saw both wealth and poverty as a justifiable reflection of merit, and towards more negative views of the very rich (Barnfield and Horton, 2009).

While public opinion remained largely opposed to redistributive policies, the intellectual groundwork that would justify this was being prepared. For example, Ruth Lister (2008) turned New Labour's rhetoric of responsibility on its head to focus on the irresponsibility of the rich (their reckless behaviour in the City and the boardroom that led to the credit crunch, their tax evasion and avoidance and the damage their conspicuous consumption causes to the environment). Some feminists have also refocused the rhetoric of responsibility by insisting that caring for others is as much a civic responsibility as working for money: from this perspective, the problem is men's 'domestic absenteeism' rather than lone parents' reluctance to enter the workplace, and it is also imperative that the ethical values associated with care should be recognised in the public sphere (see for example Fraser, 2000; Bryson, 2007). The New Economics Foundation has similarly inverted conventional understanding by redefining the 'core economy': rather than paid production and employment, it sees this as the 'human resources embedded in the everyday life of every individual (time, wisdom, experience, energy, knowledge, skills) and in the relationships between them (love, empathy, watchfulness, care, reciprocity, teaching and learning).' (Coote *et al.*, 2009: 8–9) Meanwhile Hilary Wainwright has drawn on developments in Newcastle to argue, against 'the restricted range of thought of the Westminster village', for a new model of public service reform that aims at public benefit rather than profit maximisation (although not taking taxpayers' money for granted) and that rejects 'reform initiatives done *to* [the work force] rather than *with* them, let alone led *by* them' in favour of worker-led change (Wainwright with Little, 2009: 7, 10).

Other writers and activists have launched a frontal attack on the dominant values of late capitalist society. In the 2009 Reith Lectures Michael

Sandel called for 'a politics oriented less to the pursuit of individual self-interest and more to the pursuit of the common good'. Echoing the findings of some chapters in this volume, he argued that 'Too great a gap between rich and poor undermines the solidarity that democratic citizenship requires' (2009b) and that 'Some of the good things in life are corrupted or degraded if turned into commodities . . . Health, education, national defence, criminal justice, environmental protection and so on – these are moral and political questions, not merely economic ones' (2009a). Sandel also found reasons for optimism, and he claimed that we are now at the end of an era in which 'market triumphalism' is being replaced by a healthier 'market scepticism'. This high-profile contribution to public debate was in line with Neil Lawson (the chair of Compass)'s critique of the 'turbo-consumerism' that he said breeds inequality, selfish individualism and a false value system (Lawson, 2009), and with semi-popular works on 'happiness' (Layard, 2005) and 'affluenza' (James, 2007). In 2009 Richard Wilkinson and Kate Pickett's *The Spirit Level* used international data to demonstrate that inequality is bad for the rich as well as the poor, as all groups are affected by the social problems that inequality brings, and even those in the highest-earning groups are healthier and live longer in more equal societies; this attracted significantly more media attention than Wilkinson's similar findings in earlier work.

The above ideas (and others could have been selected) are not simply 'old Labour', nor are they completely outside the mainstream of public political debate. While clearly critical of many aspects of New Labour thinking, the writers mentioned here do not generally deny that New Labour has produced a number of welcome, if limited, results (such as the minimum wage, an increase in child benefits, support for child-care costs, the introduction of parental and paternity leave, the working families tax credit and Surestart). The new ideas do not represent a coherent ideology or political programme. However, taken together, they represent an expansion of the idea of social justice to take it beyond narrowly defined notions of individual rights and responsibilities that are based in economic values and towards a more generous concept of justice that encompasses the value of human relationships and collective goods. As such,they are supportive of many of the ideas expressed in this book, and resonate with some of the micro-level experiences described in the chapters.

One of the main messages in this volume is that experiences and perspective on the micro-level of people's lives should be seen as 'political'. While New Labour sought to impose a particular model of social justice from above, this book points to a need for a wider discursive space that encourages a more critical interrogation of political rhetoric from diverse perspectives that opens up the vocabulary of social justice and critically engages with terms such as empowerment, choice, responsibilities and rights. In this context, the goal is not to develop a new political ideology but to ensure that debate continues and that ideas of social justice are informed by the daily experiences of 'ordinary citizens'. To reclaim a term that had only negative connotations under New Labour (see Jeffries, Chapter 2 of this volume), it is possible that radicalised visions of social justice can thereby emerge.

Bibliography

Barnfield, L. and Horton, T. (2009) *Understanding Attitudes to Economic Inequality*, (York: Joseph Rowntree Foundation), www.jrf.org.uk (accessed 25 August 2009).

Beech, M. (2008) *New Labour and the Politics of Dominance*, in M. Beech and S. Lee (eds) *Ten Years of New Labour* (Basingstoke: Palgrave Macmillan).

Bryson, V. (2007) *Gender and the Politics of Time* (Bristol: Policy Press).

Centre for Social Justice, www.centreforsocialjustice.org.uk/ (accessed 25 August 2009).

Coote, A., Franklin, J., and Stephens, L. (2009) 'Growing the Core Economy', paper prepared for the 'Global Economic Summit. No Turning Back' conference organised by Compass and the New Economics Foundation, London, 30 March.

Finlayson, A. (2009) 'Financialisation, financial literacy and asset-based welfare', *British Journal of Politics and International Relations* 11, 400–21.

Foucault, M. (1980) *Power/Knowledge: Selected Interviews and other Writings, 1972–1977,ed.* ed. C. Gordon (London: Harvester Wheatsheaf).

Fraser, N. (2000) 'After the family wage: a postindustrial thought experiment', in B. Hobson (ed.) *Gender and Citizenship in Transition* (Basingstoke: Macmillan).

James, O. (2007) *Affluenza: How to be Successful and Stay Sane* (London: Vermillion).

Lawson, N. (2009) *All Consuming* (Harmondsworth: Penguin).

Layard, R. (2005) *Happiness: Lessons from a new Science* (Harmsondsworth: Penguin).

Lister, R. (2008) 'The irresponsibility of the rich', *Red Pepper*, 18 September, www.redpepper.org.uk/The-irresponsibility-of-the-rich (accessed 25 August 2009).

Orwell, G. (1977/1949) *Nineteen Eighty Four* Harmondsworth: Penguin).

Robertson, C. (2001) 'Autonomy and identity: the need for new dialogues in education and welfare', *Support for Learning* 16:3, 122–7.

Rose, N. (1999) *Powers of Freedom: Reframing Political Thought* (Cambridge: Cambridge University Press).

Sandel, M. (2009a) Lecture 1, 'Markets and Morals', *Reith Lectures 2009: A New Citizenship*, http://downloads.bbc.co.uk/rmhttp/radio4/transcripts/20090609_thereithlectures_marketsandmorals.rtf (accessed 25 August 2009).

Sandel, M. (2009b) Lecture 4, 'A New Politics of the Common Good', *Reith Lectures 2009: A New Citizenship*, http://downloads.bbc.co.uk/rmhttp/radio4/transcripts/20090630_reith_anewpolitics.rtf (accessed 25 August 2009).

Wainwright, H., with Little, M. (2009) *Public Service Reform . . . But not as we know it!* (Hove: Picnic Publishing).

Wilkinson, R., and Pickett, K. (2009) *The Spirit Level: Why More Equal Societies always do Better* (London: Allen Lane).

Williams, F. (1999) 'Good-enough principles for welfare', *Journal of Social Policy* 28:4, 667–87.

Wissenberg, M. (2001) 'The "third way" and social justice', *Journal of Political Ideologies* 6:2, 231–5.

Index